Picture Palaces
of Liverpool

Published by The Bluecoat Press Liverpool
Book design by March Design, Liverpool
Printed in China by Latiitude Press

Back cover photograph: Interior of the Commodore, Bankhall

ISBN 9781872568713

Acknowledgements
The author wishes to thank Paul Bolger, Chris Clegg, David Ellis,
Roger Shone, Mike Taylor and Liverpool Record Office, for
providing photographs.

http://streetsofliverpool.co.uk

Picture Palaces of Liverpool

Harold Ackroyd

THE BLUECOAT PRESS

4

The Picture Palaces of Liverpool

Introduction

Opposite *The Paramount, London Road, 1930s.*

Merseysiders first saw exhibitions of animated pictures in 1896 when the Tivoli Palace, Lime Street, simultaneously with the Hope Hall, Hope Street, presented them during the week beginning Monday 18 May. At the Tivoli, the enterprising proprietor, James Kiernan, continually sought novel attractions to supplement his variety performances. He took the earliest opportunity in arranging for this latest craze from New York, Paris and London.

Replacing variety as the top attraction, advertisements proclaimed: *The Sensation of the Century – The Cinematographe*, on view every half hour daily from 2pm, with two performances every evening. Vincent Paul, inventor of the latest improvements in animated pictures, gave the exhibitions. In the same week, Hope Hall also presented *Edison Cinematographe*, life size moving photographs, shown hourly between 5pm and 9pm.

The next exhibition of motion pictures was to be seen under very different circumstances and in a very different setting, on 20 October 1896 at St George's Hall, Lime Street. Here, Brit Acres, another pioneer of the invention, gave a demonstration of his new machine, the Kineopticon, to the Amateur Photographer Association. Across the Mersey in Birkenhead, on 9 November 1896, a 10 minute film was shown on the Vitagraph projector by Chard and Co. In time, film replaced variety as the principal attraction at the famous Argyle Theatre. On the opening night, so eager were patrons to see the new invention, that the first house audience rushed the doors and entered without paying. Reimbursement was only obtained by means of a collection from the audience.

During the following year, 1897, pictures shown by a Bioscope projector became a twice daily attraction at Reynold Wax Works. Ironically it was the growing popularity of motion pictures which eventually resulted in the closure of the wax works in 1922.

Early in the century, a travelling showman, AD Thomas, arranged film shows in the Picton Hall, William Brown Street. For the presentation of these he engaged a local man, John F Wood, who became an important figure in connection with film exhibition in Liverpool. Eventually, Wood took over the film shows at the Picton Hall, and in 1908 rented the Queen's Hall, Birkenhead and Walton Baths for film showings. So successful were these that he decided to build Liverpool's first purpose-built cinema, the Bedford Hall, Walton. From this beginning he formed the circuit known as Bedford Cinemas Ltd (1928), which, in the Liverpool area, included three 1930s super-cinemas.

Another picture pioneer, Sydney Carter, who in 1903 was manager of the St George Hall, Bradford, worked in association with FD Sunderland to form the New Century Animated Picture Co. Shows were given at the Picton Hall, before they were transferred to the city's first permanent cinema, the New Century Picture Hall, in November 1908. At about that time film shows were also presented by Leo and Fred Weisker, the sons of a St Helens publican, who, following their successful shows at the St Helens Co-op Hall, went on to lease several Liverpool music halls for conversion into cinemas. By 1914 they had built up a circuit, Weiskers Picture Palaces Ltd, and were also film renters with an office in London Road.

Prior to this, motion pictures in the city were presented, for a limited period only, at the Prince of Wales Theatre, Clayton Square (1901) and at the Parthenon Music Hall/Theatre Moderne, Great Charlotte Street (1906-07). The suburbs also had venues for early exhibitions of motion pictures, in 1906 at the Aigburth Assembly Picturedrome, a permanent location until 1922, when it became the Rivoli Theatre. To the north of the city, George Prince, an early picture pioneer, started film shows in 1906 at Bootle Sun Hall, and in 1907 at Waterloo Town Hall. The Australian Bioscope Co's animated picture shows were accompanied by Liverpool's famous baritone, Henry Beale.

From these small beginnings, film exhibition grew rapidly and by 1918, 63 cinemas had been opened. This figure increased to 91 during the silent era of the 1920s. Although the late-1920s saw the emergence of the major cinema circuits, Gaumont British (GB) and Associated British Cinemas (ABC), the first large circuit representation in the city was the Liverpool Picture House, Clayton Square, which was opened in 1912 by Provincial Cinematograph Theatres Ltd. Confined to a policy of prestigious cinemas, in expensive city centre locations, their only other Liverpool enterprise was the Trocadero, Camden Street, which they controlled for 2 years until February 1929, when the company was taken over by GB.

Formed in March 1928, GB was the first company to justify the description of a major circuit, due to the numerous suburban cinemas they acquired at that time. Their principal rivals, ABC, having taken over three circuits, including Savoy Cinemas Ltd, then controlled the Prince of Wales (formerly the Liverpool Picture House) and the enormous Olympia Theatre, just outside the city. Two years later, in 1931, they opened their first newly-built super-cinema, the Forum, Lime Street, and added to the circuit many suburban cinemas in competition with GB.

In accordance with their policy of opening large super-cinemas in UK cities, Paramount Pictures opened Liverpool's largest super-cinema, the Paramount, London Road, in 1934. Screening first runs of all Paramount Pictures and also other notable productions, although with only one cinema, this still created a third production, distribution and exhibition organisation in Liverpool. From July 1942 it was acquired by Oscar Deutsch Odeon circuit, and from June 1948 by Circuits Management Association, with the amalgamation of the Odeon and Gaumont circuits.

The large circuits were therefore in a position to ensure that, with few exceptions, the leading attractions were screened as first runs at their cinemas in the city, then in the suburbs. The conditions of film booking, therefore, worked heavily against the many independent exhibitors, particularly in the suburbs, where showing dates were often several months later than those in the city, except for a selected number of Paramount Pictures, made available in the late-1940s to the independents for first runs in the city and suburbs. A dispute between Twentieth Century-Fox and Circuits Management Association (CMA) in 1954, led to an improvement in booking conditions.

Following the first runs of the CinemaScope productions at the Futurist and Scala, Lime Street, which were leased, any independent exhibitor who agreed to install the full CinemaScope equipment, including stereophonic sound, was offered first runs of the Fox releases. By the end of the 1950s, the Fox/CMA dispute having been settled, the advantage to the independents was lost when the Fox CinemaScope films were again booked by CMA. Many of the older cinemas had then closed, having become unviable due to the general decrease in cinema attendances.

In the new millennium, due to subsequent closures, the number of older cinemas in the Liverpool area has been reduced to only the Odeon, Liverpool (five screens), in the suburbs the reopened Plaza (former Apollo), Crosby (three screens); the single-screen ABC (former Cannon), Allerton; and the longest-surviving independent cinema, the Woolton Picture House. Multi-screen cinemas are located outside the city at Edge Lane Drive, as well as the Showcase on the East Lancashire Road, but for some time there have been announcements of plans for others in the city.

The closure of the city centre 051 triple, in September 1997, and the ABC Lime Street, in January 1998, left the ten-screen Odeon the only place of film entertainment in the city. This reinforced the opinion that the curtain had come down for the last time on the large super-cinemas, so fondly remembered by cinema-goers of earlier years.

1906
Aigburth Assembly Picturedrome • Rivoli Theatre • Rivoli Cinema
Aigburth Road, South Liverpool

The Rivoli as a kitchen shop in 1979.

Although only small, the theatre had a long and proud history dating back to 1889, the date on the stonework outside the theatre. It was built as the Sefton Park Assembly Rooms by the wealthy merchants who resided around the park. The Assembly Rooms were used for all major local ceremonies and functions, and carriages at 10pm was the order of the day on invitation cards and tickets. In the basement of the theatre, which in the 1950s housed a billiard room and boiler room, were the kitchens, and local urchins used to inhale the pleasant aromas drifting up through the pavement gratings.

The building was acquired around the turn of the century by Mr and Mrs A Scott, who introduced live entertainment, and it became known as Pa Scott's Opera House. In 1906 the upper floor was converted into a small cinema, the Aigburth Assembly Picturedrome, with seating for about 300 on wooden forms. The cinema was advertised by handbills distributed around the district:

Exclusive Animated Pictures of all the finest subjects of the day, including Filmacolour. – Complete Change of Pictures Mondays and Thursdays – Special Matinee will be held on Wednesdays at 3pm during the winter months, commencing on October 1 – Special matinee for children every Saturday at 3 o'clock – Only approved pictures shown – Seats can be booked – No extra charge – Prices, 1/-, 9d, 6d, & 3d.

To create the right atmosphere, a pianist played in front of the screen to accompany the silent films. Miss EF Graydon was the lady who performed this duty for several years. Known to all as Flo, she was also remembered for many years as a composer and for her appearances in revues.

The auditorium was reconstructed for the opening as the Rivoli Theatre in 1923, when the ground floor formed the stalls area, whilst the upper floor was converted into a balcony, giving a total seating capacity of 600. In December 1923 the Rivoli was styled as Liverpool's latest amusement centre, presenting variety shows. Among the colourful personalities who appeared were two young local men, Arthur Askey and Tommy Handley, who later became famous comedians. Another form of live entertainment came in 1925, when the Jack Fortescue Repertory Co enjoyed a successful 12 months. Advertising outside the theatre styled Jack Fortescue as 'the creator of laughter and tears', and the group produced at least one play a week before leaving to tour various parts of the country.

Since 1923 the Rivoli had been owned by the Aigburth Picture House Ltd, whose managing director, T Halliwell Hughes, had formed a small circuit of seven cinemas in Liverpool. In March 1928 this was taken over by Denman Picture Houses Ltd, part of the then countrywide GB Picture Corporation which ran the Rivoli for 28 years. Due to its small seating capacity, the Rivoli was at a disadvantage in competition with the super-cinemas which opened during the 1930s. The latter half of the decade saw the opening of the Mayfair and the company New Gaumont, in Princes Park. Films booked to the Rivoli were the later showings of the circuit releases. Each film was shown for 3 days only. Thus, admissions declined, particularly from the early-1950s, and television was also considered a major factor in the Rivoli's sudden closure only a few days into the New Year of 1957. Residents were shocked and saddened to see a 'For Sale' sign outside. The new seats were ripped out and the interior was described as having the same atmosphere as a sunken ship.

The final programme, on 5 January 1957, was *Back to Eternity,* featuring Robert Ryan, and *The High Terrace* with Dale Robertson. Despite talk of a return to a repertory theatre, about 2 years after closure as a cinema, the building was acquired by parishioners of St Charles' Roman Catholic Church. It was sold in the 1970s, when the building was converted to a fitted kitchen centre. Around 1994 it became the Grace Christian Centre. So ends the history of the theatre, which for nearly 70 years had been the home of many forms of entertainment, silent films, variety and repertory live entertainment, then the 'talkies'.

1908
Picture Palace of Bootle • Empire Picture Theatre
Knowsley Road, Bootle

This long, narrow building was originally built as the Bootle Institute in 1882, with the date engraved in the stonework at the highest point of the frontage. In 1908 it was converted into a small stadium-type cinema, with seating for about 300 people and entry from the centre of the frontage through a pair of glass-panelled doors.

The local press reported that the hall was to open as the Picture Palace of Bootle, at 8pm on 16 November 1908. It opened under the management of George Clewith, who had booked an extensive programme for the opening night. A large advertisement announced the first showing of the Empire Pictures boasting 45 miles of film nightly! The main films were entitled *An Indian's Friendship, Burglar's Midnight Surprise* and *Launch of the Laurentis*, with vocal accompaniment by Miss Gracie Davies and songs illustrated on the screen. Admission was at 1/-, 6d and 3d, with reduced prices of 8d and 4d at the early doors 7.15pm. On Saturdays there were matinees for children at 1pm and 3pm, for 1d and 2d. Parents were told to have no fear when sending their children to the matinees, as the projector, then referred to by most as 'the machine', was housed in a separate room in a fireproof box.

At that time the only other locations for film entertainment were as supporting items to variety shows at the theatres, or at the Sun Hall, where pictures were shown for whole seasons and did not become a permanent cinema until 1911. The Bootle Picture Palace was therefore regularly crowded during its early years.

There appears to have been an early change of management, since in 1915 the trade press announced that James Mawdsley had held the position for 7 years and personally selected the programmes, which included variety acts. Known as the Empire Picture Theatre from 1912, the proprietor during the war years until 1917, was William Eltoft, who also ran the Bijou at Waterloo. The Empire survived against strong competition from the Picture House, Stanley Road, the Palace, Marsh Lane and the Sun Hall. However, the end came in 1922, shortly after the opening of the Gainsborough cinema, opposite on Knowsley Road. The Empire was converted into a dance hall, when owned by W and A Cinemas Ltd, opening on Easter Monday 1922 as the Palais de Dance. The next change of use came in 1931 when it became the Bootle Trades and Labour Club, serving this purpose for over 50 years until 1984, when the building was acquired by Tetley Walker Ltd and opened as the Knowsley Social Club.

1908
Mount Pleasant Hall • Century Cinema
Mount Pleasant, Liverpool city centre

The building was originally a Wesley Chapel, erected around the middle of the 19th century, which after many years passed into the possession of the Corporation of Liverpool on the erection of the Central (Charles Garrett Memorial) Hall. In 1908 it was acquired from the Corporation for conversion into a cinema by the New Century Animated Picture Co, whose managing director was Sydney H Carter, who also had cinema interests in Yorkshire. The company operated as a picture house called the Assembly Rooms at New Briggate, Leeds and Carter was the Secretary of the huge, 3000-seat St George Hall in Bradford. Popular as the New Century Co animated pictures had been in their old home at the Picton Hall, Liverpool, it was felt that they would enjoy an even more vigorous lease of life in the highly comfortable Mount Pleasant Hall. A period of several weeks was spent on an elaborate scheme of reseating and redecoration. A 700-seat, stadium-type auditorium was formed on the first floor, reached by a staircase from Mount Pleasant.

Said to be the first organised cinema in the city centre, the local press reported an auspicious opening on Monday 14 December 1908, when the decorations and well-arranged seats elicited the enthusiastic admiration of the large audience. The entertainment was stated, both pictorially and musically, to sustain New Century's high reputation for artistic excellence and mirth. The main film, *The Destruction of Hyderabad*, was considered in every way worthy of the company and the occasion. The performances were at 3pm and 8pm, with three performances on Saturdays only at 3pm, 7pm and 9pm, to which admission prices were 3d, 6d and 1/-. There was a weekly change of pictures.

In 1915 the Mount Pleasant Hall came under joint ownership with the Lime Street Picture House Co, who in 1912 had opened Liverpool's first purpose-built cinema bearing their name. This amalgamation ceased in 1920 when the new company, Futurist (Liverpool) Ltd, was formed to take over the Lime Street House. The Mount Pleasant Hall continued under the ownership of Sydney H Carter of the New Century Co until March 1928, when it was purchased by Denman Picture Houses Ltd and managed by the GB Picture Corporation.

Becoming the Century Theatre and styled as the 'Home of Unusual Films', the cinema was given an entirely new image for the reopening on 26 December 1928. The feature film was *The Lost Moment*, supported by *Cinderella*, the famous fairy tale. The silent films were accompanied by the Salon Orchestra, under the direction of JW Smart. Performances were continuous daily from 2pm to 10.30pm, to which admission prices were: front stalls 9d, stalls 1/3 and reserved stalls at 2/4. Seats were bookable at the box office and also at Rushworth and Dreapers music store and the Adelphi Hotel.

Rare continental films during the final year of the cinema included Emil Jannings in *The Last Laugh*, Mady Christians and Willy Fritsch in *The Waltz Dream*, Emil Jannings in *Faust* and Fritz Lang's screen epic *Dr Mabuse*. However, in 1929, with the talkies becoming established in Liverpool as elsewhere, there was insufficient support for the silent films. This resulted in the closure of the cinema on 15 February 1930, then showing the German film *Conscience*, featuring Bernard Goetake.

A few months later the building was acquired by furniture auctioneers, Turner Sons and Smythe, who advertised their new rooms as the Century Auction Galleries. Their first sale was held on 30 October 1930. In the 1930s there was a change of use to a billiard hall, then to a carpet warehouse in the 1950s, before becoming well-known as the Mardi Gras Jazz Club. This was closed early in the 1970s and the building demolished to make way for a multi-storey carpark.

1908
Tivoli Palace • Grand Tivoli • Palais de Luxe Cinema
Lime Street, Liverpool city centre

In 1845 several dilapidated houses on Lime Street were demolished for road widening. Following this, the Teutonic Hall was erected to the plans of the architect, Edward Starkie Tuton. Despite its name, there was nothing Teutonic in its origins. After a decade in use as a public hall, the interior was converted into two separate areas, the ground floor being occupied by Allsopp's New Crystal Palace Waxworks and the upper floor, styled as the Teutonic Upper Hall, exhibited Hamilton Dioramas.

In 1859 this was converted into the Theatre Variété, under the ownership of Wilson and Montague, who, in April 1863 presented the first of the Charles Christy Minstrel Shows, the forerunner of what was to become the most popular and longest-surviving entertainment at the hall. A change to stage plays in 1865 introduced famous actors such as Brinsley Sheridan, Charles Wyndham and also Charles Dickens, for his second Liverpool appearance.

Continuing under the same ownership, in the spring of 1868, the theatre was renamed the St James' Hall and Operetta House, with entertainment consisting of operas, ballets and plays. However, from 31 October 1870 for over

25 years, this was Liverpool's home of the minstrels, its destiny guided by the famous Sam Hague troupe of around 40 performers, organised by him in Macon, Georgia, USA, stated then to be the only black troupe in the world.

After 4½ years of great success, on 2 May 1875, the theatre, and all of Sam Hague's property were destroyed by fire, thought to have broken out in the Green Room or a dressing room. The flames spread into the auditorium, reducing it to a charred ruin, although they were prevented from spreading to the waxworks below. Unfortunately, the property and contents, including Herr Schalkenbach's famous organ, were insured for considerably less than their true value.

After rebuilding, the new St James' Hall, with dimensions of 80' by 35', was about the same size as the old hall, but with a seating capacity of about 1000, due to the addition of a new gallery above the circle. This gallery had straight extensions along the sides of the auditorium to the ornate 25' proscenium. About a year after the fire, the new St James' Hall opened on 1 May 1876, and for 20 years Sam Hague and his minstrels successfully maintained the tradition of the hall as Liverpool's leading venue for this type of entertainment.

Early in 1896, the building was acquired by James Kiernan, one of the most enterprising figures in Merseyside's variety history, who was the fountain head of the new venture to convert St James' Hall into the Tivoli Palace of Varieties. In February 1896 the theatre was said to have been beautified and improved beyond recognition, the cream and gold relief ornamentation being enhanced by hundreds of electric globes set in three massive bronze chandeliers.

Described as the most picturesque and sumptuous theatre of its kind in the United Kingdom, the Tivoli Palace of Varieties opened on 2 March 1896, when the hall was packed for the two performances at 7pm and 9.10pm. There was an array of talent, numbering 17, headed by the brilliant queen of comediennes, Marie Lloyd. After only a short time, on 18 May 1896 the Tivoli had the distinction of being first in the city (concurrently with the Hope Hall in Hope Street) to present the new animated pictures. Arranged by James Kiernan, who continually sought novelty attractions to supplement the variety entertainment, the films were exhibited by Vincent Paul, a travelling showman and inventor of the latest improvements in animated photos. According to available information, he was not related to London instrument maker, Robert Paul, who in 1895 had devised a film projector.

In December 1896 a new company, Kiernans Palaces of Varieties, was formed with a share capital of £90,000 to acquire and take over the Tivoli Palace, the Park Palace and the Paddington Palace variety theatres, together with James Kiernan's variety agency in Lime Street. James Kiernan was offered and accepted the position of managing director on condition that he did not enter into any other similar business venture in the Liverpool area. The company wanted to retain his name as it was considered a guarantee of success. Nevertheless this proved to be a short term venture, closing as a variety theatre on 30 April 1898.

Several years later the building was demolished and the construction of the new theatre on the site was as a result of the interest of Walter de Frece, managing director of South of England Hippodromes Ltd. It was his first theatre in the north of England. The new Tivoli was erected by Brown & Sons, of Liverpool and Salford. It was built to the plans of Bertie Crewe, the well-known theatre architect, who designed the Liverpool Hippodrome in 1902. It was later known for half a century as the Palais de Luxe Cinema, with an exterior similar in appearance to that prior to modernisation in the early-1950s.

As before, the main entrance was located at the extreme right of the Lime Street frontage, parallel to the length of the building. The lower part was surmounted by a substantial iron and glass verandah with forward extensions at either end, and glass shaded electric light fittings spaced along. There were two large lanterns adjacent to the main entrance. The upper part of the frontage featured several pairs of pilasters with panels between three stone arches projected above the coping. At the extreme right was a square tower.

Internally, the planning differed from that of the old theatre, in that the stalls floor was below ground level, reached by a broad staircase from the foyer, which gave direct access to the circle from which exits to street level were provided along the side extensions. Including the gallery above, in the high ceilinged auditorium, the original seating capacity was 1,250, a remarkable number in view of the limited area.

On 8 December 1906, the famous music hall star, Vesta Tilley, wife of managing director Walter de Frece, laid the commemoration stone of the new theatre. This was preserved in the basement through the years until the end of

its life as the Palais de Luxe Cinema. But for the Grand Opening on 10 December 1906, it was the new Tivoli Palace of Varieties, described as the most beautiful vaudeville theatre in the provinces, with entertainment of the highest order provided by Walter de Frece's new company, Liverpool Theatre of Varieties Ltd. Top of the bill, making her last appearance prior to an American tour, was the famous male impersonator, Vesta Victoria. Joining the ranks of twice-nightly variety theatres, performances were at 6.30pm and 9pm, to which admission to the private boxes was 10/6, stalls 1/6 (first three rows 2/-), grand circle 1/-, pit 6d and gallery 3d.

The anticipated success of the Tivoli did not materialise, possibly due to its close proximity to Moss and Stoll Empire Theatre, where similar entertainment was presented. As a variety theatre, the Tivoli therefore again proved to be short-lived, for, by the end of 1907, cinematograph films had replaced variety as the main attraction. Presentations were by the film producers and showmen, the Weisker brothers. They were Leo and Fred Weisker from St Helens, who formed the company Weisker Picture Palaces Ltd, taking over failing music halls for conversion into cinemas.

Commencing on 30 December 1907, Weisker Bros Theatrescope and Advanced Vaudeville Co were presented at 6.50pm and 9pm, with also a matinee daily at 2.30pm. Admission prices were considerably reduced to: stalls 1/-, circle 6d, pit 4d and gallery 2d. The theatre thereafter remained open with cine-variety until 28 March 1908, then closed for 8 months. It reopened on 21 December under the management of Jasper Redfern, a Sheffield electrician who became a film showman with managerial expertise, which had earned for him an enviable reputation in various parts of the country, notably his film exhibitions at the Sheffield Central Hall and the Grand Theatre, Manchester.

Concurrently with the Park Palace in Liverpool, named the Grand Tivoli, the opening performances were on 21 December 1908, advertised as: *Great Pictures and Class Vaudeville twice-nightly at 6.50pm and 9pm*. The orchestra, led by WA Hollis, was the first in Liverpool to provide musical accompaniment to the films, which prior to this had been solely by the pianoforte. This type of entertainment was continued by Jasper Redfern until 30 June 1909, after which the theatre was closed.

On 23 November 1909, the building was reopened for the first time as a cinema, renamed the Palais de Luxe. Cinematograph entertainment was again under the control of the Weisker Bros, whose advertising boasted: *The*

Opposite *The Palais de Luxe, photographed in 1959, the year it closed down.*

finest cinematograph entertainment in the United Kingdom with Comedy, Drama, Sport, Science and Art, accompanied by a high class orchestra.

At continuous performances from 3.30pm to 10.30pm, patrons were advised that they could come when they liked and stay as long as they pleased. With admission prices similar to those of 1907, there was the additional service of providing tea, free of charge, between 4pm and 6pm, for patrons of the 6d and 1/- seats.

In September 1912, it was announced that the world's greatest pictures, together with a variety programme to suit all tastes were to be accompanied by the sweet strains of the orchestra. A notable film attraction on 12 and 13 November 1912 was *The Great Ocean Catastrophe*, of which exclusive showing rights in the city had been secured. It was described as the most thrilling and dramatic film ever to be produced and featured the sinking of the mighty liner, the Titanic.

The Liverpool Palais de Luxe Co was formed in June 1913 to take over the cinema, whose directorate included Fred and Leo Weisker and John Hickman Dovenor, another pioneer of the film trade in Liverpool. Under the new company, the Palais de Luxe became the first Liverpool cinema to have sound accompaniment to silent films, made possible by the sound-on-disc system, Edison Kinetophone. Advertisements stated: *You see the man, you hear his voice – Greatly acclaimed by their Majesties the King and Queen.* The Kinetophone was used from 19 December 1913 until 28 February 1914.

By the outbreak of war in August 1914, the son of JH Dovenor, JR Dovenor, was actively engaged with Liverpool's pioneer cinemas, including the Palais de Luxe. After war service, followed by engagement in civic affairs and trade interests, he became the manager of the Palais de Luxe in 1920. He then controlled the destinies of an important new group of Merseyside cinemas, the North Western Film Booking Agency, based at 60 Lime Street. As well as the Palais de Luxe, the Kensington Picturedrome, the Aintree Palace and St James' Picturedrome, made up the original four cinemas of the circuit.

During the 1920s a regular added attraction at the Palais de Luxe was live entertainment on the stage, and music by the popular orchestra of CV Roche. Although by the beginning of 1930 the majority of the city cinemas had changed over to sound films, the Palais de Luxe remained silent, advertising: 'The House of Golden Silence' and later 'Our Pictures are still Silent – but Sound!' thereby serving the many who still preferred an orchestra to the talkies. Finally, on 2 August 1930, the last silent film, *The Man Who Changed His Name*, was screened. Advertising 'Our Pictures Speak for Themselves', with BTH sound and projection equipment and new decorations enhanced by the Holophane coloured lighting system, the All Talking and Singing attraction, *It's A Great Life*, featuring the Duncan Sisters, opened on Monday 4 August 1930. Admission prices remained at 1/6 and 2/4 in the circle, 1/- for stalls, with admission for only 6d before 5.30pm.

Competition for patrons increased considerably during the first half of the 1930s, with the opening of two super-cinemas: the Forum (1931) adjacent on Lime Street, and the Paramount (1934) on London Road. Although mainly restricted to later showings of the circuit release films, the Palais de Luxe, with the advantage of its central location, still attracted good passing trade, with continuous performances from 1pm to 10.30pm.

During World War II the Palais de Luxe was one of three cinemas on Lime Street to suffer bomb damage, which resulted in closure from 3 May until 9 June 1941, later reopening with *Little Nelly Kelly,* featuring Judy Garland. Far more serious damage was caused in June 1951, when a disastrous fire destroyed much of the interior. Before the reopening in November 1952, there was complete external and internal modernisation. The facade was given a modern appearance by a complete covering of grey and black faience tiles. The tower was removed and the upper part was relieved only by the theatre's name in neon. Above the main entrance was a stainless steel motif of a motion picture cameraman. An almost full length new canopy, with a lettering display on the facia, was illuminated by neon tubes, which surmounted the lower part of the frontage.To the left of the main entrance were the circle exits, with still frames spaced along. A notable transformation of the interior was achieved by the suspension from the ceiling, of ranks of decorative panels across the width of the auditorium, whilst the walls were covered by modernistic decorations painted in a Merseyside studio. Fresh curtains framed a new screen and the latest type of sound equipment was installed.

The Palais de Luxe reopened at midday on Thursday 6 November 1952 with *The Great Caruso,* the film which made Mario Lanza famous. Despite the improvements, this was a period of generally decreasing attendances, and after a further 2 years during which wide screen and CinemaScope had been installed at most of the city cinemas, the Palais de Luxe had the disadvantage of an auditorium of insufficient width to accommodate the new projection systems. It had to rely, therefore, on older films and those not booked by the major circuits. Nevertheless, the cinema survived almost to the end of the decade, closing on 24 October 1959 with the double feature *Scarlet Street,* starring Edward G Robinson and *Johnny Stool Pigeon* with Dan Duryea. The Palais de Luxe was then one of four cinemas in the Liverpool area of the North Western cinema circuit, which had operated since 1920. The building was later demolished and the site redeveloped with shops and a cafeteria.

1908
Park Palace Kinematodrome • Park Palace Cinema
Mill Street, Dingle

The building was originally a music hall, the Park Palace of Varieties, erected on the site of an old coach works. It was opened by the proprietor/manager, JS Childs, on 4 December 1893, with variety performances at 7pm and 9pm. The inclusion of Charles Coburn and many other well-known artists of the time, made it one of the strongest bills seen in Liverpool for a long time.

Parallel to Mill Street, the building had quite a long frontage, the upper part in red brick relieved by a line of small windows and over the centre, a large panel bearing the theatre's name. Several curtained, plate glass-panelled doors

Park Palace Cinema, 1975.

were spaced along the lower, tiled part, providing two entrances for the pit, whilst the stalls, dress circle and gallery each had one entrance.

The auditorium consisted of the ground floor with pit and stalls providing seating for 600 people, whilst the dress circle and balcony, on one stepped floor with side extensions to the front, accommodated 500. The proscenium opening was 30' wide and of similar height, flanked by a fluted column with an ornamental capital and base supporting a cornice and pediment bearing the Royal Coat of Arms, following a visit by King Edward VII in 1904.

The proscenium opening was adorned by a deep pelmet with gold trimmings above a handsome crimson plush curtain with a deep fringe, which, when drawn up from the sides by red and gold cords with massive tassels, revealed the magnificent back-drop, painted by T Holmes, scenic artist of the Shakespeare Theatre. In front, the orchestra pit accommodated 14 musicians. At either side of the proscenium, two private boxes were draped with blue plush curtains, lined with satin and backed by white lace curtains. The box fronts were formed in fibrous plaster of Renaissance design, lit by a five-light chandelier. The front of the circle was decorated by fibrous plaster enrichments and fitted with oval bevelled mirrors with double brass ornamental gas brackets, providing a brilliant lighting effect. Decoration of the auditorium walls was by red patterned paper above a grained wooden dado and elaborate mirrors in gilt frames. The ceiling featured an attractive design in fibrous plaster in a geometrical pattern, and in the centre, a large chandelier, containing 50 gas burners, shed a flood of light on the auditorium.

The theatre was taken over in November 1896 by the new company, Kiernan Palaces of Varieties Ltd, of which James Kiernan was the managing director. Variety entertainment continued until 1907, during which time George Formby senior and many later famous artists appeared there early in their careers. Then stage plays replaced variety and continued until 1908, when a Sheffield photographer and cine showman, Jasper Reafern leased the theatre simultaneously with the Tivoli, Lime Street, opened concurrently on 21 December with similar entertainment, boasting: *Great Pictures and Class Vaudeville, twice-nightly at 6.50pm and 9pm.*

The reopening was attended by a large and enthusiastic audience, the programme was considered to be of great merit including high class pictures arranged by Redfern, among which *A Woman's Revenge* received special mention. Similar entertainment was continued by this lessee until 30 June 1910, after which the exhibition of films was arranged by the Weisker Bros.

In 1911 Kiernans Palaces of Varieties Ltd sold the theatre to the Dunn family. Peter Dunn, as managing director, marked a new lease of life as a cinema for the Park Palace, which was to last for almost 50 years, becoming Park Palace Kinematodrome. For a short time the films were supported by variety, but later it was pictures only, accompanied by a seven-piece orchestra. Then on 8 January 1930, the talkies arrived with the installation of the Western Electric Sound System, after which the orchestra was no longer required. After the death of Peter Dunn in 1934, the family continued to run the cinema and in 1941 his daughter, Sheila, became the managing director.

In 1955 attendances rapidly decreased to about 2,500 admissions weekly; 75% less than in the 1940s, and the cinema was running at a loss. The installation of CinemaScope in March 1956, opening with *Three Coins in the Fountain,* attracted some increase in patronage for a time, but television, especially commercial television, and to some extent bingo, all contributed to its eventual closure. The final programme, on 11 March 1959, consisted of *The Young Guns,* featuring Russ Tamblyn and *Hold Back the Night,* starring John Payne. Television and bingo had succeeded where Hitler had failed, in forcing the closure of the 66-year-old Park Palace. Since that time the building has been used as a chemist (1969), then a store for car spares. From 1984 it was the Mill Street Chapel.

1908
Bedford Hall • Bedford Cinema
Bedford Road, Walton

Having made a success of exhibitions of animated pictures at the Queen Hall in Birkenhead, in 1908 motion picture pioneer, JF Wood, embarked upon a new venture: the construction of Liverpool's first purpose-built cinema, the Bedford Hall. The frontage was mainly of brick, relieved by carved patterns in stone. Below the coping, a deep long panel displayed the cinema name in large white letters. In the centre a short flight of steps led up to the main arched entrance and a pair of glass-panelled doors with large poster sites at either side, whilst at the extreme sides were exits within archways at the head of a few steps. According to a reliable source the Bedford was designed by a Birkenhead architect, to provide seating for 1,200 people, including the small balcony. The stalls included forms (benches), which were replaced by seats in the early-1930s, explaining the decrease of the capacity to 1,100.

The Bedford Cinema, 1946.

The Bedford Hall was opened on 26 December 1908 by Bedford Cinemas Ltd, whose managing director was John F Wood. The cinema continued under this ownership until March 1928, when, together with several other cinemas of the company, it was acquired by the General Theatre Corporation, one of the companies amalgamated under GB. The name was then changed to the Bedford Cinema. The talkies arrived when a British Acoustic Sound System was installed for the opening, on 3 March 1930, of *On With The Show,* starring Betty Compson and Arthur Lake.

As a GB cinema, the Bedford screened the first run in the district of the company release films, becoming better attended than its opposition. A significant improvement was the construction of an extension at the left-hand side of the building, which provided a wide main entrance of terracotta and brick, flanked by still frames. Inset was a line of doors leading to a large foyer with appropriate 1930s super-cinema furnishings and fittings, including a central island paybox with a massive, overhanging, glass-shaded light fitting.

From June 1948 the proprietors were CMA, the new company formed by the amalgamation of the GB and Odeon circuits, under the control of J Arthur Rank. Despite the limited space for a wide screen, CinemaScope (minus stereophonic sound) was installed, starting on 25 April 1955 with *The Black Shield of Falworth,* starring Tony Curtis and Janet Leigh. The Bedford thereafter survived for a further 4 years of falling admissions, until closure on 23 May 1959, with *The Geisha Boy,* featuring Jerry Lewis, and *Hot Angel.* The building was sold to Abraham and Mitchell, a removal and storage firm, who continue to use it as a furniture storage depot.

1908
Westminster Hall Cinema • Doric Cinema
Smith Street, Kirkdale

The building, situated between Kirkdale Road and Westminster Road, was originally opened as a club and later converted into a small music hall by the well-known variety entrepreneurs, James Kiernan and Thomas Montgomery. It was reopened as the Westminster Music Hall on 11 April 1887. During the following year the auditorium was altered and enlarged to accommodate an audience of 650, including the balcony, with straight extensions along either side to the 26'-wide proscenium. The proscenium fronted the 25' deep stage, and five dressing rooms were also provided.

Live entertainment continued until 1908, when the Westminster was among the music halls acquired for the showing of the new animated pictures by Weisker Picture Palaces Ltd. In 1921 the theatre was taken over by the W Gordon cinema circuit of Cleckheaton, Yorkshire, who ran it for several years as the Westminster Hall Cinema. Following a period of closure there was a grand reopening on 4 April 1932, as the Doric Talkie Theatre, under the ownership of HE Radam, proprietor of the nearby Roscommon Cinema. The Doric opened with a matinee at 3pm, and evening performances at 6.40pm and 8.45pm, when the feature film was *The Criminal Code*, with Walter Huston. Admission prices were suitably low: 4d in the stalls, 6d and 9d in the circle, reduced to only 3d and 4d at the matinee.

It was claimed to be Kirkdale's 'Most Perfect Talkie Theatre', with sound equipment by the RCA Photophone System, the best procurable. The Doric continued as a cinema for about 9 years, but in 1941 it was amongst the many properties destroyed during air raids.

1909
Winter Gardens Theatre • Apollo Theatre
Pembroke Road, Bootle

Erected in the 1890s, the building was originally known as the Beaconsfield Hall. This was the Bootle Conservative Club, although it was usually referred to as the County Hall, the venue of many big social functions and concerts, including Poulson Penny Concerts. In 1909 the hall was taken over by the Suburban Entertainments Syndicate. The promoter, Ludwig Blattner, stated that he proposed to offer high class entertainment equal to any in the city. Arrangements were made to adapt the County Hall into a variety theatre to be known as the Winter Gardens, with comfortable seating for 490, including the small balcony. The Grand Opening on 4 May 1909 was attended by a large audience. The doors were opened at 7.30pm, for the performance of high class vaudeville entertainment at 8pm. This was greatly enhanced by the musical contribution of the renowned Hungarian violin virtuoso, Arnold Spiegler, the musical director and leader of the Bohemian Orchestra, which received repeated rounds of applause.

At this time, in the era of early silent films, a popular added attraction was the latest in animated pictures comprising the most up-to-date cinematograph films of both current events and entertainment. The admission prices for this programme were: 1/- in the orchestra stalls and other seats at 6d. For the next 2 years the Winter Gardens was run by several short term lessees who all presented variety with the added attraction of animated pictures. In April 1911 there was a change to purely theatrical entertainment, under JC Lodge-Percy. He reopened the theatre on Saturday 15 April, with the esteemed Charles Boult as resident manager to present Miss Joyce Marsden in the musical farce *The Girl from Chicago*.

Only 2 months later, the hall came under the direction of the new Apollo Syndicate and secured the services of Ludwig Blattner, who had been highly regarded for his successful initiation of variety entertainment at the theatre. Complete reseating and upgrading was instituted at the reopening on 19 June 1911, it became the Apollo Theatre. From this time the hall could be regarded as a cinema, since films were the main attraction. Advertised as the Electric Pictures, those chosen for the opening consisted of *A Tale of the Wild West*, also character and scenic pictures, latest productions of the Selig Vitagraph Co, Essanay and so on. But Blattner realised that good music was essential, and it was provided by La Scala Orchestra, with special praise accorded to ET Parcous, England's new violin virtuoso.

Coinciding with the coronation of King George V and Queen Mary, the reopening of the theatre was considered to be amongst the foremost of the many celebrations arranged in Bootle. In the following week the films included detailed coronation scenes, viewed by large enthusiastic audiences. Presenting films, excellent music and vocal artists, the Apollo's success continued under Ludwig Blattner's direction. His departure, in March 1914, was about 5 months prior to the outbreak of war in August and, being of German origin, his detention as an enemy alien. Thirteen years later he achieved greater distinction having bought the Neptune Film Studios at Elstree, where he formed the Blattner Film Corporation and developed the first known commercial sound recording system.

In March 1914 the Apollo came under the management of John Gaffney, with Samson Wellings as acting manager, who later became the lessee and manager. The Apollo was styled as the Home of Cinema and Music with films accompanied by the Apollo Orchestra, performances nightly at 8pm, and a children's cinematinee every Saturday at 3pm. Admission prices were: 3d, 6d and 10d (entertainment tax was extra). In June 1920 Wellings made an application to the local authorities for permission to construct a new projection room outside the main hall, so that, in addition to providing a slight increase in the seating, it would serve the more important purpose of protecting the public in the event of fire, always a danger due to the use of inflammable films. The improvements were only to be enjoyed for a short time, during the last 7 months of the Apollo under the control of a company which included Harry and Stanley Pennington, whose family was well-known locally for its establishment of the Royal Muncaster and Metropole Theatres.

The Apollo was taken over from Samson Wellings in December 1922, when it was announced that the entertainment policy would continue as previously. However, this proved to be short-lived, for the Apollo finally closed as a cinema on 22 July 1923, with the western, *The Strength of the Pines*, starring William Russell, with *Fireside Brewers* and *Eve Review*.

Structural alterations were carried out during August and September 1923, after which the building reverted to its former use and name, the County Hall. Opened in October 1923, it was stated to be the finest and most up-to-date hall in the district, available for receptions and dances in the large ballroom. The hall's chequered history ended abruptly in 1941 when it was severely damaged during an air raid, and remained partly demolished until 1950 when the site was cleared. For many years this has been occupied by part of St Winifred's Girls School playground, near Bootle Oriel Road Railway Station.

1909
Bijou Theatre • New Pavilion • Bijou Electric Palace • Bijou Cinema
East Street, Waterloo

Designed by Richard Waddington, the building was erected as a Methodist Chapel in 1840. It was the birthplace of many religious societies and churches of different denominations were nurtured within its walls. At the turn of the 19th century it became a Salvation Army HQ, after which, in the early-1900s, it was a venue of live entertainment – the East Street Assembly Rooms. In 1909 the buiding began a new lease of life when it was acquired by Weber, Son & Arnold who completely converted and redecorated the once dingy theatre. Three hundred seats were added, with red tip-up seats at the front, separated from the cheaper rear seats by a wooden partition.

The joint lessee, Arthur Weber, was an accomplished entertainer whose magnificent voice and musical skill had won him a reputation in places of much greater prominence than Waterloo, whilst Professor Weber mystified his audiences with his ventriloquism.

The opening of the district's first permanent live entertainment venue was a significant event in the quiet suburb and took place on Saturday 5 June 1909 at 8pm. Admission was 3d, 6d and 1/-, to the programme of variety entertainment and the contributions of Arthur and Professor Weber were the most vigourously applauded. Music was provided by an orchestra under the direction of Ernest Wilinski. Animated pictures on the cinematograph – *Coney Island at Night*, *A Convict's Comic Escape* and *A Sound Sleeper* – concluded the performance.

In 1910 the theatre was renamed the New Pavillion, under the brief control of the Empire Enterprise Company. The name Bijou was reinstated in 1912 by new lessee and manager William Eltoft, who ran it as a cinema, the Bijou Electric Palace, and later the Bijou Cinema. It thrived, despite being off the beaten track and its proximity to Queen's on South Road, which had become the leading cinema in the district. After William Eltoft's retirement, Walter Jackson became the cinema's last lessee and ran it until closure in November 1922. Brady's Taxi Cabs acquired the building and it later became a motorcycle repair business until the late-1980s, when it was demolished and the site used for new housing.

1909
New Picture Hall • Waterloo Picture Playhouse • Winter Gardens Cinema
Church Road, Waterloo

According to available information, the building was probably erected in the 1870s. It passed through many changes of use, the first being as a gymnasium in 1890 when it was owned by Alfred T Davies, political agent of Lloyd George, then MP for Caernarfon. Later it was a billiard hall, where various types of entertainment were held, until it became the district's first cinema in 1909. The cinema was to be run by lessees W Weber and Weisker Picture Palaces Ltd, the former was well-known locally and had appeared at the hall as host and entertainer in a series of concerts and legerdemain exhibitions.

The local press advertised the cinema as: 'New Entertainment for Waterloo and district, All Pictures superior and up-to-date at the New Picture Hall'. It opened on Monday 13 December 1909, starting promptly at 8pm. Admission prices were: side seats 3d, centre seats 6d, balcony (reserved seats only) 1/-, with children under 12 years 2d, 3d, and 6d, with a matinee every Saturday at 3pm, with specially reduced prices for children.

After about 2 months, the hall was closed and reopened by the same lessees, with a change of name to the Winter Gardens on 28 February 1910, when at 8pm, the World in Motion Entertainments was supported by live entertainers, comedians and dancers. The full admission prices were the same but the 1/- seats were in the front stalls, the pit stalls 6d, and the balcony 3d.

The Weisker lease terminated in April 1913 and the new lessees were the Waterloo Winter Gardens Co, and the cinema was managed by the experienced and enterprising Jack Wellings. The hall was closed on 28 July for one week for complete renovation, incorporating tasteful redecoration in shades of green, as well as new carpets and plush tip-up seats. An increase in the seating capacity to

The Winter Gardens Cinema, 1960s.

450 was achieved by moving back the stage to provide a larger stalls area, and the plans also included a lounge and bar. The management announced that only pictures of the highest class would be shown, with the support of live entertainment by artists who had made their reputations in vaudeville.

In response to numerous requests, the opening on Monday 5 May 1913 was *Monte Cristo*, an adaptation from Dumas' famous novel. The musical programme was provided by the Viennese Orchestra under the direction of Herr Weingarten. The Winter Gardens then reverted to its original, once-nightly policy at 8pm, later for some time running performances at 7pm and 9pm.

In February 1914 the cinema was under the new management of John Carr and from 20 April of that year it was acquired by new proprietors, Kinema (Waterloo) Ltd, who changed the name to the Waterloo Picture Playhouse. Regular live entertainment ceased in favour of a feature film supported by comedy and interest shorts and regular serials, among which the famous *Perils of Pauline* was included in 1916. By this time admission prices were: balcony 11d, stalls 7d, front stalls 4d. The policy of once-nightly at 8pm, with a Saturday matinee for children at 3pm, was kept.

After a further 8 years as a cinema, the building entered another phase of its long and varied history when the Playhouse closed on 29 July 1922, then showing the silent feature film *The Carnival of Truth* and the serial *The Lurking Devil*. The change to a live theatre, known by its former name, the Winter Gardens, was instigated by Frederick V Ross, a well-known local figure in variety entertainment. The theatre would be a venue for first class concert parties and light musical plays by the best companies, but no films.

To the plans of Liverpool architect Colin S Brothers, the outline of the old building was completely changed and modernised, and virtually rebuilt by contractors, JM Milestone and Son Ltd. Parallel with the length of the building, the long frontage to Church Road had three distinct elevations, the largest of these, in both width and height, to the left side. Three storeys included the stage block and large door for taking in scenery, whilst on the roof was a large name sign in neon tubes. Between this and the two-storey elevation at the opposite end of the frontage, a single storey splayed section provided the main entrance with two pairs of glass-panelled doors to the foyer.

The entire frontage, like the side elevation, was extremely plain, having a dull, white stone facing, without ornamentation and relieved only by numerous small windows. Shelter was provided by a full length metal and glass canopy. Extensive internal alterations increased the capacity from 450 to 650 by the construction of an entirely new straight fronted balcony, seating about 170 patrons with new entrances and exits. The stalls accommodation was increased to 480 by widening the lower part for the side gangways, the upper section of the walls being supported by plain columns.

At the reopening as the Winter Gardens Theatre on 22 September 1922, a large crowd assembled outside and the auditorium was soon filled to capacity, leaving many disappointed people outside. The ceremony was performed by Alderman TS Ashmole of Wallasey, who, during a short speech, congratulated the architect and builders on a wonderful transformation in only 7 weeks. He also congratulated Ross on his new venture and trusted that the high class of entertainment would be supported by local residents. Fittingly, the new theatre was inaugurated by a variety performance at 8pm entitled *Harry Leslie's Famous Nobodies*. Additional performances were to be presented at a Saturday matinee at 3pm and twice-nightly on Saturdays and bank holidays at 6.40pm and 8.40pm, to which admission was: 9d, 1/3 and 1/10.

This began the theatre's 9 year life, during which various types of live entertainment were presented. Apart from revues and variety during the late-1920s into the 1930s, many comic and dramatic plays were produced. Most notable were those of Edward Banstan's talented repertory company, whose attractions during two seasons in 1930 varied from Shakespeare's The Taming of the Shrew and King Lear, to the drama Interference and the hilarious Hawleys of the High Street. A variety show The First Army Follies ended on 28 June 1930, after which the theatre was closed until 4 August and reopened with The Road Show of 1930, advertised as: 'Everything that is best in vaudeville — performed by sixteen artistes'.

The year ended with a return visit of Sydney Monckton, Esme Lewis and full London company in the West End farces *Rookery Nook* and *Love at Second Sight*, after which, in January 1931, the last theatrical manager, Max Wakeman, instituted a twice-nightly entertainment season and reduced admission prices, continuing the previous entertainment policy.

The final closure as a theatre on 27 June 1931 was at the end of a week of nightly changed productions by the Godwin Opera Co. It was then announced that the Winter Gardens was to be closed for extensive redecoration and reconditioning, also to be equipped with BTP sound system for the reversion to a cinema, catching up with the latest craze, the talkies.

The new venture was under the management of Horace C Lewis, who had been connected for many years with both the exhibition and rental side of the cinema business, originally the managing director and chairman of the Alhambra Cinema of London Road. The Winter Gardens reopened as a cinema on 26 December 1931 with *Let Live and Laugh*, featuring Ronald Frankau, an appropriate choice since the star had appeared in 1930 on the theatre stage in his show *Cabaret Kittens*. The supporting programme consisted of the comedy *Interest*, and the *Newsreel*, to which the popular admission prices were: 7d, 9d and 1/3, at the two separate performance times of 6.30pm and 8.40pm. Sunday to Friday, the performances were continuous from 6.30pm and matinees were on Monday, Wednesday and Saturday at 3pm.

The use as a cinema was continued by Winter Gardens Talkie Theatre (1933) Ltd, with A J Willett as manager. For 20 years, from 1945, it was continued by the Heyes family, one of whose directors, Henry Derek Heyes, aged 21, was the youngest booking manager on Merseyside. Although a cinema for over 30 years, the stage was quite regularly used for the productions of the Waterloo and Crosby Amateur Operatic Society. These stopped in the early-1960s when the stalls seating was removed to accomodate 'beat' dances on weekend evenings, after bingo sessions had failed. With a flexible film booking policy, including a large proportion of X certificate horror films, changed three or four times weekly, as well as other attractions, the Winter Gardens survived as a family cinema for many years after many larger cinemas had closed. It was the last privately owned cinema in north Merseyside. Finally, rising costs, dwindling audiences and stiff competition from the remaining circuit cinemas, resulted in the closure of the Winter Gardens, after almost 56 years as a place of entertainment. The final performance was the matinee on 4 September 1965, showing The Train, with Burt Lancaster. Although the building had been offered for sale to the local authorities, it lay unused until 1982, when it was acquired by the Kingsway Christian Fellowship. The entire frontage was then demolished and replaced by the present one of red brick with the entrance way projecting forward at the extreme left, leaving only the reconstructed former cinema auditorium beneath the original roof. The building was opened as a new church centre in April 1983 and remains in this use to date.

1910
Coliseum Picturedrome • New Coliseum
Paddington

Originally opened in 1890 as the Paddington Palace of Varieties, this small music hall was in Edge Hill, about a mile from the city centre. It was constructed lengthwise to Paddington, with a tall, gabled frontage to Upper Mason Street, in brick relieved by stone, with a glass and metal canopy along both elevations, necessary in view of a lack of internal waiting space. A small venue, a year after opening it was enlarged to accomodate 650. In the centre of the fontage, the main entrance gave access to a small, rectangular foyer with stalls entrance opposite and white marble balustraded stairway on the left. The stairs led up to the small gallery at the rear of the auditorium, which narrowed towards the front, with boxes at either side of the tall, slim proscenium.

The theatre was opened by enterprising music hall owner James Kiernan, on 2 September 1890. Performances were at 7pm and 9pm, with admission at: 1/- and 1/6 for the best seats, 6d for the orchestra stalls, 4d for the pit seats and 3d for the gallery.

In November 1896 a new company used a capital of £90,000 in shares to take over, from Kiernan, the Paddington Palace, the Park Palace and the Sefton Palace, as well as his United Kingdom musical and dramatic agency. Due to Kiernan's reputation in the sphere of music hall, the new company retained the name Kiernan's Palaces of Variety Ltd and Kiernan agreed to remain as managing director for 10 years, precluding him from taking any such position elsewhere.

The Paddington continued successfully into the early-1900s, when there was a gradual change in public taste towards legitimate theatre. Accordingly, in 1906 a change was made to twice-nightly dramatic plays. In 1910 it was one of several former music halls to become a cinema, the Coliseum Picturedrome, leased by Weisker's Picture Palaces Ltd. They terminated the lease in 1919, the cinema continuing under the control of the Coliseum (Liverpool) Ltd.

Temporarily closed in 1926, it was then acquired by the Regent Enterprise circuit of Stanley Street, Liverpool. Extensive alterations included the removal of the theatre boxes and replacement of the gallery by a waiting room, with two entrances into the new, 300-seat balcony which extended over the stalls to half the auditorium length, increasing the capacity to 876.

The Grand Opening as the New Coliseum Picture House took place on 18 November 1926. The company emphasised the new improvements, boasting a comfortable balcony. The matinee was at 2.45pm, with continuous performances from 6.40pm to 10.45pm, with the feature film *His People,* featuring Joseph Schildkraut. Admission was: balcony 1/-, stalls 6d, pit stalls 4d, reduced to 6d, 4d and 3d respectively at matinees.

In 1935 the last change of ownership was to ABC. During the peak cinema admissions of the 1940s, performances were continuous from about 2pm, with double feature programmes plus *Pathé News*, to which admission was only 7d, 10d and 1/6. The films were the last on the circuit. Strong competition in the early-1950s reduced performances to evenings only. CinemaScope was installed on 3 October 1955, commencing with *Bad Day at Black Rock,* starring Spencer Tracy. Due to the narrow proscenium, the picture was shown with reduced height.

The New Coliseum was among the first three cinemas closed by ABC in 1956. The final programme on 8 December was *Miracle in the Rain*, starring Jane Wyman, and also the *Square Jungle*. The building was not reused and was later demolished.

1910
Moulton Picture Palace • Tivoli Cinema
Roscommon Street, Everton

Originally a small public hall known as Moulton Hall, it was converted for use as a stadium-type cinema with a 25' proscenium, small stage, and seating capacity of 700. Councillor John Walker was granted the first cinematograph licence on 5 April 1910. In 1920 the cinema was leased by the circuit Haigh and Son, whose managing director, Edwin Haigh, was also a director of the city Futurist and Scala cinemas. He was also the founder and first chairman of the Cinematograph Exhibitors Association in Liverpool, and a city councillor. It was then closed for complete renovation, reseating and the installation of an up-to-date heating system.

During the late-1920s films were occasionally supported by variety and despite its comparatively humble status as a cinema, in 1929 it was one of the few halls outside the city to install sound equipment (RCA Photophone System). The opening as the Tivoli Talkie Theatre was on 9 December 1929 with *The Singing Fool,* starring Al Jolson. Following the termination of Haigh and Son's lease, the lessee became Alfred Levy, managing director of the company which controlled the city's Futurist and Scala cinemas. In 1930 the cinema was operated by NTP Ltd. In the early-1940s there was a final change of ownership to B and S (Bateman and Speakman) Cinemas (Lancs) Ltd, whose managing director was WJ Speakman. The Tivoli was run by this company until 16 January 1954, when the last film was *Sorry, Wrong Number,* with Barbara Stanwyck. It was later demolished during the redevelopment of the area.

1910
Garston Picture Palace • Wellington Picture Palace
Wellington Street, Garston

From 1867 the building was a church for the English Congregationalists, and in 1889 it was also a monthly Petty Sessions Court. A Penny Savings Bank was established in 1880, which was open in the building on Saturday evenings. A music, singing, dancing and other public entertainments licence was granted on 27 October 1903. Following annual renewals, this was granted in September 1909 to Roger Abel, contractor and secretary of the Garston Reading and Lecture Room. Apparently Abel became the licensee with the intention of showing films, although this is unconfirmed, but he did apply for a cinematograph licence on the first day that they were issued, 11 January 1910. Prior to the Cinematograph Act of 1909, films were shown at various locations, including cafés in town, irrespective of suitability and without appropriate alterations. The premises then became known as the Wellington Picture Palace, where between 5 May and 6 June 1912, alterations were carried out, details of which are not available. On 22 January 1913, plans were received by the City Building Surveyors Department for a proposed new projection room, as well as a men's toilet. Permission was granted and the work was carried out under the supervision of Roger Abel, between 28 April and December 1913. The gallery was closed to the public, and the existing projection box was removed and replaced by a new one on the ground floor at the rear of the 338-seat hall.

The Wellington Picture Palace remained open under the direction of several proprietors, with an annual change, until 31 October 1918, when Edmund Houghton's licence expired and was not renewed because the city surveyor considered that the building was unsuitable for the purpose. The property was next used in 1921 as the Garston Citizen Institute. The following year saw the beginning of a long period of use as a location for clubs – 1922-1925 the Reading Room Men's Club, 1926-1938 the St Michael's Church Club and from 1939, the Garston Boys' Club, located there until the early-1960s. After later reversion to a reading room, the interior was renovated as a commercial centre.

1910
Garston Picturedrome • Rink Cinema
Heald Street, Garston

Due to the roller skating craze which reached its peak in 1909, the Garston Skating Rink Co was formed for the purpose of erecting a suitable building in Heald Street. On behalf of the company, local architect, T Townson, submitted plans to the City Building Surveyor, which were approved on 19 October 1909. George Atkin was managing director and the shareholders seven local tradesmen. Atkin applied for a music and other public entertainments licence on 11 January 1910, but the application was withdrawn as the building was not ready, on the understanding that another application could be made at the next sessions in March. The successful application was dated 24 May, when the architect was Robert Wylie, and on or about that date, the skating rink opened.

After a few months, the roller skating craze having ended, Atkin applied for a cinematograph licence, for which a second application was successful on 27 September 1910. The interior had then been converted into the Garston Picturedrome; a stadium-type auditorium with a seating capacity of 586, for performances of pictures and variety. Between 2 and 10 May 1912, alterations to increase the seating capacity, were carried out by J Williams, who was either the owner or the builder. At this time the Picturedrome was also known as the Rink Cinema. Nearly 3 years later, under the ownership of the Garston Empire Ltd, the capacity was again increased, to 886, by 20 August 1921.

The cinematograph licence expired on 31 October 1923, and was not renewed, the cinema closed on or just before that date, marking the end of the building's use as a cinema. It continued to be associated with leisure activities for which a dancing, music singing and other public entertainments licence was granted on 14 December 1923, for the new enterprise opened as the Winter Gardens. The proprietors, Winter Gardens (Garston) Ltd, 19 Castle Street, operated the dance hall until the early-1940s, but in 1943 it was closed, and the building used as an ARP depot. Retaining the name Winter Gardens, it was reopened for dancing in October 1950 by the Garston and District Co-op Society Ltd, 80 St Mary's Road, Garston, and remained open for this purpose until November 1966. Plans were submitted on 11 January 1967 for conversion into a discount store, the Garston and District Co-op Society. By April 1982 the building was sold with vacant possession, and the following year it became a Government YTS centre. Since 1993, the building has become the property of a furniture manufacturers.

1910
Electric Picture Palace
Bridge Road, Litherland

The premises was erected as a furniture auction room by Peter Blackburn, who founded the auctioneers continued by Outhwaite and Litherland. The assembly rooms served two main purposes: to conduct regular sales of furniture by auction and to provide a spacious room for mission services by Peter Blackburn, who, as well as being an auctioneer and estate agent, had considerable talent as an evangelistic preacher. Meetings of various kinds were also held there and it was frequently used for live entertainment, until 1910, when the building was acquired by the popular proprietor, William Allert. He formed the Electric Picture Palace Co, and expended much care and money in renovation; fitting tip-up chairs, electric lighting and a modern heating system. Every fire precaution was taken, principally by siting outside the main hall the latest bioscope, which apparently produced a picture of maximum clarity with the minimum of audible machine noise.

The opening of the Electric Picture Palace took place on Saturday 17 December 1910, with a programme of first class entertainment, including guest appearance by Madame Georgina Johnson, late of the Geosen Opera Co. The manager, WJ Moxon, who 3 years later was to become the popular, long-serving manager of Seaforth's new cinema, the Palladium, was congratulated on having secured an excellent film programme. The performances began with a 3pm matinee, followed by evening performances at 7pm and 9pm. There was to be a matinee each Wednesday, at popular prices of 3d and 6d, with a change of programme every Monday and Thursday. The cinema soon become a favourite rendezvous due to the high standard of the programmes.

Although in November 1912 advertisements in the local press implied great success, a fall in numbers was indicated by the fact that performances had been reduced to once-nightly at 8pm and matinee on Saturdays only. At that time a third admission price of 9d was introduced. The Electric Palace proved to be Liverpool's shortest surviving cinema for, after little more than 2 years, it was destroyed by fire in the early hours of Sunday 13 July 1913.

1910
Kensington Picturedrome • Kensington Cinema
Kensington

Kensington Cinema, photographed when vacant in 1977.

Although the trade press *Kinematograph & Lantern Weekly,* in December 1910, said this was another cinema added to Liverpool's lengthy list, it was nevertheless only the second purpose-built cinema, erected exactly 2 years after the opening of the Bedford Hall, Walton.

The plaster-faced facade had a central main entrance, with two pairs of glass-panelled doors below a substantial metal and glass verandah, which extended full width of the frontage. This was surmounted by the imposing architectural feature of a massive dome, supported by columns. The stadium-type auditorium was described as effectively decorated, with tip-up seats fitted throughout to seat 1,050. The plans included special kitchen arrangements to serve tea to patrons of the 6d and I/- seats at the matinees.

The enterprise of the Liveroool Picturedrome Ltd, the cinema opened under the management of Rex Dooley on 26 December 1910. Performances were at 3pm, 7pm and 9pm, with admission prices at 3d, 6d and I/-.

The expensive installation of Liverpool's only 'Mirroroide' screen was announced in December 1910. Having a mercury quicksilver amalgam surface, it was claimed to provide not only the largest picture in Liverpool, but also the most brilliantly illuminated.

In 1914 the Picturedrome was taken over by the Weisker Bros, film renters and exhibitors at Kinema House, London Road, Liverpool. The cinema was later run by the proprietor and resident manager, Mrs Dooley. In 1920 it became one of the four cinemas controlled by the North-Western Film Booking Agency, also known as the Dovenor Booking Circuit. This was formed by Leo and Fred Weisker in association with John Hickman Dovenor, who was also a pioneer of the film trade in Liverpool. By the outbreak of war in 1914, his son, John Reginald Dovenor, was also actively engaged with the Kensington. After the cessation of hostilities, following a period of management at the Palais de Luxe, Liverpool, as a partner in the company, he then controlled an important group of Merseyside cinemas.

As at the company's other cinemas, in 1930, BTH sound system was installed, and on 2 June the Kensington advertised – 'The Talkies are Here!' presenting Gloria Swanson's first 'All-Talking Dramatic Sensation' – The Trespasser. From 1923, the nearby larger and more modern Casino, a GB cinema from 1928, had provided strong opposition. The Picturedrome was re-named the Kensington Cinema in 1937, and screened alternative products, including many ABC circuit releases with normally single feature programmes twice-nightly and daily matinees.

The showing of CinemaScope films began on 27 June 1955, with River of No Return starring Marilyn Monroe and Robert Mitchum. The cinema survived for 3^1/$_2$ years of generally decreasing patronage until closure on 6 December 1958, then showing Wonderful Things starring Frankie Vaughan, and also Johnny Bravo featuring Clint Walker. The building was sold to a television sales company, Stuart and Dorfman, but was later used as an amusement arcade. The premises are currently a public house and restaurant.

1911
Sefton Park Picturedrome
Smithdown Road, Wavertree

The building was built as stables for horses pulling the city tramcars before electrification. It was converted into a small stadium-type auditorium with seating for about 300, of mostly forms with a few tip-up seats at the rear. Admission prices were originally 1d and 3d. It was among the halls leased by the Weisker Bros, to whom the first cinematograph licence was issued on 11 January 1911. The silent films were shown with musical accompaniment by Miss Allison Holden, pianist and violinist, and in 1915 sound affects appropriate to the action of the film were provided by the Linlater Bros, well-known for this novelty attraction. In August of that year the trade press reported that the Picturedrome was the enterprise of Sydney, who was congratulated upon the completion of the artistic renovations.

The lease and management of the Picturedrome was taken up c1917 by Will Hughes, who ran it until March 1928 when it was acquired by Denman Picture Houses Ltd, one of the companies which formed the GB Picture Corporation. Hughes was then appointed as general manager of the Palladium, Southport, also a GB cinema which had come under the control of the GTC. Apparently the Picturedrome did not measure up to the standards of GB, both for reasons of size and scope for improvement, and not surprisingly, in 1929, it was the first of the company's new acquisitions in Liverpool to close. The interior was converted for use as a penny bazaar, but later, as a DIY store for many years. A horse's head remains on the frontage to provide a reminder of its original purpose.

The Sefton Park Picturedrome as DIY store, 1974.

27

1911
Sun Hall • Imperial Cinema
Stanley Road, Bootle

The building was erected in the 1890s, mainly for religious purposes, by Richard Waddington, but was also used for public meetings and various other functions. It became known as the Sun Hall, and although still available as a public hall, seasons of animated pictures began in 1906, presented by film producer and showman, Sidney Prince. It was first advertised in the *Bootle Times* on 1 June of that year. The Whitsun attraction was described as: '40 miles of pictures with talking pictures including The Train Wreckers, also Pictures Dramatic and Comic never before shown in the annals of Animated Photography'.

At that time, several years before sound-on-disc, the talking was provided from behind the scenes by a man who read the film's story as it was shown and also provided all the sound effects. There were pictures of the May Day procession and the occasion was attended by the Mayor and Mayoress of Bootle, Dr and Mrs RE Roberts. The pictures were supported by the Prince Edward choristers who rendered telling vocal accompaniment with grand organ effects. Performances were nightly at 8pm, and a matinee at 3pm on Whit Monday and Tuesday. Admission prices were: back seats 2d, chairs 4d, balcony 6d, reserved seats 1/-, and for children, a matinee every Saturday at 3pm, admission 2d and 3d.

The seasons of Sidney Prince pictures continued with great success, and the Sun Hall became known as the home of animated pictures. This was justified to an even greater extent in March 1911, when it became a permanent cinema under the ownership of Sidney Prince's successor, George Prince, also a picture pioneer whose period of control totalled almost 40 years. During the week beginning 5 March 1911, the feature film *The Blue Bird* was described in the local press as a magnificent production of the charming fairy story. When he acquired the Royal Muncaster Theatre, Irlam Road, Bootle, which he reopened as the New Prince Theatre in August 1912, Prince declared that it would in no way interfere with the Sun Hall. However, he was forced to announce its closure on 28 March 1914, due to greatly increasing film rental charges. He then concentrated his attention on his increasingly popular Prince's Theatre.

Lovers of cinematograph entertainment were pleased to learn that the cinema was shortly to reopen with the highest possible expectations of success, under the ownership of J Leslie Greene, a well-known local journalist, who had been interested in cinematography from the birth of the art, and who was, in every sense, an expert on the subject. Sun Hall was reopened on Saturday 4 April 1914, by popular demand, after complete redecoration and new seating arrangements. The exclusive opening attraction, *Detective Finn*, at a very high rental, was advertised as one of the most sensational dramas to have taxed cinematographic ingenuity. Supporting this, a number of the latest dramas, comedies and scenic subjects made up an attractive programme with musical accompaniment by Arthur Davies' Orchestra, under P Jordan, with performances at 3pm and 8pm.

The cinema continued under the control of J Leslie Greene until February 1922, when he became managing director of a syndicate which took over Bootle Metropole. The Bootle Cinema Co was then formed, with £28,000 capital, to acquire the Sun Hall and the four shops and offices on the Stanley Road frontage. The principal directors were John Henry Liptrott of the Victoria super-cinema in Anfield as chairman, and Alfred Smith, director of several North West cinemas, as managing director.

The company prospectus was published on 24 February 1922, giving local people the first opportunity of subscribing to the new venture by the purchase of 28000 shares at £1 each. The experienced new directors stated their intention to continue the showing of the same class of films, and J Leslie Greene agreed to act as booking agent for 5 years. There was another change of ownership in December 1922, when the cinema, together with the Apollo in Bootle, was acquired by the Bootle Cinemas and Entertainment Syndicate, whose directors included Harry Pennington, former proprietor of the Metropole Theatre.

Early in the New Year of 1923, they decided upon a change of name from the Sun Hall to the Imperial Cinema, and in September of that year, George Prince, after 9 years, resumed his connection in the position of managing director of the company. Following his first installation in the district of sound equipment by Western Electric at the Palace Cinema, Bootle in July 1929, George Prince similarly equipped the Imperial for the opening on 2 December of *The Singing Fool,* starring Al Jolson. There were three performances daily: 2.45pm, 6.30pm and 8.45pm.

In order to satisfy demand for higher standards of comfort, the proprietors of the Imperial instituted, in January 1931, an extensive scheme of internal structural alterations. AO Chatterley was the architect, and the structural work and decorations were carried out by George Parr Ltd, Stanley Road, Bootle. Although resulting in a decrease in seating to 785, the removal of the balcony sides provided an uninterrupted view for the entire audience and gave the impression of greater spaciousness. A new stage and 40'-wide proscenium were constructed, the latter having a curtain of tangerine silk trimmed with blue, whilst the front of the stage was given a colourful jazz effect, and 9' oak panelling to conform with that around the walls. The walls above were in blue with panels in flame colour between the pilasters, above which the ceiling curved to the central straight section. Colours of cream and buff were selected for the ceiling, and at the front of the auditorium, an effective sunray design surmounted the proscenium. At either side was an Indian window, all brightly lit. In order to produce a restful atmosphere, an indirect lighting system was provided by glass shades suspended from the ceiling, and in addition, individual light shades on the walls created a warm glow. An important innovation for the comfort of patrons was a new waiting room in the basement, with room for 500 people. The walls were in buff colour and the woodwork dark brown.

The costly alterations and improvements resulted in increased patronage, and the Imperial entered the1930s as one of the premier local places of entertainment. During that decade, competition increased from the cinemas of the major circuits ABC and GB, the Imperial then having to rely to a great extent on B movies from producers such as Republic and Monogram, not booked by the circuits. However, 'House Full' signs were quite regular during the showings of British films starring Gracie Fields and George Formby, which were then ignored by the circuits.

At the time of generally decreasing audiences in the 1950s, George Prince, the picture pioneer, still remained in control of the Imperial and the nearby Palace, Marsh Lane. He had been the first to bring the talkies to Bootle, and at this difficult time, especially for independent cinemas, he quickly seized the opportunity to secure the leading first run films. He achieved this by taking up Twentieth Century-Fox's offer to supply their CinemaScope films to any exhibitor who agreed to install the complete equipment, including magnetic stereophonic sound and the Mirroroid screen. Over a month before the nearby Essoldo, Litherland, the Imperial began a long run of Twentieth Century-Fox CinemaScope films on 12 September 1954, with *The Robe*.

The novelty of the much wider screen was not particularly long lasting and the Imperial finally succumbed to circuit opposition, where CinemaScope minus stereophonic sound except for the Essoldo, had been installed by the end of 1954. The Imperial survived until 1959 when it was among the many cinema closures. The final performance on 7 March was not by CinemaScope, being *Kings Go Forth* featuring Frank Sinatra, Tony Curtis and Natalie Wood. Bootle Council acquired the premises, including shops and offices on Stanley Road from the proprietors, Bootle Amusements Ltd, in 1960, at a cost of £11,350. With plans for conversion into a public hall, also to be used for dances, an application was made for a £25,190 loan from the Ministry of Housing and Local Government. The application was refused and the only subsequent use of the building was as a DIY store with frontage in the former cinema's main entrance. Towards the end of the 1970s the building was demolished.

1911

Electra Palace • London Road Picture House • Alhambra • King's Picture House • Essoldo • Curzon Club Cinema • Tatler Club Cinema • Classic • Eros Club Cinema
London Road, Liverpool city centre

This cinema, with the distinction of the greatest number of name changes on Merseyside, originated as a stadium-type hall, which although quite narrow, was considered to be quite deep, providing a picture throw of 98'. Outside, the tall, London Road frontage was of red brick relieved by stonework around a large advertising display panel. Under a canopy, the almost full width entrance had a white tiled floor and several doors giving access to the medium-sized foyer.

The first cinematograph licence was granted to Tarton on 29 May 1911, and on 30 May the cinema opened with the name Electra Palace. Performances were continuous from 2pm to 10.30pm, with admission prices 3d, 6d and 1/- and children at half price. Musical accompaniment was by the Blue Hungarian Band and, like many other cinemas, patrons of the 6d and 1/- seats were served with tea free of charge.

The opening in that part of the city in June 1914 of the Majestic Picture House provided strong competition, but despite this it was reported in December of that year that the Electra continued to be well attended. A change of proprietor occurred in 1917 to John Henry Phillips, and a few years later it was known as the London Road Picture House, under the ownership of the company of the same name, who renamed it the Alhambra. This name was retained until 1932 when the cinema was taken over by Regent Enterprises Ltd, whose circuit office was at 1-3 Stanley Street, Liverpool. Liverpool architects, Gray and Evans, drew up plans for the partial reconstruction of the hall at a cost of £15,000, including reseating, refurbishment and redecoration. Capacity was increased from 580 to 820 by reconstruction of the auditorium in which an unused upper floor was removed and replaced by a concrete balcony with 290 seats, whilst the stalls were altered to seat 530. The work was completed in about 4 months, and with a new name – the King's – it was styled as Liverpool's latest luxury theatre.

The grand reopening, in the presence of the Lord Mayor of Liverpool, Alderman JC Cross, took place on Thursday 13 October 1932, at 2.45pm. The film was *The Silent Voice* featuring George Arliss with a supporting programme. Performances thereafter were continuous from 12.45pm. Admission prices were: balcony 1/3, stalls 1/- and front stalls eight and a half pence. Despite the considerable improvements, due to the strength of competition from the major circuits in the city centre, to which was added the new Majestic in 1937, the King's was not among Liverpool's best attended cinemas. Bookings were later runs of the circuit release films and B films, a policy which of necessity was continued from March 1938 by the Southan Morris cinema circuit. The Newcastle-based Essoldo circuit gave its name to the cinema on takeover in October 1954, and the following year installed CinemaScope, thereby securing second runs in the city of Twentieth Century-Fox releases, beginning on 30 May 1955 with *Broken Lance*, starring Spencer Tracy. Before the end of the decade, the dispute between Fox and the Rank Organisation having been settled, the Fox releases were again booked by Odeon and GB, the Essoldo then reverting to its former type of programmes, but with the addition of many off circuit X certificate films.

Essoldo closed the cinema on 1 April 1972, with *Chisum* featuring John Wayne, and *Cosa Nostra* with *Arch Enemy of the FBI*, opening again on 4 April as the Curzon Club Cinema, showing uncensored films. The Tatler Club Cinema transferred from its Church Street location from 22 December 1972, and continued until 18 November 1979, after which the hall was run by the Classic circuit with X certificate double feature programmes until 24 August 1980. Uncensored films then returned for the final 12 months as the Eros Club Cinema until August 1981, when it was closed by the council because of the type of films being shown. Several years later the building was demolished.

The Eros Club Cinema, photographed soon after closure in 1981.

1911
Adelphi Picture Palace • New Adelphi Cinema
Christian Street, Liverpool city centre

As a location for entertainment the site dates back to 1795, when the Christian Street Circus was opened. Later, in 1805 it was known as the Olympic Circus and then the Adelphi Theatre in 1862, which was a venue for drama until early in the century. After use by the Liverpool Gymnastic Club from c1906, the interior was converted into the 650-seat Adelphi Picture Palace, for which a cinematograph licence was granted on 1 August 1911 to a Mrs A Tarshish, whose husband was the proprietor of the Roscommon Picture Palace. By 1920 Mrs Tarshish had become the proprietor. At that time the admission prices were among the lowest, being only between 3d and 5d.

The building was demolished in 1921 and replaced by a larger cinema named the New Adelphi, with a seating capacity of 1,134 and a proscenium of 40' width. The plaster faced frontage had a central main entrance, above which the principal first floor windows were surmounted by the cinema's name and year of erection. The New Adelphi was opened on or about the date of the licence, 13 February 1922. The Adelphi was sold in July 1929 to Mortimer Dent of Standard Cinema Properties, Birmingham, shortly after he had disposed of his considerable cinema circuit in the Midlands to ABC.

In the early-1930s British Acoustics Sound System was installed, and the cinema continued under this ownership until 1936, then acquired by Byrom Cinemas Ltd, 1 Stanley Street Liverpool, who, in 1936, had taken over the Prince of Wales cinema in the city from ABC. The Adelphi continued under this ownership until 1941, when the building was destroyed during an air raid.

1911
Prince's Picture Palace • Prince's Picturedrome • Prince's Picture Hall • Lytton Cinema
Lytton Street, Everton

The situation of this small cinema was inconspicuous, being midway along Lytton Street, between Everton Road and Radcliffe Street. The painted, plaster faced frontage was relieved by several first floor windows above the central main entrance. Therein, two pairs of glass-panelled doors led into the small, rectangular foyer from which two entrances gave access to the 580-seat stadium-type auditorium. There was a 6' stage for live entertainment and one dressing room. Whilst the building's origin is obscure, it can be confirmed that c1911 the proprietor was George Prince, then well-known as Bootle's picture pioneer, due to his seasons of pictures at the Sun Hall. He named his new venture the Prince's Picture Palace, later the Prince's Picture Hall, and then, in 1915, the Prince's Picturedrome, before the final name change to the Lytton Cinema in 1918, under the ownership of the company of the same name.

In 1929 it was sold to Arthur Dolan who presented pictures and variety. The cinema continued as a family concern retaining the company's name, Lytton Cinema (1918) Ltd, by whom a BTH Sound System was installed c1930. The Lytton was the smallest of Liverpool's independents, where CinemaScope was installed in 1955 to show Twentieth Century-Fox releases. These were shown in the new wide screen format which began on 4 April with *The Robe*, when for the first time the cinema advertised in the local press. With the inclusion of *The Fox* and other CinemaScope films, the Lytton, surprisingly for a cinema of such modest size, remained open until 1959, despite strong nearby opposition from Rank Hippodrome. At some time later the building was demolished.

1911

Prince Picturedrome

Myrtle Street, Liverpool city centre

Proprietor – Picturettes (Liverpool) Ltd. Seating capacity – 750. Opened – c1911 (pictures only). Closed – c1916.

1911

Roscommon Picture Palace • Roscommon Cinema

Roscommon Street, Everton

Roscommon Music Hall, named after the street where it was built, was converted in 1892 from two spacious dwellings to a small music hall, under the supervision of a Mr Tomkinson. The auditorium seated 600 people comfortably on forms on the ground floor, and in excess of that number, in a lesser degree of comfort, seating was available for an admission price of 3d. The red upholstered balcony seats, with backs, cost 6d. For 1/- patrons could have a seat in one of the two attractive and comfortable boxes at either side of the stage, with white colourings and white lace curtains. The ceiling and walls were painted in bright colours, and the Liverpool coat of arms appeared above the decorative proscenium. The orchestra pit accommodated eight members and the stage area, 30' by 20', included up-to-date requirements such as gas, lime-light and commendable drop scenes.

The theatre was opened by Mr Tomkinson, on 16 May 1892 as the Roscommon Music Hall. It was said to be the latest of the working class variety theatres, and its low prices suited local people, who could not afford a visit to the more prestigious city centre theatres.

Early in the century the hall became known as King's Theatre of Varieties with Frank Calden as manager for the lessee. In 1907 music hall entertainment was continued for a short time under Frederick Wilmott, who was part owner, as well as a performer, doing a star turn as an Irish comedian. Wilmott later made a change to twice-nightly drama, preferred by the majority of patrons. Dramatic plays were continued until 1911, when the growing popularity of silent films resulted in its reopening as the Roscommon Picture Palace, commencing a considerably longer phase in the over 60 years of the hall. As a cinema it continued under the ownership of Tarshish, who was also the proprietor of the Adelphi Picturedrome, Christian Street.

The Roscommon underwent extensive alterations in 1915 to make it more suitable for a cinema. There was a change of ownership c1920 to G Wilson, who was the proprietor and resident manager, opening for two performances of the films, changed twice-weekly. Wilson was succeeded as proprietor by HE Radam, of Princes Road, Liverpool, who booked films for the Roscommon and for the Doric Cinema, Everton, which he also owned.

In the early-1930s the Roscommon was equipped with BTP Sound System and continued during the decade, under the control of Radam, to maintain the policy of the Roscommon from its theatre days. Entertainment was provided at very low prices, from 3d to 6d. In the early-1940s, the Roscommon Cinema was taken over by the small circuit B and S Cinemas Ltd, of which the managing director was WJ Speakman, whose leading Liverpool cinema was the Capitol, Edge Hill. Their regime ended suddenly due to severe fire damage to the auditorium during an air raid in 1941, after which the cinema was closed until 1947, then reopened by Duncan Entertainments Ltd, London.

After repairs and refurbishment, as well as reseating the auditorium almost to its original capacity of 600, low prices were maintained at 7d to 1/3. At the reopening of the Roscommon admissions were at their peak, and although these decreased annually in the 1950s, the cinema survived against strong opposition. However, the final show was on 13 December 1958, when the feature film was the CinemaScope western *White Feather*, with supporting film *Overnight Haul*. The building was used by a firm of construction engineers before demolition during major redevelopment of the area.

1912
Premier Picture Palace
Smithdown Road, South Liverpool

Proprietor – ML Monkhouse. Seating capacity – c500. Ground floor of former billiard hall converted to cinema. Licence granted – 18 April 1912. Performances – Continuous from 7pm to 10.45pm. Matinee daily at 3pm. Admission prices – 5d to 1/-. Opened – c1912. Closed – c1924

1912
Lathom Hall Picture Palace
Lathom Avenue, Seaforth

A long, narrow building, built in 1884, which, for many years was Seaforth's only social centre. In June 1912 it was announced in the local press that in order to exhibit motion pictures, the hall had been transformed into the most elaborate picture palace in the district. The auditorium walls were buff-coloured, contrasting with the comfortable seats and lounges in blue plush. Electric lighting was installed and, during performances, subdued light was provided by shaded globes. For the safety of patrons, an entirely fireproof operating box was made to comply with the Cinematograph Act of 1909.

On the Saturday evening of 8 June 1912, at the Lathom Hall Picture Palace, with seating for over 200, a large audience witnessed the opening performance, arranged by proprietor and manager GH Sewell. The varied programme included: *A Red Cross Martyr* (a story of the war in Tripoli), *The Last of the Cartrouche Gang*, *Burglar Proof Villa* and *Her Saint's Day*, comedies with piano accompaniment and songs by Miss E Dunville.

The popular prices were: 1/-, 6d and 3d, children half price, for whom there was also a Saturday matinee at 2.30pm. The motto of the management: 'Come once and you're a regular patron', was justified by the fact that the hall was regularly crowded for the twice-weekly change, Monday and Thursday, of pictures.

Although until near the end of 1913 it was the only cinema in Seaforth, the Lathom Hall nevertheless had a rather short life, closing in 1916 under the ownership of GR Lloyd. The building was later used as a factory by the Icilma Face Cream Co and as a stained glass windows workshop. During World War II it was a NAAFI storeroom and after the war, a school kitchen. Conversion into a dance hall took place in the 1950s, but disorder in February 1958 resulted in its closure. The hall was later used as a Royal Naval Association club, and in the 1990s became another club, The Lathom.

1912
Picture House • Broadway Cinema
Stanley Road, Bootle

The exterior and interior of the Broadway Picture House, Bootle, photographed in 1912.

The building was originally designed as a roller skating rink, which was opened in 1909 by P Alberti, managing director of the Bootle Roller Rink and Public Hall Co, who had anticipated a great demand in the borough for the sport, following its success at the Ardwick Palace, Manchester. But the venture was short lived, and in 1912 a syndicate, The Bootle Picture Palace Ltd, acquired the building. They spent about £2,000 on extensive alterations and furnishings to convert the hall into what was described as one of the finest and most luxurious picture houses in the provinces, including a billiard hall at the rear, containing 26 tables.

The stone built frontage, spanned by a shallow gable, had a wide central main entrance with supporting square columns, beyond which a broad vestibule gave access via four pairs of glass-panelled doors to the spacious high-ceilinged foyer and central island paybox. From this, two short flights of stairs with ornamental balustrades led up to two pairs of doors to the rear of the 1,200 seat stadium-type auditorium. This extravagant venue was described as a feast of art, decoration and luxurious comfort, with upholstered seats of red plush in the grand lounge and stalls, arranged in three sections across the hall, with the front stall seats separated by a crossover gangway. Supporting an elaborately carved frieze along the side walls was a line of white fluted columns, beyond which were unusually wide gangways, formerly used as lounges, from which people watched the skaters. Due to the large dimensions of the hall, 190' by 75', the straight ceiling appeared rather low and restricted the size of the screen, which was as large as possible within the confines of the proscenium. At either side of the screen, curved long walls were adorned by pilasters and panelled plasterwork.

The Picture House opened at 3pm on 25 July 1912, when hundreds of invited guests attended and among whom were councillors Ellis Pennington and JR Barbour. The programme consisted of *Paris, the City of Charms*, three dramatic films: *Lottery Ticket No 13*, *Her Face* and *Exposed by the Dictograph*, and a comedy, *A Helping*

Hand. The picturesque Pathé-colour production showing a village in Borneo received special praise for the clarity of the photography. Appropriate music to the films was provided by the Elite Gold & White Ladies Orchestra. The evening performances were at 7pm and 9pm, and matinees at 3pm on Wednesdays and Saturdays, with a complete change of programme every Monday and Thursday. Seats in the grand lounge, at the rear, were 9d, with the stalls and pit stalls at 6d and 3d respectively.

In 1921 the cinema was closed for further improvements due to being added to the Bedford cinema circuit. In the redecoration scheme the foyer ceiling was adorned by two large oval areas of cherubic paintings, framed by carved plasterwork, whilst a Grecian-style frieze decorated the upper part of the walls. The auditorium was reseated with grey tip-up seats on a luxurious new carpet, and a polished mahogany screen behind the rear seats.

Renamed the Broadway Cinema, the reopening was on 26 December 1921 at 2pm, with a huge holiday film programme accompanied by the popular 1920s Grand Orchestra, under the direction of Alfred Delmonte. After the matinee at 3pm there was a continuous evening performance from 6.30pm to 10.30pm, with admission at 6d, 9d and 1/. The Broadway was taken over by the GTC and became a GB cinema in May 1929, after which the company soon installed sound equipment, commencing on 30 September 1929 with the first British sound film, *Blackmail*, starring John Longden and Anny Ondré. The performances were continuous from 2pm to 10.30pm and admission prices increased to 6d, 1/- and 1/6. During the 1930s, with first showings in the district of the GB circuit release films, the Broadway was the best attended cinema, not only of Bootle but of the surrounding areas.

The last patrons visited the Broadway on the evening of 8 May 1941 to see *Third Finger, Left Hand*, featuring Myrna Loy and Melvyn Douglas, also *March of Time No 11* and *British Movietone News*, after which the auditorium was destroyed in the May blitz. Surprisingly, the frontage was barely damaged and with the shutter pulled down over the main entrance, it stood until several years after the war with the appearance of a closed cinema. The Gaumont Cinema was built on the site and opened on 23 January 1956.

1912
New Prince's Theatre • Strand Cinema
Irlam Road, Bootle

Construction of the building, originally known as the Royal Muncaster Theatre, began in 1888 when there was a pressing need for a purpose-built permanent theatre. It was the enterprise of the Penningtons, who could trace their family tree back to a time before the Norman Conquest and who, for many centuries, resided at Muncaster Castle, their principal residence from which the theatre name was derived. Completion of the theatre was delayed by Harry Pennington's death in August 1888. Work was resumed the following year by his sons, James and John, and was finished in 1890.

Penningtons, the architects, were praised for the design of what was considered one of the finest buildings in the borough; James Pennington was especially recognised for his supervision of the structure throughout. The tall, gabled frontage was stone-faced with two central entrances, and an exit at either side, whilst a line of first floor windows was surmounted by arches, with panels below the almost full width gable. The spacious auditorium had a proscenium opening 24'-wide and 20'-high fronting the stage, with a depth of about 25'. The interior, being practically divided into two parts by solid brick walls, iron doors and a safety curtain, was considered effective in resisting fire, wherever it might occur. The auditorium ceiling, rising from picturesque pilasters and arches in the walls on either side, was divided into bays by panelled beams, painted in light colours to give a brilliant appearance. The front of the balcony, which gracefully curved towards the proscenium, was decorated by panels and medallions. At each side of the stage were four canopied private boxes. Notable among the scenery, painted by Sam King, then an eminent artist of the Star Music Hall, was the drop scene depicting Muncaster Castle. The Muncaster coat of arms was incorporated in the richly designed pediment above the proscenium, a reminder of Bootle's old traditions.

Although all credit for Bootle's first purpose-built theatre must go to the Penningtons, the theatre was leased for the opening to HT Denyer and Harris Fineberg, the son of Isaac Fineberg, proprietor of the Star Music Hall in the city. The lessees secured some of the country's leading variety artists in addition to popular local artists for the Grand Opening of the Royal Muncaster Theatre on 6 October 1890. The performance at 7.30pm was under the patronage and presence of His Worship the Mayor of Bootle, Alderman B Cain, the Right Honourable Earl of Derby KC, members of the Bootle Town Council and many other VIPs. Following the playing of the National Anthem by the orchestra of 15 selected musicians directed by Edward Jonghmans, and sung by the Liverpool Quartet, the overture was played as the iron curtain rose to reveal, inch by inch, the magnificent backdrop in old gold of Muncaster Castle. The variety performance was enthusiastically received by the large audience, which packed the house at popular prices of: stage boxes 10/6 to 32/-, orchestra stalls 2/-, centre circle 1/6 and side circle 1/-.

The Muncaster was run as a variety theatre until 1893, when Denyer severed his connection, after which Pennington took over the management and instituted a change to drama for 3 weeks of every month, with variety in the remaining week. Finding that drama was then of greater appeal to the public, the change was made to purely theatrical entertainment until just after the turn of the century. After a period during which the theatre was closed for the installation of electric light, the reopening on 5 August 1901 was at 7.30pm for the presentation of The New Muldoon Picnic. The private boxes were 3/- each person, orchestra stalls 2/-, circle 1/- and pit stalls 6d. In the same year a new attraction was introduced, animated pictures as at the Hippodrome and other principal London theatres by the American Phono Bioscope Co. The presentation at the Muncaster in the week beginning 16 December 1901 was the first outside the city centre and with sound by disc, patrons were advised that they would see and hear great artists, including Vesta Tilley, Lil Hawthorne and Alec Hurley. It was advertised that over 40,000 pictures were shown, including the spectacular production of The Seven Castles of the Devil, as well as scenes of the Boer War. The admission prices were 2/- for orchestra stalls, 1/- for circle and 6d in the pit stalls.

Although mainly the home of drama, further motion pictures were shown in 1904 and 1905 by the New Century Animated Picture Co, 3 years prior to their opening of the Mount Pleasant Hall Liverpool. After the inauguration of twice-nightly drama by a stock company on 1 August 1907, followed by control by a short term lessee who reopened on 1 August 1911 with high class variety, supported by the latest animated pictures, the theatre was acquired in 1912 by George Prince, the highly esteemed picture pioneer and manager of Sun Hall. Complete redecoration was carried out with no expense spared to make it an attractive, comfortable entertainment venue.

Appropriately renamed the New Prince's Theatre, the reopening was on 19 August 1912, when films formed the principal attraction of the performance at 8pm. By request, the feature film was the sensational picture drama *A Victim of the Mormons*, supported by the unique film, *The Robbery at Old Burnside Bank*. Humour was provided by live entertainment with Farrow and Fiske in a vocal pot-pourri, and also Adken, the motoring ventriloquist. At this time the admission prices were reduced to 3d, 4d and 6d.

Another short period as a variety theatre began in July 1920 under Turner and Smith, from whom the Prince's was acquired in the following year by the Bedford cinema circuit, which then controlled several cinemas on Merseyside. Sparing no expense or artistic skill, the auditorium was completely restyled by architect, AE Shennan, for its new lease of life as a cinema. The old boxes and circle were demolished in the conversion to a 750-seat stadium-type auditorium. The new, handsomely upholstered tip-up seats were fitted to the carpeted floor, and there was a new electric light installation and heating system. With the latest and best type of projectors and screen, the management aimed to show the clearest picture in Bootle.

The new enterprise opened as the Strand Cinema on 19 September 1921, with a continuous performance from 6.30pm to 10.30pm, with popular prices of 5d, 9d and 1/-. Instead of naming the feature film, press advertisements were intriguing: 'What is the Picture? Come and see, be surprised and delighted'.

In March 1928 the Strand became a GB cinema, being among those of the Bedford circuit which were taken over by the GTC. Surprising, then, that the talkies arrived rather late, the reason being that the newly appointed manager in August 1929, Norman Stancliffe, announced that the cinema was 'The House of No Talking', insisting that patrons preferred good silent productions presented with good music. Stancliffe had extensive experience of the film industry, in which he had been engaged for 22 years, for almost nine of these as a manager with Provincial Cinematograph Theatres Ltd, which in 1929 was also taken over by GB. Nevertheless, by the latter half of 1930, when the majority of cinemas had been equipped for sound films and there was little interest in the silents, the Strand opened with its first all talkie programme on 11 August 1930 with *The Street Girl*, starring Betty Compson, with supporting films. At the performance continuous from 6.30pm to 10.30pm, the admission prices were 4d, 6d and 8d.

GB relinquished control in 1942 when the cinema was taken over by the Strand Cinema Co, Liverpool, within the small circuit of WJ Speakman, Capitol, Edge Hill. As an independent cinema, the programming consisted of later runs of the circuit releases and B pictures, with which it survived for nearly 6 years. The final programme, on 26 December 1947, was the double bill, *Secret of the Whistler*, featuring Richard Dix, and *Medicine Man*. The building was later used by Cork Industries Ltd until July 1954, when it was destroyed by fire, thought to have been started by an intruder.

1912
Lime Street Picture House • City Picture House • Futurist
Lime Street, Liverpool city centre

The city's first purpose-built cinema, having been open for almost 70 years at the time of closure in 1982, was the leading cinema of the circuit. It was controlled by Edwin Haigh, who formed the Lime Street Picture House Co Ltd, which was registered in 1911 with an authorised capital of £20,000.

The Georgian-style frontage was about 60' wide and included a shop at either side of the central main entrance, surmounted by a metal and glass verandah with the name, Picture House, on the facia in large letters formed by white opaque glass. Along the front edge were mounted several torch-style, shaded electric light fittings. Extending above the stone balustraded apex at the sides, the curved, recessed centre was bordered by a tall arch which extended above the second floor circular windows, whilst those of the first floor were of considerable height with metal balustrades set on stone ledges. At the head of a short flight of white stone steps, the main entrance with two pairs of glass-panelled doors led to the foyer with flooring of black and white square tiles and walls of Sicilian marble and Saxe blue colour scheme. At each side was an enclosed turning staircase to the first floor, and at the rear of the foyer, doors within archways led to entrances at either side of the stalls, in which 700 seats were fitted in two sections with centre and side gangways.

A café lounge was provided on the first floor, from which a continuation of the winding stairs led at either side to a landing, with entrance doors to the rear of the circle and accommodation for 350 patrons. A lift from the foyer up to this second floor level was also provided. The auditorium was notable for the abundance of architectural features, embellished by plaster mouldings, the whole effect being reminiscent of a live theatre, although it was never used for this purpose. Extending considerably over the stalls floor, the circle curved around the sides, providing access to the front exit doors, and terminating on the splayed walls either side of the proscenium. These featured a balconet with a curved front enriched by plaster mouldings, in the style of a theatre box. The area above had decorative infilling, spanned by an arch and flanked by fluted columns with carved capitals, all surmounted by a classic architectural feature. The lower part of the walls had a dark, wood-panelled dado between the fluted pilasters with carved capitals, whilst light coloured panels with attractive gold painted borders adorned the upper part of the walls on both floors. The unusually wide cornice was supported by large consoles spaced along the side walls, and from these rose the curved ceiling, spanned by carved ribs containing further decoration by panels. Suspended electric lamps, within large glass-shaded fittings, provided the principal illumination.

In the announcement of the Grand Opening on 16 September 1912, the Lime Street Picture House was described as the finest in the kingdom, including a luxurious café lounge, and a full orchestra to accompany the silent films at a continuous performance from 1pm to 10.30pm, to which admission was at 6d and 1/-, with children half price until 3pm. The film programme was designed to satisfy every mood with comedy, tragedy, sensationalism and domesticity. Other pictures portrayed historical events and in this category, in beautiful colours, was the film *Caesar Borgia*, whilst in complete contrast the comedy, *One Round Brian*, provoked unrestrained laughter.

The opening of the Liverpool Picture House in Clayton Square just over 2 months later resulted in the change of name of the Lime Street cinema to the City Picture House from 14 August 1916 to avoid confusion among intending patrons. A new company, Futurist (Liverpool) Ltd, was formed in October 1920, to purchase the cinema and the two shops for the sum of £167,000. The property was leasehold from the Corporation of Liverpool for 75 years from 1920, subject only to a peppercorn rent. From this time, the Futurist and adjacent Scala cinemas were both controlled by the Levy cinema circuit, whose similarly-named Birmingham halls were recognised among the greatest early successes of the picture house business. The company was fortunate in having a board of directors with exceptional experience in the running of picture theatres, having appointed Alfred Levy, the brother of Sol Levy, who had opened the Scala, Liverpool in 1916, and John Arthur Williams, cinema proprietor, as joint managing directors; Edwin Haigh, vice-chairman of the Scala company, was among the first directors.

During the 1920s, Sol Levy's original pictures only policy, the best of them with full orchestral accompaniment,

brought music from the greatest composers to his patrons. A new attraction was introduced at the Futurist, for the first time in Liverpool, concurrently with the Scala Cinema, as a supporting attraction for 6 days commencing 29 November 1926, when De Forrest Phonofilms was advertised as The Amazing Talking Picture – The Invention of the Age. Seat reservations were: 1/10 and 3/- in the stalls and circle respectively, whilst admission before lpm was at 1/3 and 2/4.

Following the death of Sol Levy in July 1929, his younger brother, Alfred, who had been co-managing director of individual companies within the group, took over as managing director of the circuit. 1929 was also the year which saw the end of silent films at the Futurist, where Western Electric Talking equipment was installed for the opening on 2 September, with the All Talking, Singing, Dancing feature film, MGM's *Broadway Melody,* starring Anita Page, Bessie Love and Charles King. This was shown at four distinct performances daily at 2pm, 4.15pm, 6.30pm and 8.45pm for 6 weeks until 12 October. Although the talkies provided a boost to attendances, which had been in decline for silent films, Levy cinemas soon faced increased competition.

In addition to the GB first run cinema, the Trocadero, Camden Street, two super-cinemas were added: the ABC Forum, Lime Street, in 1931 and the Paramount, London Road, in 1934. This resulted in mainly second runs of the leading films at the Futurist and the Scala. In addition to the detrimental effect of the early war years on cinema attendances, the Futurist and Scala sustained bomb damage, which forced closure in May 1941. The Futurist was the first to reopen, the date being 16 June with the programme *The Ghost Train,* featuring Arthur Askey, and also *The Man at the Gate.* The Futurist regained its former status as a first run cinema in 1954, when it was leased by the Twentieth Century-Fox Film Corporation for the first showings in Liverpool of their Cinema Scope films following the producer dispute with the Rank Organisation.

After closure on 15 May 1954 with *The Outlaw,* starring Jane Russell, extensive alterations were carried out to accommodate the huge Miracle Mirror CinemaScope screen, behind which and along the walls of the auditorium were mounted numerous speakers for the reproduction of stereophonic sound, with improved sight lines for the audience due to raising the circle seats by 7".

The Futurist reopened on 20 May 1954, with continuous performances from 12.30pm of *King of the Khyber Rifles* starring Tyrone Power, heralding first runs in Liverpool of Fox CinemaScope films which continued for nearly 6 years until the producers relinquished control of the cinema, closing on 2 April 1960 with *Journey to the Centre of the Earth,* featuring Pat Boone. ABC Ltd then took over from Alfred Levy at a cost of £135, 000 and spent a further £50,000 on modernisation and equipment. New seating reduced the capacity to 870, whilst in the projection room, Phillips DP 70 (35mm and 70mm) projectors and sound equipment replaced the Kalee 11s and Western Electric sound system. The proscenium and architectural features of the flanking splayed walls were engulfed by the even larger Todd-AO screen. In front of this the deep red curtain and pelmet extended to each side of the circle.

Advertised as Liverpool's latest luxury Todd-AO theatre, ABC reopened the Futurist on 10 July 1960 with the Rodgers and Hammerstein musical *Oklahoma!,* starring Shirley Jones and Gordon Macrea. The film ran for 20 weeks until 26 November, at two performances daily, 2.30pm and 7.30pm, and one on Sunday at 7pm. Prices were: stalls 3/6 and 5/6, circle 7/6, all seats bookable in advance. *Oklahoma!* and the films which followed in 70mm with magnetic stereophonic sound, were shown at separate performances known as 'Road Show' presentations,

This policy attracted excellent business to the Futurist, and notable among the longer runs was the 70mm reissue of *Gone With The Wind,* which ran from 15 September 1968 until 1 March 1969. The company policy for Road Show theatres was the provision of a licensed bar in order to boost normal refreshment sales in the 15-minute intermission in the film. In the Futurist, the first floor lounge was converted for this use and opened in June 1969.

By the mid-1970s, due to the shortage of new Road Show films, there had been a gradual change to normal circuit releases at continuous performances, but early in 1975 the novelty attraction, Sensurround, brought a return to the former policy. At the rear of the circle equipment was installed to provide the vibratory special effects for the film *Earthquake* in 70mm, starring Charlton Heston and Ava Gardner, which began a 16-week run on 23 February 1975. Performances on Sundays were at 4.45pm and 7.45pm, weekdays 2pm, 4.45pm, 8pm, and seats were bookable for the evenings only.

Less successful films in Sensurround over a 4 year period were: *Battle of Midway, Rollercoaster* and *Battlestar Galactica.* The mixed film bookings included circuit releases and reruns of former successes during the remaining years. An almost 70-year long history of the Futurist ended on 17 July 1982, when about 100 patrons attended for the double feature programme, *History of the World Part 1* and *Blazing Saddles.* The closure was the result of the conversion to a triple-screen cinema of the ABC Forum on the opposite side of Lime Street. The Futurist was the first to close so that the 70mm equipment could be installed in the new ABC 1. No alternative use has been made of the building which remains in a deteriorating condition.

1912
Everton Electric Palace • Everton Palace
Heyworth Street, Everton

Everton Electric Palace, 1920s.

An early, purpose-built suburban cinema at the corner of Heyworth Street and Rupert Lane, an exceedingly well populated area. At a cost of £6,000, the building was under the supervision of the well-known Liverpool architects Campbell and Fairhurst, who, it was stated, had displayed great taste in the internal and external ornamentation of the building. The white, stone-faced frontage was splayed in keeping with the curve at the road junction. In the centre, flanked by fluted stone columns, several steps led up to the main entrance from which two pairs of doors gave access to the foyer. Above the entrance were the cinema name, performances times and admission prices, surmounted by the first floor windows below a stone arch, whilst at the highest point of the frontage a large dome was supported by several pairs of columns as well as pilasters, panels and vases. The internal fittings were arranged to create maximum enjoyment and ensure the safety of the public. The Wedgewood blue decorations were complemented by the 900 dark blue seats in the auditorium.

The cinema was opened by Everton Electric Palace Ltd, on 28 September 1912, managed by GW Pettigrew. Performances were at 3pm, 7pm and 9pm, to which the admission prices were: 3d, 4d, 6d and 1/. In 1921 the cinema was an addition to the four of the North-Western Film Booking Agency, who called it the Everton Palace. For the opening of the talkies on 9 June 1930 a sound system was installed, the first sound film being the William Fox production *The Girl from Havana*, starring Lola Lane and Paul Page.

The next significant attraction, CinemaScope, was included in the film booking policy from 30 June 1955 with *River of No Return* starring Marilyn Monroe and Robert Mitchum. Despite increased competition during the 1930s from larger, modern cinemas, the Palace survived for a further 30 years, presenting almost entirely single feature programmes with a matinee daily at 2.15pm and a continuous evening performance from 6pm. The Everton Palace was the last of the North-Western circuit cinemas on Merseyside, and closed on 12 March 1960, with the feature film *Idle on Parade*, featuring William Bendix. The building was later demolished as part of a redevelopment scheme.

1912
Granby Cinema • Prince's Cinema
Granby Street, Toxteth

It was announced in 1912 that the well-known Granby Hall, a billiard hall since 1909, following use as a public hall, was being converted into a 400-seat cinema. A cinematograph licence was granted on 27 September 1912, to the proprietors Granby Cinema Ltd. The cinema opened on 2 October, presenting *The World in Educational Pictures* at a continuous performance from 6.30pm to 10.30pm. Admission prices were 3d, 6d and 1/-, reduced to 4d and 6d at the matinees on Monday, Wednesday and Saturday. The Granby Cinema was run by the same company until December 1931, then taken over by the circuit Regent Enterprise Ltd, 1-3 Stanley Street. Liverpool architects Gray and Evans drew up plans for the reconstruction of the auditorium and the addition of a balcony, increasing the seating capacity to 600.

In the absence of press advertisements, the date of reopening as the Prince's Cinema is unknown, but it can reasonably be assumed that it took place early in 1932, then equipped for sound films with the RCA Photophone system. Regent Enterprise operated the cinema until March 1938, when the company cinemas were taken over by the country's largest independent circuit, Southan Morris Associated Cinemas Ltd, whose managing director was W Southan Morris. At this time admission prices remained low, being only 7d to 1/-. All the cinemas of Southan Morris were acquired by the Newcastle-based Essoldo circuit in October 1954, and in the following year the Prince's became another CinemaScope location starting with *King of the Khyber Rifles*, starring Tyrone Poweron on 1 August 1955.

In a thickly populated area, the Granby/Prince's cinema was open for nearly 53 years, surviving for a year after the closure of its strongest local rival, the Rank-owned Rialto, Upper Parliament Street. The final performance at the Princes was on 27 February 1965 with the double feature programme Ladies' Man, starring Jerry Lewis, also Conquest of Space. The front of the building was later converted for use as shops.

1912
Derby Picturedrome • Derby Cinema
Scotland Road, Liverpool city centre

Situated about a mile north of the city centre, in an area once referred to as 'Mile End', the building was originally the United Methodist Free Church. In January 1912 permission was granted to Edwin Haigh of Edwin Haigh & Sons, cinematograph and billiard hall proprietors, for conversion to a cinema. The original church front was substantially altered by the construction of a forward extension of the central section to provide two separate entrances, each with one pair of glass-panelled doors. Above this the extension was faced with brick and terracotta, the latter forming a large frame enclosing a space for poster advertising. The front entrances were provided for admission to the stalls and balcony, whilst the front stalls were reached via a covered area along the left-hand-side of the building. From the foyer, a staircase led up to a landing with a double door to the rear of the balcony, which extended over the rear stalls in the auditorium. The seating capacity, including forms in the front stalls, was approximately 750', the proscenium was 33' in width, and to provide for live entertainment, there was a 9' deep stage.

Derby Cinema, Scotland Road, 1967.

The first cinematograph licence was granted to Haigh & Sons on 14 October 1912, which, in the absence of press advertisements, may be taken as the probable date of opening. On 12 December 1912 the *Kinematograph Weekly* reported that under the management of HG Edmonds, the cinema's popularity was due to the presentation of good films in comfortable surroundings. Also, the admission prices were low, ranging from 4d to 8d.

From 1915 until the end of the silent film era in 1929, an added occasional attraction was live variety, booked by Edwards and Elliman of Bold Street. Since about 1920, Edwin Haigh had become either proprietor, director or managing director of many Liverpool cinemas, including the Futurist and Scala in the city centre. Haigh continued to control the circuit, including the Scotland Road hall, from 1922 known as the Derby Cinema, until 1936, when it was acquired by Byrom Picture Houses Ltd of 1-3 Stanley Street. The managing director, Stanley Grimshaw, was also vice-chairman of the Cinematograph Exhibitors Association's north-west branch, and was connected with several Liverpool cinemas including the Prince of Wales, which he had taken over from ABC.

The Derby had a final change of proprietor in 1942, when it came under the control of Regent Enterprise Ltd, whose managing director was Phillip M Hanmer, who also booked the films. Considering the fact that this was an old, converted building, the Derby had a comparatively long life of 48 years, remaining open until 14 May 1960. The final programme consisted of Carry on Teacher, featuring Ted Ray and Kenneth Williams, supported by The White Cliffs Mystery, a Scotland Yard series film with Edgar Lustgarten. Coyne Bros, wedding and funeral directors, converted the building for their use, which continues to date.

1912
Bootle Picture Palace • Palace Cinema
Marsh Lane, Bootle

This was the first local building to be erected especially for cinematograph exhibition. It was designed by architect George Tonge of Southport, who in later years was responsible for many fine cinemas in the North West. The building was situated in the midst of a vast population, near to the main thoroughfare, Stanley Road, and within a one minute walk of Marsh Lane railway station. The elevations were designed in accordance with the latest ideas of cinema construction, and neither time nor trouble was spared by the builders, Woods of Bolton. An imposing, wide entrance in the centre of the facade led, by two pairs of swing doors, into a luxurious lounge, which provided ample waiting room for early doors patrons. The auditorium was entered from the lounge by three double swing doors. Due to the well-raked floor, there was an uninterrupted view of the screen from every seat. Except for the forms in the front stalls, the seats were the acme of comfort and luxury, being tip-up with arm-rests, upholstered in crimson velvet. Eight exits meant that the 1000-seat auditorium could be emptied in 2 to 3 minutes.

The decor was in white and crimson and coloured lights gleamed from the stage, shedding a warm glow through the building. The main hall was ventilated by large grids. Impure air was extracted by a large electric fan in the centre of the roof, effecting a complete change of air every 10 minutes. The heating was scientifically installed to give a constant temperature even on the coldest day. The operating room was one of the largest and best equipped in the country, and patrons were ensured of pictures shown under perfect conditions.

The Mayor of Bootle, Councillor JWE Smith, was present, accompanied by a large party at the opening on Saturday 19 October 1912, and seemed gratified to find that the borough had received so admirable an addition to its public buildings. Before the Mayor's speech, Yates Baxter, chairman of the Bootle Palace Co Ltd, praised those involved in building the hall, but apologised for two unfinished items: a verandah for use in wet weather which would improve the look of the frontage, and the mosaic floor inside the entrance.

The opening performance was a delightful series of pictures repeated on the following evening at 7pm and 9pm. The public crowded into the building and frequently applauded during the show. The Lady Diver was the favourite, with its attractive water scenes shot with powerful realism. Admission prices were 3d, 6d and 1/-, children, 2d, 3d and 6d. Tea was served free of charge to patrons of the 6d and 1/- seats. Matinees at 3pm were on Wednesdays and Saturdays.

Against competition from the Picture House and the Sun Hall on Stanley Road, the Palace was popular for many years, but attendances fell with the opening of larger, more imposing cinemas in the early-1920s, such as the Gainsborough, Bootle and the Coliseum, Litherland. But, under the ownership of George Prince, well known for his early showing of motion pictures at the Sun Hall, the Palace was the first cinema in the district to be equipped for sound. The silent era at the Palace ended on 27 July 1929 with Scaramouche, starring Ramon Navarro.

The talkies, by Western Electric sound system, opened on 29 July with the Fox Movietone feature In Old Arizona featuring Edmund Lowe and Warner Baxter. Supported by an all talkie programme including British Movietone News, there was a matinee at 3pm and continuous evening performance from 6.30pm to 10.30pm. The increased strength of circuit oppositions ABC and GB in the early-1930s greatly limited the number of first run films available to the Palace, it being restricted to those not booked by the circuits (for example British productions starring Gracie Fields, George Formby and Frank Randle, and American B pictures from Republic and Monogra). The Palace was also noted for Roy Rogers and Gene Autrey westerns, and gangster pictures from Warner Bros starring Cagney, Robinson and Bogart, although the latter normally had first run on the ABC circuit.

Still under George Prince's control in the 1950s when attendances were dropping, the Palace was equipped with CinemaScope and stereophonic sound, which in September 1954 was the first in the district together with the Imperial, Bootle. The Palace was closed for a week for the installation and reopened on 18 July with the CinemaScope film, *Sitting Bull,* featuring Dale Robertson. Additional circuit opposition was provided by the opening of the New Gaumont, Bootle in January 1956, after which the Palace survived for a further 2 years, closing on 26 April 1958 with *River of No Return* and *Copper Sky*.

Later into 1958, negotiations began for the purchase of the building at a cost of £7,500 by the trustees of the Bootle Social Centre For Children building fund. The centre opened in December 1959 after extensive internal alterations, although the exterior of cream faience tiles, a post-war modernisation, remained unchanged. After the closure of the Social Centre, the building was not used and was demolished in the Autumn of 1997.

1912
The Liverpool Picture House • Prince of Wales • Liverpool News Theatre • Gala International Film Theatre • Jacey Film Theatre
Clayton Square, Liverpool city centre

This was among the first 15 cinemas to be called Picture House, opened by the rising Provincial Cinematograph Theatres Co, who formed in 1909 with a capital of £100,000. The company originally restricted their operations to city centre sites, and became known for its exceptionally high standard of luxury, elegance and comfort; a notable feature being all tip-up seats, with no forms at the front. The Liverpool Hall was erected on the site of the Prince of Wales Theatre, centre of dramatic delights in Victorian times, and the location of a very early appearance of the famous dramatic actor, Henry Irving.

The new building, designed by George L Alexander, ARIBA, and Matthew Watson, Landless and Pearse architects, was described as an ornamental and notable addition to the existing cinemas. The tall, imposing frontage was of classic design, in Marmor stone by the Leeds Fireclay Co. The lower part was in horizontal stone bands with a central main entrance flanked by fluted stone columns, surmounted by an iron canopy with the cinema name on the glass facia, extending to almost full width. At first floor level a line of six tall windows was surmounted by a similar number of small windows below the coping. At the highest part of the frontage, a stone pediment gable was supported by square columns with an iron balustrade. The main entrance had a paybox at either side, where two pairs of glass-panelled doors led into the oak-panelled foyer, with doors to the rear of the stalls, and stairways to the Wedgewood café on the first floor, serving light refreshments to both the audience and the general public.

The whole building was designed with some pretensions to grandeur. Oak panelling was used for the lower part of the walls, whilst pilasters extended up to the carved cornice, the areas between decorated by murals. Bordered by a considerable area of black masking, the rather small screen was set quite high in the tall proscenium, surmounted by the Liverpool Coat of Arms. Flowers adorned the front of the stage and were also in vases mounted upon the polished wooden side exits. The high, steeply-curved ceiling, from which elegant light fittings were suspended, was spanned by carved plaster ribs, and the areas between decorated by panels of classic design. No attempt was made to maximise the floor space for seating, the stalls floor was raked, whilst the slightly curved fronted circle was stepped, providing a total seating capacity of 700 with unobstructed view of the screen. The modern ventilation system gave a change of air every 5 minutes and ensured an even temperature.

The Liverpool Picture House was opened by private reception at 3.30pm on 25 November 1912, by JJ Newbould, director of the proprietors, Provincial Cinematograph Theatres Ltd. He stated that the company's cinemas were being erected in practically all the leading cities, and were acknowledged to be superior. He drew attention to the rigorous censorship exercised by the company over subjects of questionable taste. Comedy, drama, travel, natural history and the news of the day in pictorial form, were embraced in the varied programme which was educational and entertaining. Especially interesting were three of the company's own series, wherein Sir Beerbohm Tree appeared in scenes from *The Merry Wives of Windsor* and *Trilby*, also Gerald Lawrence in an excerpt from *David Garrick,* all accompanied by the strains of a competent orchestra.

The Picture House was open to the public at 6.30pm, when admission was: 6d to the stalls, 1/- to the balcony, with children half price before 5pm. After the opening day, performances were continuous from 2pm to 10.30pm, an arrangement favoured by PCT, then practically unknown, although not for the first time in Liverpool, the Picture House on Lime Street having opened 2 months earlier with a similar policy. The cinema was renamed the Prince of Wales in April 1914, and continued under PCT until 1923, by which time the company was in decline, despite opening their newly-built cinema, the Trocadero in Camden Street, in April 1922.

The Prince of Wales was then taken over by Savoy Cinemas of Oxford Street, London, which, in 1928, was one of the three circuits which amalgamated to form ABC in 1929. The acquisition of the Prince of Wales and the Olympia, West Derby Road, Liverpool, also from Savoy Cinemas, began ABC representation in Liverpool with concurrent screenings of the company release films. BTH sound system was installed for the opening of the talkies on 30 September 1929 with *The Trial of Mary Dugan,* featuring Norma Shearer and Lewis Stone, screened at four separate performances daily at 2pm, 4.15pm, 6.30pm and 8.40pm. All seats were bookable at 1/6 in the stalls and 2/4 in the balcony, unreserved at 1/3 and 2/-.

In May 1933, ABC created a subsidiary company, the Regent Circuit Ltd, based at Heddon House, 149-151 Regent Street, London W1, to take over what they regarded as their poorer, loss-making cinemas. The Prince of Wales was among the seven Liverpool locations which formed part of the new circuit. This proved to be very detrimental with regard to film bookings, the more attractive of which had, since May 1931, been lost to the ABC new super-cinema, the Forum, in Lime Street. The concurrency of the other company release films with the Olympia ceased in September 1934, when this was shared with the Forum, and in the final 18 months of ABC control, the mixed film booking policy included older attractions, and others of often a lower standard.

The Regent circuit was disbanded in 1935 and its cinemas returned to direct control by ABC. The company disposed of the Prince of Wales and their last film booking was *Forsaking All Others* starring Joan Crawford and Clark Gable, finishing on 15 February 1936. The cinema was then taken over by Stanley Grimshaw, managing director of Byron Picture Houses Ltd, 1 Stanley Street. He was connected with several Liverpool suburban cinemas and vice-chairman in the north-west branch of the Cinematograph Exhibitors Association and set out to make internal alterations, improve the sound apparatus and brighten the front of house with neon lighting.

As to future film programmes, Grimshaw styled his new venture as a news and feature theatre, with bookings consisting of later runs of star feature films supported by the newsreels, *Pathé Gazette*, GB, Universal and *British Movietone News*. The grand reopening was on 17 February 1936. With a continuous performance from noon to 10.45pm, consisting of short films and newsreels, and admission prices: stalls 6d, and balcony 1/. The first feature film was *East Meets West,* starring George Arliss, also there were three newsreels which began on 24 February.

This type of programme continued until 14 November 1946, when the Prince of Wales closed for alterations prior to reopening as the Liverpool News Theatre on 17 December 1946, in direct competition with the Tatler News Theatre, Church Street. The seating capacity had, by 1946, been reduced to 561 during internal alterations by the new proprietors, Jacey Cinemas Ltd of 37 Temple Street, Birmingham. As the Gala, Liverpool's International Film Theatre from 20 September 1962, there was a complete change to continental X certificate films, starting with *Les Liaisons Dangereuses* featuring Jeanne Moreau and *Street of Shame*. Performances were continuous from 12.30pm.

After 12 months it was renamed the Jacey Film Theatre, with a similar film booking policy until closure on 7 July 1972 with the programme *Don't Deliver Us From Evil* and *The Subject is Sex*. This could hardly have been in greater contrast to the films of 60 years previously. The building was then converted into a church – The Shrine of the Blessed Sacrament. In 1986 it was demolished in a major redevelopment scheme including the Clayton Square shopping precinct.

1912
Dingle Picturedrome
Park Road, Dingle

The first cinematograph licence was granted on 6 December 1912, to T Halliwell Hughes, managing director of the Dingle Picturedrome Ltd. This 850-seat hall was the first of a small circuit of cinemas in Liverpool opened by the company during the ensuing 10 years. A brief reference in the *Kinematograph* and *Lantern Weekly* of 30 January 1913, stated that the cinema had been open for about 5 weeks and was very popular.

In March 1928 the Halliwell Hughes circuit was among many countrywide taken over by Denman Picture Houses Ltd, then becoming a GB cinema. Its existence was very short lived, as was the Sefton Park Picturedrome. Sound film equipment was not installed, and the Dingle Picturedrome was closed towards the end of 1929.

The building was demolished in 1935 and the site, including the area of Dingle Lane previously occupied by the South End Motor Co, a private hire and weddings concern, provided the much larger site for the New Gaumont, for which construction began in 1936, opening in 1937.

1912
King's Hall Cinema
Oakfield Road, Anfield

The cinema, with 1000 seats including a balcony and a billiard hall, was opened by John F Wood, managing director of Bedford Cinemas Ltd, to whom a cinematograph licence was granted on 20 December 1912. After only 3½ years, the balcony was closed, as the local authorities required that the ceiling over this part of the auditorium should be raised and the balcony was reopened in mid-August 1915. Except for its last 5 months, the King's screened silent films with musical accompaniment, originally by a piano, and later by an orchestra. During the late-1920s, Jazz Nights were an added attraction, presented by an orchestra of eight players who travelled around the cinemas of the Bedford circuit.

In the takeover by GB, the King's was acquired by the GTC in March 1928, and was equipped for sound films, opening with the All Talking, Singing, Dancing sensation, *Mirth and Melody*, starring Lola Lane, on 14 July 1930. Sadly, the talkies were for a limited time, the cinema was closed in October of that year and then demolished to make way for the New Gaumont Palace which opened in December 1931.

1912
Warwick Picturedrome • Warwick Cinema
Windsor Street, Toxteth

The first reference to the cinema appears in the *Bioscope Annual* of 1912, as the Picturedrome, 101 Windsor Street, for which a cinematograph licence had been applied for by A Leitch for Toxteth Picturedromes Ltd. The main entrance gave access to the stalls and the balcony of the 437-seat auditorium. The balcony had straight extensions along either side with several long rows of seats parallel to its front. In the middle of the balcony were six rows of seats on a stepped floor with a gangway at either side, whilst above, visible girders supported the ceiling, and over the rear, columns supported the projection box.

The planning indicated its original use as a 'live' theatre or music hall, although it does not appear in *Annals of the Liverpool Stage* by RJ Broadbent (1908). The only early official information appears in the *Kinematograph* and *Lantern Weekly* of 17 April 1913, stating that the Warwick Picturedrome was open for two evening performances and matinees: Monday, Wednesday and Saturday. The Warwick was leased to SR Coleman in 1914, and in 1918 the lease was taken up by the Liverpool cinema circuit, E Haigh & Sons Ltd. In 1921 a long period of ownership by the Wilkinson family, former funeral directors, began with JJ Wilkinson as proprietor. From 1926, ownership passed to other family members until the early-1950s, during which time it became known as the Warwick Cinema.

The Warwick was operated by lessees Westman Enterprises Ltd, a company associated with the Capitol, Edge Hill, whose managing director was WJ Speakman. Unfortunately, the only reference to the cinema in the local press dealt with an incident in October 1955, when about 60 square-feet of the ceiling collapsed onto the balcony, caused by the weight of seats stored above, resulting in injuries to several members of the audience.

After the repairs, the cinema reopened for 3 more years up to November 1958, when the trustees managing the estate of the former proprietor wound up the company, realising the assets and paying off creditors. Television and bingo contributed to the decline in admissions, eventually resulting in closure.

1912
Hope Hall Cinema • Everyman Cinema
Hope Street, Liverpool city centre

On the site of the present Everyman theatre, this building was originally Hope Street Chapel, erected in 1837, becoming the Anglican Church of St John the Baptist in 1841. This was converted in 1853 to a public leisure and concert hall, run by RA McFee, and became the main venue for Mersey concerts. Next it became a cinema, reported in the trade press *Kinematograph* and *Lantern Weekly* of 26 August 1915. Hope Hall also appeared in the *Bioscope Annual* of 1912, which stated that the hall, with a seating capacity of 1,500 and under the control of JA Thompson, was available for pictures.

Hope Hall, 1973.

The history of the building as a cinema during its first 3 years is obscure, but it must have been closed in 1915 because Edwin Haigh had to apply for a renewal of the licence, the cinema having been acquired by his circuit. Despite objections from the trustees of the Masonic Hall and Notre Dame College, who felt that a cinema was out of place in the neighbourhood, the licence was granted. The Hope Hall cinema was reopened on Saturday 19 August 1915, in the presence of a large, specially invited audience. The management was represented by a Mr Gibson, the former assistant manager of the Smithdown Picture Playhouse. The auditorium was entirely renovated, reseated to a capacity of 960. The tall proscenium arch was about 20' wide, with an 11' stage and two dressing rooms provided for occasional variety acts during the early and mid-1930s. At the time of opening, in 1915, there was a daily matinee and one evening performance, with low admission prices from 4d to 9d.

Still under the control of Edwin Haigh, in 1929, the Hope Hall was one of the first Liverpool's cinemas to be equipped for sound, but by installing the BTP sound system, Haigh challenged the stranglehold of the US Western Electric Co. The monopoly insisted that only cinemas equipped with their own sound system could be supplied with American films, by producing companies under their control. After a trial at London Rialto, Coventry Street, and then at the Stamford Hill cinema, when it was agreed that there was nothing to choose between the two systems, Haigh challenged J Bryson of Universal Pictures to show their feature film, *Broadway,* at the Hope Hall. Although he reported that the BTP system was not up to standard, it won universal praise. Parliament later resolved the matter.

The Hope Hall opened with the talkies on Monday 17 June 1929, when the feature film was *The Moulin Rouge,* with gorgeous French stage scenes and the latest camera angles. The second film, *At The Dentist,* was an all talkie made by BTP, also with vaudeville acts by well known artists, recorded at the Wembley studios. Performances were at 3pm and continuous in the evening from 6.30pm.

Edwin Haigh relinquished control in 1936 when the chairman of the company, J Leslie Greene, a former journalist and proprietor of the Metropole Theatre in Bootle, took over the Hope Hall. With a film booking policy of mainly older circuit release films, the Hope Hall eventually closed on 11 July 1959, with *Floods of Fear,* starring Howard Keel and *Blazing A Trail to the Stars*. It was then taken over by the J Leslie Blond circuit, who introduced continental X certificate films, shown previously at the Continental in Wallasey.

The Hope Hall was reopened on 8 May 1961 with Ingmar Bergman's *So Close to Life* and *The Little Island*. However, the new venture, from 10 December 1961 renamed the Everyman Cinema, was short-lived due to falling audiences, as people were relocated to make way for new University buildings. The cinema closed on 12 January 1963 with the film of DH Lawrence's *Sons and Lovers,* starring Dean Stockwell and Wendy Hiller. Then, for a short time, it was a venue for dances.

August 1964 began the conversion into a theatre, which opened on 28 September of that year, retaining the name The Everyman. It was closed in January 1977 and almost entirely demolished to make way for the present theatre, which opened on 21 September 1977.

1912
New Premier Picturedrome
Prescot Road, Old Swan

The New Premier Picturedrome, photographed when in use as a record shop in the 1960s.

This was the first purpose-built cinema in Old Swan, with a capacity of 900 in a stadium-type auditorium. The stage was 10' deep, with two dressing rooms used for variety acts in the supporting programmes before sound equipment was installed in 1929. Typical of the older stadium-type halls, the rectangular auditorium was decorated by wood panelling over the lower part of the walls, along which were spaced pilasters extending up to the carved cornice, with decorated plasterwork panels between. The first proprietors, New Premier Picture House Ltd, were granted a cinematograph licence on 31 December 1912 and the opening date was probably in early January 1913.

In 1919, the cinema name was changed to the New Premier Picture House, and soon after the opening of the Clubmoor cinema in 1925, the two cinemas came under the same ownership. In 1929 they were among the first suburban cinemas to install sound equipment, which was by Western Electric, for the opening on 19 August 1929 of *The Doctor's Secret*, starring Ruth Chatterton and John Loader, with three separate performances at 2.30pm, 6.30pm and 8.30pm. Admission prices were 6d and 1/-, bookable at 1/6. For many years both cinemas often screened the same films. Known as the New Premier, the cinema was well attended during the 1930s. As with other independent cinemas, it suffered increasing competition from the super-cinemas and the disadvantage of later showings of the leading films.

In the mid-1950s, a modernisation scheme included a restyled plain frontage of black faience tiles over the lower part, and contrasting plain white surface above, with a small, modern canopy over the main entrance, relieved above by several windows. Upon the stark white plaster facing was spaced the cinema name. A new screen was fitted for the opening of CinemaScope on 15 September 1955, with *Rough Company*, starring Edward G Robinson and Barbara Stanwyck.

The cinema survived a further 4 years and was one of many closures in 1959. The last picture show was on 6 June, when *The Young Invaders*, starring James Garner and *Black Patch* with George Montgomery, were shown. Retaining many of its original features, the building was later reopened as a record and music store, Premier Records. Following subsequent use as a furniture store, the entire frontage has been demolished for its present use as a public house, appropriately named The Premier.

1913
Queen's Picture House
Walton Road, Walton

Just over 4 years after the opening of Liverpool's first purpose-built cinema, the Bedford Hall, Walton, the opening of a second in the same area was expected to provide strong competition, particularly as it was on a main road, about $2^1/_2$ miles from the city. At that time it was quite a large hall, orginally seating 1, 200, with a stadium-type auditorium, but there was a reduction to 960 seats c1930, arranged in two sections with centre and side gangways.

The walls had panels above a wooden dado with pilasters spaced along. These extended up to the carved cornice from which the curved ceiling was spanned by ribs between the pilasters. The frontage, of painted plaster and brick, featured a gabled centre section with the name in the triangle, and below, first floor windows in groups of three. The substantial, full-width, metal and glass verandah also carried the cinema name on the fascia above the main entrance. For patrons of the lower priced seats in the front stalls, there was a covered way with a central handrail along the left-hand-side of the building.

The opening of the cinema was briefly reported in the trade press, which announced that a cinematograph licence had been granted on 18 February 1913. It was also stated that the hall was tastefully decorated, and that the projection box was equipped with Gaumont machines.

During the early-1920s the cinema came under the ownership of Wirral Picturedromes Ltd, one of the five which made up the Queen's circuit. Although enjoying a large patronage in the early years, by 1930 it was one of six cinemas in the district, four of which, by the mid-1930s, were controlled by the large circuits. Most films were therefore second runs in the district, with the exception of several Paramount pictures, which, during the late-1940s, were made available to independent exhibitors. Of necessity, the booking policy continued until early-1955. The company was then in a position to book first showings of Twentieth Century Fox CinemaScope pictures due to their agreement to install CinemaScope and stereophonic sound, to which the major circuits were not agreeable at suburban situations. *The Robe* began on 24 January 1955 for 6 days, and Twentieth Century Fox CinemaScope films were the principal item of the company's film bookings during the 4 years prior to closure. The last advertised CinemaScope film was *These Thousand Hills,* featuring Don Murray, which ended a 6 day run on Saturday 20 June 1959. This cannot be confirmed as the closing date, since the only press adverts were for Fox Cinemascope Films. The front of the building was converted for use as a post office, then a store, which was vacated during the 1970s. The building was demolished in 1980.

Queen's Picture House, 1976.

1913
Queen's Picture House
South Road, Waterloo

Queen's Picture House, 1930.

This was the first purpose-built cinema in the Waterloo/Seaforth area. Having a stadium-type hall seating 660, the cinema was designed by Joseph Pearce and built by JA Milestone & Son Ltd. The site was in the middle of a row with shops on either side and, although not very wide, the brightly-painted, plaster-faced frontage stood out prominently, surmounted by a central tower with small arched windows and a silver painted dome above. At either side of the tower, glass fronted panels displayed the cinema name in two sections. The first floor windows were in two groups with a central window flanked by pilasters. Extending across the entire frontage, whose lower part was lit by a row of electric light bulbs, was a metal and glass verandah. The entrances were separated by a large, curved poster site, with access via glass-panelled doors to a small foyer with a paybox opposite and at either side a short flight of stairs, with doors at the head to the rear of the auditorium.

The seating was in two sections with centre and side gangways. The decoration, mainly in white, was relieved over the lower part of the walls by a wood-panelled dado in pale crimson. A row of pilasters extended up to the carved cornice, with the intervening spaces relieved by plasterwork panels of increasing depth towards the front of the auditorium, consistent with the raked floor which descended to the front stalls exits at street level. From the pilasters, broad ribs of carved plasterwork spanned the curved, extensively panelled ceiling, from which the hall was illuminated by six electric fittings with large, multi-coloured, circular shades. Instead of the usual proscenium, a splayed wall extended from the dark brown side drapes to the front of the small stage, with footlights along the front row illuminating framed sections of coloured glass separated by crowns. The colours toned with the screen curtains, deepening towards the sides. The projection room was equipped with the latest Gaumont machines, with which, it was claimed, the pictures were shown with beautiful clarity and steadiness.

Queen's Picture House, 1949.

Queen's Picture House was opened on 17 March 1913 by the Waterloo Picture House Co Ltd, whose general manager was E Angers and resident manager, WS Taylor. There were large crowds for the 3pm matinee, and the continuous evening performance from 6.30pm to 10.30pm, for which the film programme consisted of the dramas: *His Western Way, Cry for Help* and *Nemesis*; two comedies, *Polidor and Priscot* and *Tweedledum*; and a travel film accompanied by a string orchestra. Admission prices were higher than average: 6d, 1/- and 1/6, with children half price except Saturdays and Bank Holidays. As at many cinemas, ladies attending the matinees were served trays of tea and biscuits by the usherettes during the intermission.

The Queen's soon became the focal point for fans of silent films and the élite of the district made it their rendezvous. Previously, film entertainment in the district had been limited to the Winter Gardens, a former gymnasium, and as a support to variety at the Bijou Theatre. After the outbreak of war in 1914, the latest war reports were made available during the performances, a service which was very much appreciated by patrons.

There was a change of ownership in 1920 when the cinema, and the Queen in Walton, came under the control of Wirral Picturedromes Ltd. During the 1920s the Waterloo hall advertised a symphony orchestra, under the leadership of A Rigby, to accompany the silent films, which ended on 17 May 1930 with *Interference,* starring Evelyn Brent and William Powell.

The Grand Opening with talkies by Western Electric sound system was on Monday 19 May 1930 with the film *Smiling Irish Eyes,* featuring Colleen Moore. The cinema was normally quite well attended during the 1930s, showing a good selection of the circuit release films, although following the ABC and GB cinemas in Crosby, but from 1939 the new Plaza, in the same district, provided stronger and more immediate competition.

Equipped for CinemaScope in 1955, the Queen presented some first runs in the district of Twentieth Century-Fox releases for 6 days, Monday to Saturday, starting on 21 March with *Three Coins in the Fountain*, with Clifton Webb and Dorothy MacGuire. Surviving until the late-1950s, the Queen closed on 22 August 1959 with *I Only Arsked* starring Bernard Bresslaw, and *Buchanan Rides Alone*. The general manager, RP Rutherford, who had worked there as a very young operator during the silent era, ran the last reel.

The building was acquired by Thomas Hall Ltd for conversion to a furniture store, later enlarged with the addition of an adjoining large drapery store, Pearson's Ltd. The frontage was completely rebuilt and the roof and rear wall are now the only reminders of the former cinema.

1913
Palladium
West Derby Road, Tuebrook

The Palladium, photographed during the week the cinema closed in 1967.

This was a most favourable situation, being in a well populated area on the main road served by several tramcar routes. The building, parallel to the main road, provided a reasonably long, stone-faced frontage, which at ground floor level included two large windows for film advertising. This elevation extended to the curved corner where the main entrance, flanked by columns, was surmounted by the cinema name. This, and the gabled side elevation made mainly of brick, were fitted with a steeply-roofed metal verandah with a narrow facia of white opaque glass, and the name, Palladium, adjacent to the main entrance.

The auditorium had a seating capacity of 905, including about 250 in the curved fronted balcony which extended over the rear stalls. The side walls were decorated by several large panels with smaller panels inset, framed by carved gilt plaster mouldings. The panels were separated by pilasters with carved capitals, which extended up to the frieze below the carved cornice. In line with the pilasters, carved plaster ribs extended across the curved ceiling. Suspended by chains, glass-shaded electric lights provided the principal illumination. Flanked by fluted pilasters with capitals, the curve of the proscenium arch accorded with that of the ceiling, and at either side the exits were festooned with carved architectural features. In front of the stage there was an orchestra pit for musicians accompanying the silent films, shown by GB projectors in the box at the rear of the balcony.

Advertised as the most palatial and comfortable picture house in Liverpool, the Palladium was opened under the management of a Mr Harcourt, formerly of the Bradford Hall. It opened on Whit Monday, 10 May 1913, with an all-star programme headed by the feature film *The Penalty* (exclusive for Liverpool), with full musical programme by the Palladium orchestra. The popular admission prices were 3d, 6d and 1/-. The managing director of Liverpool Palladium Ltd, Don Ellis, later famous for his Old Time Music Hall shows, occasionally presented variety acts, while afternoon tea was being served in the stalls. Among the guest artists was Ted Ray, later to become a famous comedian, also appearing as Nedlo, the Gypsy Violinist, Nedlo being his own name (Olden) spelt in reverse.

In 1915 the manager was Samuel Eaton, for many years a popular Liverpool cinema manager, who instituted repertory programmes at the Palladium, with music specially arranged and magnificently played by a popular band of artists. Orchestral accompaniment continued for a further 15 years, until the silent era ended on 17 April 1930, with a special farewell night by Sam Bonner and his Number One Dance Band. The feature film was *While the City Sleeps*, starring one of the most famous actors of the silent screen, Lon Chaney. On Easter Monday, 21 April, patrons were treated to the perfect Talking Picture by Western Electric sound system, which opened with *Fox Movietone Follies of 1929*, starring John Breeden and Lola Lane.

Twice during the 1930s improvements were carried out, the first without closure in January 1935, when the Palladium was styled as 'The Town House of the Suburbs' with alterations including new carpeting, making it the most comfortable cinema in Liverpool. It was closed on 12 April 1939 for almost 3 months, during which many costly improvements were carried out, including new seating, carpeting and decoration, as well as the installation of projectors with the very latest Western Electric Mirrorphonic sound system.

The grand reopening was at 2pm on Monday 10 July 1939, with the double feature *Broadway Musketeers,* featuring Margaret Lindsay, and James Ellison in *Next Time I Marry.* There was a matinee daily, Monday to Saturday, and a continuous evening performance from 6.15pm. The Palladium was among the more popular independently owned cinemas in the Liverpool area. It has been described as a typical family cinema, with good local patronage, continuing as a family business under the ownership of Liverpool impresario Don Ellis and Dr Ray Ellis of Durham.

The decrease in attendances during the early-1950s was counteracted by the Palladium being among the few suburban cinemas to be equipped for CinemaScope and magnetic stereophonic sound. First screenings in the district of the Twentieth Century-Fox CinemaScope pictures began on 26 September 1954 with *The Robe* starring Richard Burton and Jean Simmons. The Palladium became known for epic films, but the closest opposition cinemas being the Rank-owned Hippodrome and Savoy, many dates were allocated for films of ABC circuit release.

After a further 13 years, closure was by compulsory purchase order, issued in connection with the road widening scheme. The owners and hundreds of patrons were desperate to keep it open and signed a petition which was taken personally to 10 Downing Street by the manager, Geoffrey Manders. Sadly, this was unsuccessful and the Palladium took its final bow on Saturday 1 July 1967, when hundreds of pensioners, parents and children crowded into the auditorium for the last time to watch the epic *The Ten Commandments,* starring Charlton Heston. There was a 1.30pm matinee and evening performance at 7pm, with admission prices: balcony 3/6, stalls 2/6, children 2/- and senior citizens 1/-. So ended the Palladium's 54-year history, with the impression that it would be sadly missed, especially by the older regulars who had enjoyed reduced access to any performance at only 1/.

1913
Gaiety
Scotland Road

The first and only reference to this cinema, situated on the main road a short distance to the north of the city, is apparently that which appeared in the trade publication *Kinematograph Weekly* of 13 May 1913, which stated that the Gaiety was to open to the public within a few days. The frontage, flanked on either side by other properties, was of white, glazed stone with carved adornments, spanned by an iron and stained glass verandah. The central main entrance was in the form of a broad, open arch to a waiting area divided in the centre by a hand rail and at the opposite end, doors to the foyer. The auditorium, including the balcony overhanging the rear stalls, had an original capacity of about 1000.

The Gaiety was the enterprise of an independent exhibitor, of whom no details appear to have been recorded, but it can be confirmed that in 1915 the company, Gaiety (Liverpool) Ltd, was formed in association with the cinema circuit of Councillor Edwin Haigh. It was operated by the company until 1936, the RCA sound system was installed c1930. The new proprietor was Stanley Grimshaw, managing director of Byrom Picture Houses Ltd, who in 1936 had taken over the Prince of Wales, Liverpool, from ABC Ltd.

The normal policy for suburban cinemas was continued with two shows nightly, a matinee daily, two programme changes weekly and low admission prices (4d to 9d). During the early-1940s an association was formed with the Regent Enterprise cinema circuit, with film bookings under the control of the managing director, Phillip M Hanmer, who maintained a similar operational policy. By 1950 prices had risen, although still below average at 7d to 1/-. The cinema was large enough to boast 966 seats.

In the 1950s the film booking policy continued with later runs of GB/Rank releases, with various off circuit releases as well as B movies. The last show was on 14 May 1960, with *That Kind of Woman* starring Sophia Loren and *Thunder in the Sun* featuring Robert Mitchum. The building was demolished during major redevelopment of the area.

1913
Cabbage Hall Picture House
Lower Breck Road, Anfield

It would be difficult to find another cinema in the country with this unusual yet rather demeaning name, but at the time of opening in 1913 it was described as the latest addition to Liverpool's many palatial cinemas. The proprietors were known as Cabbage Hall Picture House Ltd, for whom the architect, EA Aldridge of Liverpool, designed a small, stadium-type hall with about 600 seats. Although small, the frontage of white painted plaster presented a striking appearance. Entry to the small, Tudor-style, oak-panelled foyer was by two pairs of doors. The auditorium was decorated in sapphire blue and cream above oak wood panelling. The comfortable blue plush seats were arranged with a centre and two short side blocks, and near the screen the seating was by forms. Two Pathé projectors were fitted in the fire proof operating room.

It was reported that a large crowd attended on 15 November 1913 for the silent programme with piano accompaniment to *No Riches Like Love* and *The Marusc's Child*, as well as comedies and *Pathé Gazette*. Patrons paid 3d, 6d and 9d for admission to the continuous performance from 7pm to 10.30pm. Programmes were changed every Monday and Thursday, and for a penny, patrons could buy a programme of forthcoming attractions. In its early years, the Cabbage Hall was well attended by fans of Charlie Chaplin, Tom Mix, Harold Lloyd and the like. Supporting programmes included the serials of Pearl White and her cliff-hanger adventures.

In 1943 the cinema came under the control of the Bedford circuit, but with numerous large cinemas in opposition, it only screened later runs of the circuit release films. During its last 6 years, from 1953, there were evening performances only. Closure was on 31 January 1959, with a double feature *Up The Creek* featuring David Tomlinson, and *West of the River*. The building was later bought by Liverpool Football Club for its supporters' club.

1913
Crosby Picture House
Liverpool Road, Crosby

The building was St Luke's Parish Hall, which in 1913 was converted into Crosby's only cinema. With 500 seats, it opened under the management of WS Taylor, who was formerly resident manager at the Queen, Waterloo. First advertised on 15 November 1913, performances were on Monday, Wednesday and Saturday evenings at 8pm, with admissions at 3d, 6d and 1/- and a children's matinee on Saturday at 3pm for 1d and 2d. The films were shown to the accompaniment of musical items by soprano vocalist Miss Dunville.

The reopening took place on 6 December 1913, after redecoration. Under the new management of JF Askew, the cinema was stated to have the latest and best pictures, open 4 days weekly with the addition of Thursday, and admission prices reduced to 3d, 4d and 6d. Large audiences attended and the booking of seats was advised. After another period of closure in 1915, with further redecoration including the exterior, a grand reopening was announced for 26 July, managed by HB Turner. The feature film was *The Morals of Marcus* with short films and *Pathé Gazette*, accompanied by an orchestra under the direction of Stanley Ade. The performance was continuous from 7pm to 10.45pm, all seats bookable and prices which had risen to 6d and 1/.

In November 1915, the cinema secured sole rights in the Crosby/Waterloo district for all new Charlie Chaplin films, which probably increased attendances for a considerable time, as the comedian was then a favourite with cinemagoers. The cinema advertised in the press until 22 July 1916, and appears to have closed at about that time, since it was later advertised as St Luke's Hall, available for dramatic society plays. The building still stands next to the Regent, also a former cinema.

1913
Grand Cinema
Smithdown Road, Wavertree

A purpose-built cinema, with 824 seats, it was designed by Liverpool architects Campbell and Fairhurst, and was built near the electric tram sheds. Although not a large building, the position of the auditorium, at an angle to the main road, allowed quite a wide frontage of white cement. Surmounting the frontage, an elaborately-carved feature projected considerably above the main building line, whilst the extreme ends were adorned by domes. The entire width of the frontage was spanned by an attractive stained glass and wrought iron verandah bearing the cinema's name.

Two pairs of doors in the main entrance led into the foyer, decorated with Wedgewood blue panelling. In the auditorium, the stalls, seating, carpets and curtains were of a similar colour. From the foyer, a wide, green, carpeted staircase led up to the luxurious lounge at the rear of the balcony, where the prevailing colour was red. Lighting was from bowl-shaped shades suspended by chains from the ceiling, whilst gas secondary lighting operated red pilot lights during performances. The operating box had GB projectors with a throw of 85' showing a 17' picture. The screen was set in the centre of gold-embroidered curtains, above a stage decorated by flowers and plants. In front of the stage, a piano provided musical accompaniment when the cinema opened, as an orchestra was engaged later.

The Grand Cinema, 1946.

The proprietors, Grand Cinema (Liverpool) Ltd, who had 8 months previously opened the Dingle Picturedrome, formed the Halliwell Hughes circuit which, by 1922, consisted of seven cinemas. The Grand Cinema opened at 2pm on 26 July 1913, with evening performances at 7pm and 9pm. Thereafter, there were three matinees weekly on Monday, Wednesday and Saturday. Less than 2 years later the Grand was one of the few Liverpool cinemas to show Edison Kinetophone Talking Pictures, a sound-on-disc system introduced on 26 April 1915, when special posters advertised that the human voice could be heard in synchronisation with the pictures. However, apart from this temporary novelty, silent pictures and the orchestra continued until the talkies opened with *The Desert Song*, starring John Boles, on 30 March 1930, when there was a matinee at 2.30pm and evening performances at 6.30pm and 8.40pm.

The Grand became a GB cinema in 1928, having been acquired by Denman Picture Houses Ltd (a subsidiary of GB), together with others in the Hughes circuit. Being one of the GB small cinemas, the Grand showed later runs of the circuit releases for 3 days only, and by November 1952 declining admissions resulted in performances restricted to the evening.

Although it had insufficient width for CinemaScope, the system began on 4 August 1955 with *The Black Shield of Falworth* starring Tony Curtis, but did little to improve declining admissions. The Grand was one of the first three Rank suburban cinemas to close, its last performance on 29 September 1956 with *Indian Scout*, starring George Montgomery and also *The Lyons in Paris*. The site is now a petrol station and car showrooms.

1913
The Palace
Warbreck Moor, Aintree

The Palace, 1925.

A purpose-built, 960-seat stadium-type cinema, the Palace had a white stone frontage. Above the central main entrance was an elaborately-carved, arched section, including the cinema name. Between this part of the frontage and the auditorium, a separate elevation housed the projection box. On the lower side walls of the frontage posters were displayed within tall, stone-framed surrounds, and in front of the building, wooden fencing enclosed an area decorated by potted plants. Two pairs of doors in the main entrance led to the foyer with a paybox on the left and entrance doors on either side to the rear of the auditorium. The seating was arranged in two blocks with central and side gangways. Like many halls of the time, there was a curved ceiling, spanned by decorative carved plasterwork ribs, between the pilasters along the side walls, with panels above a dark dado. Until modernisation in the early-1950s, there was no proscenium, only a deep pelmet surmounting the screen and side drapes, with a screen curtain in front of the orchestra pit.

The proprietors were The Aintree Picture Palace Co, and the cinema was opened on 20 November 1913 at 2pm, by Councillor RC Hermann, but in the absence of press advertising, details of the programme are unknown. The trade press reported that there was to be a continuous performance each evening from 6.30pm to 10.45pm with popular prices from 4d to 1/-. There were matinees on Mondays, Wednesdays and Saturdays.

Conveniently situated for local tramcar routes and the Cheshire Line's Warbreck railway station, the Palace was well attended without significant competition until 1922, when the Walton Vale Picture House opened nearby. Being situated in a well populated area, both cinemas continued to draw the crowds until the early-1950s, regularly having queues. Until 1953 seats could be booked for Saturday evenings at admission prices of 1/-and 1/6.

In 1954 the upper part of the frontage was modernised with a straight-topped, vertical ribbed construction, and a plain modern canopy over the pavement. Glass entrance doors led into the modernised foyer with a new paybox between the stalls entrances. A proscenium was constructed incorporating the widest possible screen, but the height was not covered when CinemaScope films were shown; the first of these, *Three Coins in the Fountain*, shown on 11 April 1955, began a run of Twentieth Century-Fox releases in this format. Film bookings also included ABC and Rank circuit releases with normally single feature programmes until 1957. The films were late showings, the cinema being barred by the Reo, Fazakerley, an ABC cinema which played a similar run of films.

From the mid-1950s admissions continued to fall, with performances in the evenings only. Apparently the closure of the nearest opposition, the Walton Vale, in January 1959, made little difference, the Palace closing 6 months later on 27 June with the film *Bell, Book and Candle,* starring James Stewart and Kim Novak. Following closure, the building was a supermarket for many years, but more recently has been a shoe store.

1913
Palladium
Seaforth Road, Seaforth

An announcement was made in the local press of December 1913 that a distinct acquisition to the district's places of amusement had been made with the opening of this new, purpose-built, 905-seat cinema. The Palladium was described as the finest in the locality, handsomely furnished with all the latest appliances. The frontage was constructed entirely of cream-coloured, glazed stone, with coping and pedimented gable in which was carved the year of erection, 1913. The ground and first floor windows were grouped in threes with stone-framed surrounds, and carved, floral festoons below, and in the centre, the circular first floor window was similarly adorned. Spanning the frontage was a heavy, glass-fronted verandah with the cinema name in white opaque glass in the centre. On the left side were the words, 'Latest Pictures' and on the right, 'Drama, Topical, Sport'. The frontage lighting was entirely from the verandah, which had a lantern-style central fitting, whilst underneath were electric bulbs within globular shades.

The Palladium, 1930s.

Recessed in the main entrance, a central revolving door was flanked on either side by a single swing door leading into the richly-carpeted foyer with panelled walls in blue and white. The central paybox against the rear was used by patrons of the stalls and balcony. A covered extension along the left-hand-side of the building led to the front stalls paybox. At each side of the foyer a broad white marble stairway with a wrought iron balustrade led up to a small landing with doors to the rear of the balcony, where approximately 200 seats were fitted in three sections. Extending over the stalls to about one third of the length of the auditorium, the balcony had a curved front adorned by carved plaster mouldings. The auditorium was also painted in blue and white, with panels along the side walls between the pilasters which extended up to an attractively-carved cornice, from which patterned ribs of plasterwork spanned the curved ceiling. Spaced along the side walls were three circular curtained windows. The proscenium arch was nearly ceiling height with plants at the foot, and the light screen curtain had a multi-coloured floral base. Six light fittings were shaded by opaque glass bowls, suspended by chains from alternate ceiling ribs. Projection was by the latest GB machines, installed in the fireproof operating chamber between the balcony entrances.

It was reported that large numbers attended the opening performances on Christmas Day 1913 at 2.45pm and 6.45pm by the proprietors, the Seaforth Palladium Picture Palace Co, who appointed WJ Moxon as manager, who had had 3 successful years at the Electric Palace, Litherland. He was praised for his good taste in securing the opening programme. Drama was provided by *The Midnight Message*, *Seeds of Wealth*, *The Railroad Inspector's Peril*, and *A Temporary Truce*, which was a story of western life. The humorous side of the programme was provided by *After the Honeymoon* and *Stronger than Sherlock Holmes*. Musical accompaniment was performed by a fine orchestra under the leadership of Ellis Morris, formerly of the Royal Court Theatre, Liverpool. The popular admission prices were 3d, 6d, 9d and 1/- and matinee performances on Monday, Wednesday and Saturday, when patrons received tea free of charge.

Situated a short distance from the northern end of the Liverpool docks, the Palladium, with no immediate opposition, was well attended during its earlier years, but in the early-1920s, three larger cinemas opened nearby. In 1922 the cinema came under the management of J Langham Brown, formerly London manager of the Albany

The Palladium, c1935.

Ward circuit, with vast experience of the industry, who announced his intention to provide the finest shows in the district with live entertainment as an added attraction. From the previous once-nightly performance at 8pm, on 3 April 1922 the programmes became continuous from 7pm to 10.30pm, during which all films except the main feature were shown twice.

The Palladium was among the last cinemas in the district to show sound films. Western Electric sound system was installed for the opening of the talkies on 8 December 1930, when the feature film was *Disraeli*, with George Arliss. There were three performances daily: 3pm, 6.30pm and 8.30pm. Admission was at: 6d, 9d, 1/- and 1/3, reduced at the matinees to 5d, 6d and 9d.

Due to the large number of cinemas in the area, during the 1930s feature films with supporting programmes including *British Movietone News* arrived rather late at the Palladium. In about 1935, under the ownership of Gilbert Dewhurst, an attempt was made to increase attendances by bringing the large stage back into use for amateur talent contests on Tuesday and Friday evenings. With film bookings including many off-circuit B pictures, the cinema was not particularly well attended when, in 1949, it was taken over by Crosby Entertainments Ltd, whose managing director was Phillip M Hanmer, who, in 1939, had opened the new Plaza, Crosby.

The Palladium closed on 19 February with *Ellis Island* and *Death from a Distance*. In the following week there was complete reupholstering of the balcony and rear stalls seats and also reseating in the front stalls. The projection room was re-equipped with the latest GB Kalee 21 projection and sound equipment.

The reopening was on Monday 28 February 1949 when the feature film was *To The Ends of the Earth* starring Dick Powell, with full supporting programme and a matinee at 2.15pm, and a continuous evening programme from 6.15pm. Despite the improvements, generally decreasing admissions during the 1950s, and opposition from numerous cinema circuits, left Seaforth without a cinema from mid-1959, the Stella having closed the year before. The Palladium closed on 10 June 1959, when the final programme was *Rockets Galore*, with *Wild Heritage*. The building was next used as a wholesale tobacco store and, from 1982, was unused until, in early-1985 it became a store for secondhand furniture, with a sauna solarium on the first floor. For a considerable time known as The Fitness Connection, the building remains a health and fitness club.

1913
Wavertree Picturedrome
High Street, Wavertree

Known locally as 'Old Ryme's' cinema, this was a wooden structure near the old Prince Alfred Road tram depot, at the back of land now occupied by Wavertree Gardens, it had a small auditorium on one floor, with seating mainly on forms. The cinema opened in 1913 and an advertisement in the Wavertree Magazine announced: 'The best and most refined pictures in Liverpool'. Films were mainly educational, covering travel, historical subjects and the arts. One of their first films was the drama, *Still Alarm*, featuring Fireman Jack. There were two shows each evening at 7pm and 9pm, with matinees on Wednesday at 3pm and Saturday at 2.30pm. At the opening the admission price was 6d, this being laid down by the General Manager, CM Riby, but thereafter admission was at 2d, 4d and 6d. The building was destroyed by fire in 1919.

1914
Belmont Road Picture House • Lido Cinema
Belmont Road, Anfield

This was described in the trade press as one of the most handsome halls in Liverpool, with a frontage set quite far back from the road, and a beautifully laid out forecourt adorned by flower beds, making a pleasant entrance approach. The white plaster-covered facade had, above the central first floor windows, a large wooden-framed gable and pediment in the Old English-style of vertical black beams on a white background. Towards the sides, a small window was surmounted by a carved architectural feature, extending above the upper part of the frontage. Across the full width of the frontage was a wrought iron and glass verandah, with, on the facing of the curved centre section, the name in white opaque glass. Two pairs of glass-panelled doors led into an attractive lounge with comfortable plush settees, rich tapestries and thick carpet. The same level of comfort was also to be found in the stadium-type auditorium, which had 780 seats on a raked floor. Stepped seating at the rear rose to the height of a balcony. The attractiveness of the interior was increased by indirect lighting from elegant, glass-shaded fittings.

The Belmont Road Picture House, 1930s.

The proprietors, Belmont Road Picture House Ltd, appointed as manager WA Leak, formerly associated with the Picture House, Southport. The local press on 17 January 1914 announced:

> *Opens tonight at 7pm and 9pm – Belmont Road Picture House*
> *Something new in Picture Theatres,*
> *Luxurious, Artistic, Splendid Orchestra under the leadership of Mr B Brassey-Eyton.*
> *Next week at 3pm, 7pm and 9pm.*
> *Afternoon teas at matinees – The World from An Armchair.*

The occasion was marked by a special ceremony at 3pm, after which the capacity audience watched films supplied by the well known Liverpool film renters, the Weisker Bros, but the titles were not advertised. Musical selections by the orchestra were popular at the Belmont, where it was retained longer than at the majority of cinemas. BTP sound system was later installed for the Grand Opening of the talkies on 15 December 1930, with *Not So Quiet On The Western Front* featuring Leslie Fuller, and *After the Fog* with Mary Philben.

A few months later, in 1931, the cinema was leased to ABC Ltd who ran it until 20 November 1937. Their last programme was *Please Teacher* starring Bobby Howes and Jack Holt in *North of Norme*. A few weeks before it had been announced that the Belmont had been acquired from ABC by Councillor A Levy, director of the Futurist and Scala cinemas. The cinema was closed for just over 2 months, and at a cost of £15,000, improvements were made including an increased seating capacity to 800, redecoration and refurnishing, and the installation of a new British Acoustics sound system.

Renamed the Lido Cinema, the grand reopening was on Monday 24 January 1938, with a continuous evening performance from 6.30pm. The feature film was *One in a Million* starring Sonja Henie, with a full supporting programme including up-to-the-minute news. Thereafter, there was a matinee daily at 2.45pm, with reduced prices of 5d and 9d, whilst evening admission was at 6d, 9d and 1/-, bookable in advance without extra charge.

Due to circuit opposition, the Lido had a mixed film booking policy of later runs and B pictures, with which attendances decreased during the 1950s when performances were reduced to evenings only. The only change was at the end of January 1957, when advertisements carried the line on the wide screen and on the final 3 days, ending on 6 June 1959, with a continuous performance from 6pm. The last films were *Streets of Laredo* featuring William Holden, and *The Buckskin Lady*. The building received a newly-styled frontage as a theatre club and cabaret, which opened in 1960 as the Wookey Hollow. It was closed in 1982 due to fire damage but reopened a year later styled as a fun bar, which later became known by its former name, the Wookey Hollow.

1914
St James' Picturedrome
St James' Street, Dingle

St James' Picturedrome, 1960.

A purpose-built, stadium-type cinema with 870 seats, and a frontage similar to the Kensington Picturedrome, surmounted by a large white dome supported by columns. Faced entirely in white plaster, there were three semi-circular windows on the first floor and a black wrought iron and glass verandah spanned the entire width. On the facia, in the centre, was the name, in white opaque glass. Front stall patrons entered via a covered extension along the right-hand-side of the building.

The first cinematograph licence was granted to the St James' Picturedrome Co Ltd on 6 March 1914, this being the only indication of the opening date. Silent pictures, accompanied by a small orchestra, were presented, but 3 years before the talkies arrived it was announced that the manager, WH Lennon, had successfully applied for a singing and dancing licence which permitted four variety acts per performance. A gaily-coloured, well-lit stage was constructed, together with a dressing room.

The cinema was advertised as 'The Hub of the North'. Live entertainment, accompanied by a small band, supported the films on Thursdays and Fridays from October 1927. Admission prices were: 4d, 6d and 1/-, with reductions to two and a half pence, 4d and 6d at the matinees. Strong competition came from the Rialto Cinema, Theatre and Ballroom, which also opened in October 1927.

On 9 June 1930, St James' announced the arrival of the talkies, with Gloria Swanson in *The Trespasser*, which, as at most cinemas, ended variety entertainment. Admission prices were: 3d to 9d, with a matinee daily at 3pm and continuous performance from 6.30pm.

Having survived the bombing of the early-1940s, modernisation in the 1950s completely changed the cinema's appearance. The central dome and the old glass verandah disappeared, replaced by a plain modern one, with a covering of glazed black and white faience tiles. A neon cinema sign and modern canopy, with lettering display on the facia advertising current attractions, were added.

The St James' closed on 5 March 1960, with a double feature: *The Mating Game*, starring Tony Randall and Debbie Reynolds, and *Frontier Rangers*. Matinee was at 2.15pm and evening shows, continuous from 6pm, continued the policy of the North Western cinema circuit, who ran the cinema for 40 years. The building was later demolished due to a new road system.

1914
Rice Lane Picture House • Atlas Cinema
Rice Lane, Walton

A main road situation about 4 miles to the north of the city, the long, tall frontage of this cinema was constructed parallel to the road, with the auditorium at an angle. The intervening triangular space was used for the main entrance, first floor lounge and other internal areas. The construction was of ordinary brick, relieved by terracotta, with horizontal and vertical designs, which formed three tall architectural features projecting above the apex. Extending over the full length was a stained glass verandah, brilliantly illuminated by electric lights and topped by the cinema's name in large letters, providing an attractive frontage.

The Picture House was built by J & G Chappell of Walton, to the plans of Nagington and Shennan. It was described as one of the most up-to-date picture theatres in the north of Liverpool, with seating for almost 1000. At the extreme right of the frontage, the main entrance, with walls of buff-coloured tiles and the paybox on the right, gave access via two pairs of glass-panelled doors to the mosaic-tiled foyer. A separate entrance to the front stalls was at the extreme left of the frontage. From the foyer, a wide, white marble staircase led up to the sumptuous lounge with comfortably upholstered settees in blue, tastefully decorated with flowers. From here there was an entrance to the rear balcony with nearly 300 seats on a stepped flooring, from where all patrons had an uninterrupted view. In the midst of embroidered curtains, set quite high in the approximately 25'-wide proscenium, a picture 16' in width was obtained at a distance of 85' from the projection room at the rear of the balcony. The tall proscenium was flanked by splayed walls which extended to the front of the curved balcony. The auditorium had Wedgewood blue panels and blue tip-up seats, and a cosy appearance was achieved by the rich red curtains and carpet. Electric, glass-shaded dimmer lights were suspended from the curved ceiling, whilst red pilot lights provided illumination during performances.

As the Gordon cinema company's first venture, under the able manager, Eric Thornber, the Rice Lane Picture House was described as one of the most modern cinema theatres in the north of England. It opened with an afternoon performance on Saturday 16 May 1914, by special invitation only. Several directors and the chairman, G Gordon, formally opened the theatre, and the all-star programme featured the great Pathé film, *Honesty*.

The Grand Opening took place on Monday 18 May 1914, with a continuous performance from 6.30pm to 10.30pm for an exclusive showing of the sensational drama *Detective Finn* and a full programme of the very latest dramatic, comic and scenic films. Top class music, including audience requests, was provided by the Picture House Trio, under the direction of Edward C Price. On Saturday evenings, performances were twice-nightly at 6.45pm and 9pm, with admission prices at 3d, 4d and 6d in the stalls, and 9d in the balcony. Children were not admitted unless accompanied by adults.

The Picture House continued under the Gordon circuit until c1929, when the new proprietors were the Rice Lane Picture House Co of 14 North John Street, Liverpool. They opened with their first sound film, the All Talking dramatic sensation *Hearts in Exile* starring Dolores Costello, on 20 October 1930. It was closed in the summer of 1932 for major refurbishment. The auditorium was redecorated in an Egyptian-style and reseated to a reduced capacity of 800, providing more comfort and the latest lighting and heating systems.

The Grand Reopening of the cinema, then renamed the Atlas Super Talkie Theatre, was on Monday 5 September 1932, when it was announced that the latest Western Electric sound system would provide the most perfect sound in the Liverpool area. It was presented to great advantage, the opening attraction being the world famous operetta *The Beggar Student*, starring Shirley Dale and Lance Fairfax, with full supporting programme at 2.15pm and at the continuous evening performance from 6.30pm to 10.30pm.

In March 1938 the Atlas came under the ownership of Southan Morris Associated Cinemas, Britain's largest independent circuit, who ran it until October 1954, when all their cinemas were taken over by the Essoldo circuit. Due to its narrow proscenium, the Atlas was unsuitable for CinemaScope and wide screen film, which restricted bookings during its last 4 years.

With small audiences at evening performances only, the cinema survived until 1 March 1958, when the last programme was *Man Without A Star*, featuring Kirk Douglas, and *Francis Joins the WACS*. The building lay derelict until November 1981, when it was demolished leaving a vacant site, recently redeveloped with flats.

1914
Majestic Picture House
Daulby Street, Liverpool city centre

Erected on a corner site, the building fronted onto Daulby Street and Boundary Place with the main entrance on the curved corner. The frontage was faced with terracotta with a dome on top supported by columns interspersed with glass, illuminated from within by electric lamps. Spanning the main entrance was a canopy, on which were several globular light fittings. The building was triangular, with increasing width towards the rear providing a waiting room at either side of the stalls. The capacity of 870 included about 200 seats in the small balcony, which was supported by pillars. On the right-hand-side at balcony level, were three boxes, each containing five seats.

The proprietors, Majestic Picture House Ltd, were a private company, whose chairman was Alderman John Gordon, a pawnbroker. The opening was advertised in the local press on 10 June 1914, as a continuous performance from 2pm to 10.30pm, with a first class programme at the popular prices of 3d, 6d, 9d and 1/-. The next day began a 3 day showing of *A Terrible Night At Sea*, a thrilling picture in four parts.

About 12 months after the opening, the trade press stated that since taking over the management of the Majestic, Percy Hamer had introduced many innovations, including a new and capable orchestra, whose selections were a

great feature of each programme. Hamer also booked all comedy programmes for one afternoon and evening, Charlie Chaplin being the most popular, a type of show relatively new to Merseyside cinemas.

In about 1920, the longest surviving, and possibly the cinema's best remembered manager, Ellis Williamson, arrived. In the 1920s the Majestic was styled as the city's super-cinema, making a speciality of double features, rarely seen in those days. Musical accompaniment with the big programmes was then by the Majestic Grand Symphony Orchestra, consisting of ten instrumentalists with HS Cropper as musical director. It was emphasised that parents could safely bring their families, as objectionable and sensational pictures would not be shown. The success of the double feature is indicated by the fact that, in 1927, a larger seating capacity was required, achieved by replacing the waiting rooms with a block of seats at either side, and by the removal of the boxes at the right-hand-side of the balcony, providing an extra 350 seats. Towards the end of the 1920s, the symphony orchestra was led by CV Roche, who in 1930 was the leader of the city's last cinema orchestra at the Palais de Luxe, Lime Street.

March 1930 saw the end of the silent era at the Majestic, the orchestra being replaced by the talkies, and the cinema being equipped with Western Electric sound system on 24 March. *King of the Khyber Rifles*, featuring Victor McLaglen and Myrna Loy was shown. Performances, as usual, were continuous from 2pm to 10.45pm and prices little different from those in 1914: balcony 1/3, stalls 8d and 1/-, and at only 6d and 9d up to 4.30pm.

During the 1930s, against strong competition from the new super-cinemas in the city, the Paramount and the Forum (ABC), the independently-owned Majestic's policy was to book second runs of both circuit releases, which included the productions of Paramount, Metro-Goldwyn-Mayer and Warner Bros. Retaining the policy of double feature programmes introduced during the 1920s, the Majestic normally presented a continuous performance from 12.30pm to 10.30pm. Early in 1937, the proprietors submitted plans to the Liverpool justices for the erection on the site of a new, 1,800-seat super-cinema. The plans having been approved, the cinema closed on 3 April 1937 with the all-star Paramount feature *The Big Broadcast of 1937* featuring Jack Benny, George Burns and Gracie Allen.

Demolition began almost immediately, followed by the construction of the new building, both being completed within a record 6 months.

1914
Homer Cinema
Great Homer Street, Everton

The Homer Great Homer Street, 1967.

The location of this purpose-built cinema was a thickly populated area about one and a half miles from the city. The stone-faced frontage closely resembled that of the recently opened Palladium, Seaforth, with a similar sized, rectangular auditorium and a balcony above the rear stalls. Although not particularly large in area, it nevertheless originally had a seating capacity of 1000 in the early-1930s, reduced to 950 when tip-up seats replaced front stalls forms. This was a W Gordon circuit venture, closely following the opening of their Rice Lane Picture House, the first licence being granted on 21 August 1914. The opening was not advertised in the local press.

The Homer was acquired c1920 by the Liverpool cinema circuit of Edwin Haigh & Son and prices ranged from 4d to 1/-. In May 1933, the cinema was leased to the Regent circuit, a subsidiary of ABC, and was then purchased in December of that year. Their period of ownership was short, for in May 1934 the Homer, and several other Regent circuit cinemas on Merseyside, were sold to local cinema circuit, Regent Enterprise Ltd, Stanley Street, Liverpool. The next change of ownership came in March 1938, when the company's cinemas were added to Britain's largest independent circuit, Southan Morris Associated Cinemas Ltd, London, SW1.

From October 1954 until closure, the owners were the Newcastle-based Essoldo circuit. From the time of opening, the Homer was one of many older cinemas in the area. More cinemas were added nearby in the early-1930s: two cinemas of the major circuits, the Astoria Walton, an ABC cinema, and the Gaumont Palace, Anfield. Except at the start of 1930s, film bookings were therefore fairly restricted to later showings of the circuit releases. With the exception of the Astoria, the Homer was the longest-surviving cinema in the area immediately to the north of the city, the closing date being 20 January 1962. The double programme was *Two Rode Together*, starring James Stewart and Richard Widmark, and *A Question of Suspense*. The building was demolished during a major redevelopment of the Great Homer Street area.

1914
Magnet Cinema
Picton Road, Wavertree

In a prominent position on the main road, the mainly plaster-faced front elevation had a slanting tiled roof visible above the facade. This consisted of a wide central section, flanked on each side by a curved top section, bounded vertically by stone with recessed divisions, and providing lower level areas for poster advertising. A central short flight of steps led up to two pairs of glass-panelled doors, separated by a column. Above the upper part of the frontage featured a semi-circular window and the cinema name. A large magnet, illuminated by electric lamps of 10,000 candle power, made a striking image.

Inside, a rectangular foyer led to the rear of the stadium-type, 1,038-seat auditorium, with a raked floor, providing every patron with an unobstructed view. Following the opening of the Grand Cinema, Smithdown Road, in the previous year, the Magnet was an addition to the circuit of T Halliwell Hughes. The company, Magnet (Wavertree) Ltd, with a capital of £6,000, was registered on 6 May 1914. After completion of the building, a cinematograph licence was granted on 11 December 1914, at about which time the cinema opened, apparently unannounced in the local press.

Like other cinemas of the TH Hughes circuit, the Magnet was taken over in March 1928 by Denman Picture Houses Ltd, a subsidiary of GB. Equipped with British Acoustics sound system, the talkies opened on 21 April 1930 with *Sunny Side Up*, starring Janet Gaynor and Charles Farrell. Admission prices were:

5d to 1/-, slightly above those of earlier years (4d to 10d).

Before the shrinking audiences of the early-1950s, the Magnet was well attended, screening first runs in the district of the company release films, although from 1939 the strongest possible competition came with the opening of the new super-cinema, the Abbey. CinemaScope was installed and opened on 21 March 1955 with *Sign of the Pagan,* featuring Jeff Chandler. In the last 4 years before closure, evening performances were continuous and at the final performance on 23 May 1959, the programme consisted of *Man of the West,* starring Gary Cooper, and *Hong Kong Confidential.* The building was sold to VM Gaskin & Son Ltd, of Low Hill, manufacturing upholsterers, and later became a badminton and squash club.

1914
Tunnel Road Picturedrome • Avenue Cinema
Tunnel Road, Edge Hill

The opening of this cinema was announced in the *Kinematograph Weekly* of 24 December 1914, as the first of two picture houses which had opened that week, the other being the Savoy, West Derby Road. The Picturedrome had an imposing structure, with a tall, wide frontage, the upper part of which was of red brick relieved by broad horizontal bands of buff-coloured stone, and a line of small windows below the coping. The white stone lower level had a full width iron and glass verandah, below which were several entrances and exits. With white marble floors, the spacious vestibule gave access to a large and comfortable waiting room with entrances to the luxurious auditorium, with prevailing colours of blue and red, and comfortable tip-up seats for 500 persons. From the vestibule, wide carpeted staircases led up to the balcony which extended considerably over the stalls, which held 340 plush seats. Such seating capacity was exceptional considering its modest size and the era of construction. The auditorium featured a 54' proscenium, within which a clear picture was projected onto the screen, distanced about 80' from the projection room, equipped with two GB machines.

The Tunnel Cinema, 1977.

The first cinematograph licence was dated 15 December 1914, with the manager S Hope Phoenix. The opening performance, accompanied by an orchestra under the baton of HE Mason, was attended by over 800 persons invited by the directors of Tunnel Road Picturedrome Ltd, whose chairman was John Gordon CC.

In accordance with normal policy of that time, there was a daily matinee and continuous performances in the evening. Admission prices were from 6d to 1/-. In its early days, the 'House Full' signs were often used for film favourites such as Charlie Chaplin and Harold Lloyd, and serials including Pearl White and her cliffhanger adventures. Orchestral accompaniment to silent films was replaced in the early-1930s by Western Electric sound system, but the cinema still faced increased competition from the new super-cinemas. Still, 'the Old Tunny', as it was nicknamed, was among the longest surviving of Liverpool's suburban cinemas and, except for a short period of closure due to bomb damage in September 1940, it was open for a total of 54 years. Due to circuit opposition, the mixed film booking policy included later showings for 3 days only of the more popular attractions, and also off circuit releases and B pictures, among these thrillers and westerns were the most popular.

Having survived the television and bingo boom of the 1950s, the cinema continued into the 1960s, from 10 July 1961 renamed the Avenue. The final blow to its fortunes was the demolition of practically all the surrounding houses. A compulsory purchase order was served, but the Avenue was kept open as long as possible, but the great reduction in the local population was responsible for the eventual closure on Saturday 7 December 1968. This was attended by the chairman and managing director, Duncan French, who was there for sentimental reasons, his father having been present on the opening night in 1914. Some patrons turned up to see Cliff Richard in *Finders Keepers* and *Ambush Bay.* The hall reopened for bingo and then as the Tunnel Club until 1984, after which it was not used and was damaged by fire in 1995, leaving only the frontage and outer walls which were later demolished.

1914
Savoy
West Derby Road, Tuebrook

The Savoy, 1946.

On a main road just beyond the city area, was the Savoy, on a corner site at the end of Brougham Terrace, between Liverpool's two largest theatres, the Hippodrome and the Olympia. Although not very wide, the three-storeyed frontage, surmounted by a central tower, nevertheless presented an imposing appearance with a facing of buff-coloured terracotta, relieved by horizontal green bands. There were three tall central windows at first floor level and three circular windows above. At ground level, beneath a full width iron and glass verandah, two separate flights of steps led up to the entrances, each with a pair of doors with circular glass panels. These provided access to the handsome, oak-panelled vestibule, from which grand staircases led up to the balcony with a line of windows on either side.

In the *Kinematograph Weekly* of 24 December 1914, it was reported that, from the balcony, the size of the hall appeared surprisingly large, considering that the total seating capacity was only 890, indicating that the comfort of patrons had been a top priority. Lighting from glass-shaded electric lamps was on a dimmer system. A bower of plants and flowers on the orchestra pit screened the musicians accompanying the silent films. The projection equipment consisted of two Tyler Indomitable projectors, installed by the electrical department of Fennings, Liverpool.

The first cinematograph licence was granted on 15 December 1914 to the W Gordon circuit, with offices on West Derby Road, and the Savoy opened under the management of a Mr Evans of the Electric Palace, Rock Ferry. The opening programme was headed by the film *Called Back,* booked and projected by Fenning representative, Mr Moser. The admission prices were from 4d to 9d at continuous performances from 6.30pm to 10.30pm, with separate shows on Saturday at 6.50pm and 9pm, and a matinee daily at 3pm.

The Savoy was among the few Liverpool cinemas to present Edison Kinetophone Talking Pictures, advertised as 'The Latest and Greatest Marvel of the Age', which on Monday 3 May 1915 followed on from a week at the Grand, Smithdown Road. The cinema was taken over in 1923 by the Liverpool circuit of Edwin Haigh & Son, opening with music by the New Savoy Symphony Orchestra under W Jones. In 1926 there was another change of ownership to First Federated Cinemas Ltd, associated with John F Wood Bedford Cinemas Ltd, by whom it was run until March 1928, when this was another of the local circuits taken over by the GTC in the amalgamation of companies under GB.

In the early-1930s, the Savoy, sandwiched between the Olympia, an ABC cinema, and the Hippodrome, suffered with regard to film bookings, when in 1931, the latter also became a GB cinema, resulting in the Savoy having to rely on a mixed film booking policy of older films. Surviving for a further 25 years, it was then among the first three of Rank Liverpool's suburban cinemas to close in 1956, when the final performance, on 29 September, ended a 3 day showing of *The Brave and the Beautiful,* starring Anthony Quinn, and *The World in my Corner* featuring Audie Murphy. Since then, the building has been used as a lino store, a car showroom and later as offices.

1915
Empress Picture House
West Derby Road, Tuebrook

This purpose-built cinema was the latest addition to the small circuit of T Halliwell Hughes, who in the *Kinematograph Weekly* was congratulated on his enterprise. On a main road, about 4 miles east of the city, the building had a frontage of white-painted plaster, with an iron and glass verandah extending across the full width. The upper part had a curved central section supported by columns, the lower part in front of the first floor windows being enclosed by metal railings between the columns. At ground level, several steps led up to three sets of doors. Separated by square columns, the entrances led into the rectangular foyer with maple flooring, handsome fireplaces and tapestries forming an elegant frieze. At either side of the paybox, short, richly-carpeted, Sicilian marble stairways led up to the rear of the stadium-type auditorium. The seating accommodated close to 1000, arranged in two sections with central and side gangways. Tip-up seats were provided, except for several rows of forms at the front. The lower half of the walls was covered in dark, patterned wood with panels above. Flanked by walls on which large glass-shaded electric fittings were set within panels, the tall proscenium was adorned by a deep red pelmet and

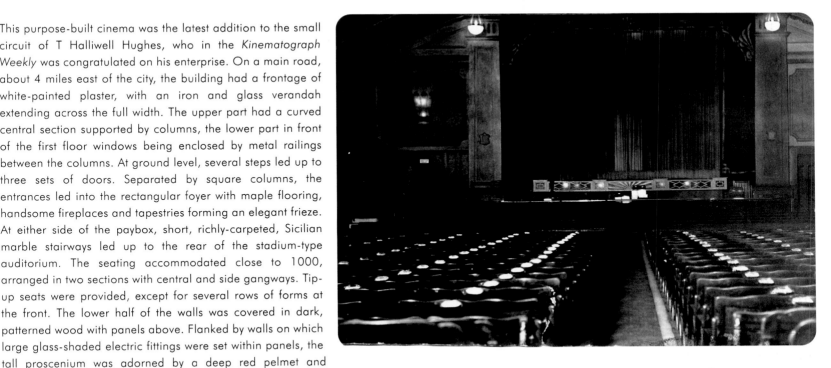

curtain relieved by gold designs in front of the pale screen curtain, illuminated by electric lamps within the lighting trough. A central sunray design surmounted the proscenium and the orchestra pit was separated from the front gangway by a dark curtain hanging from a brass rail. Lighting was by electric lamps within glass globes suspended from the curved ceiling.

The *Kinematograph Weekly* reported that this picture hall was the latest and one of the most artistic in Liverpool. It was opened on Saturday 20 February 1915, under the management of a Mr Bell, who previously managed the Derby Picturedrome. Pictures were projected by GB machines under the guiding hand of Mr Jones, late chief operator of the company's Grand Cinema, Smithdown Road. The 2pm matinee was followed by evening performances at 7pm and 9pm and the first main feature was the silent version of the film *Kismet*.

The Halliwell Hughes circuit was bought in March 1928 by Denman Picture Houses Ltd and the Empress then became a GB cinema. Two years later, like several other of the company cinemas at that time, British Acoustics sound system was installed for the opening of the talkies on 31 March 1930 with *The Great Gabbo*, starring Eric von Stroheim and Betty Compson. In June 1932, the opening of ABC's nearby super-cinema, the Carlton, represented extremely strong competition. However, screening first runs in the district of GB circuit release films, the Empress continued to be quite well attended during the 1940s, apart from the general effects of the war early in the decade.

Despite rather limited space for the wide screen systems, the showing of CinemaScope films began on 20 March 1955 with *Sign of the Pagan*, starring Jeff Chandler and Anthony Quinn. During the last 5 years, with declining attendances, performances were mainly continuous in the evenings only. From 21 December 1959, performances were reduced to once-nightly, until closure on 12 March 1960 with *House of the Seven Hawks*, featuring Robert Taylor, and *Tarzan, the Ape Man*, starring Denny Miller. The building was demolished for the construction of a dual carriageway.

The projection room of the Smithdown Picture Playhouse.

1915
Smithdown Picture Playhouse
Smithdown Road, Wavertree

Reporting the opening of this latest Liverpool cinema, the *Kinematograph Weekly* of 25 February 1915 stated that, the exterior of the building showed evidence of many months of labour. At the head of several steps, the entrance was supported by fluted columns and illuminated by electric bulbs in ruby-coloured shades. Extending across the full width, the stained glass verandah, also lit by electric lamps, displayed the cinema's name on the facia. The main entrance led into the spacious foyer which had a mosaic floor. Tapestries decorated the walls, with an ornamental ceiling sporting elegant light fittings. The 900-seat auditorium, was also decorated by tapestries, which splendidly harmonised with the red, plush, tip-up seats and blue carpets and curtains of the 27'-wide proscenium.

A cinematograph licence was granted on 19 February 1915, to the Smithdown Picture Playhouse Ltd. The next day a private show for the directors preceded the Grand Opening on Monday 22 February 1915, with a 3pm matinee and continuous performances from 6.30pm. The cinema was leased c1921 to the Bedford circuit, whose managing director, John F Wood, Liverpool picture pioneer, ran it until March 1928, when the company's cinemas were acquired by the GTC under GB.

The lease on the Playhouse was terminated and it reverted to independent ownership by the company of the same name with offices at 1-3 Stanley Street Liverpool. Little more than 2 years later, BTH sound system was installed, and the first talkie, *The Last of Mrs Cheyney* starring Norma Shearer and Basil Rathbone, was shown for 3 days beginning on 2 June 1930. On a main road, in a well populated area, the Picture Playhouse continued to be one of the better attended independents, with a booking policy including the leading attractions of the ABC and GB release films, shown normally for 3 days only, at separate matinee and continuous evening performances.

The next notable improvement was the installation of a wide screen for CinemaScope, which began on 7 July 1955, with *Ring of Fear* starring Clyde Beatty and Pat O'Brien. Performances continued to consist of a 2.30pm matinee, with continuous performances from 6pm. Principally, double feature programmes were shown after May 1960, and 2 years later these were in the evenings only until closure on 11 September 1963 with *Woman of Summer* starring Joanne Woodward and Richard Beymer, and *Hand of Death*.

A gala opening as the Smithdown Bingo Club was immediately announced, and this took place on Tuesday 17 September 1963 at 8pm, in the presence of *Coronation Street* characters Minnie Caldwell and Martha Longhurst. The building was later acquired and converted by Tesco for use as a supermarket.

1915
Empire
James Street, Garston

At the junction of James Street and Church Road, the building was originally constructed as a live theatre by R Costain and Son for £7,500, including the site. The exterior was almost entirely of ordinary brick, relieved by red brick on the James Street frontage. This comprised of three storeys, the upper part of which was recessed, whilst the lower part, adjacent to the road, included the main entrance surmounted by an iron and glass verandah. The foyer had a short flight of marble steps to the waiting room with three entrances to the rear of the stalls. At the extreme left of the foyer, an enclosed marble staircase, with metal balustrade, ascended to the first floor lounge, from which there was a door to the rear balcony. The seating was arranged in two blocks, with central and side gangways on a stepped floor descending to the curved front, terminating with a box at either side of the proscenium. This balcony and boxes provided 336 seats of the total 1,040. The circle front had plasterwork panels in which brackets suspended shaded electric lamps. The boxes had circular fronts and were similarly decorated, flanked by substantial marble columns with carved capitals at either side of the tall, arched, 30' proscenium. A feature of the auditorium was the gold fittings, whilst the principal illumination was from electric lamps concealed within large glass shaded fittings, suspended from the carved ribs spaced along the curved ceiling. Full theatrical facilities included an orchestra pit, a full-sized stage with fly tower, eight dressing rooms and, to provide for cine-variety, a Biograph box equipped with a cinematograph, appropriate to the licence granted on 1 June 1915 for Theatre, Music Hall and Cinematograph.

The Empire, 1980s.

The Grand Opening of the Empire, under the management of Charles Locke, took place on the afternoon of Saturday 5 June 1915. A large crowd attended for the programme of comedy, variety and pictures, which were also shown at 6.45pm and 9pm, with prices at: stalls 6d, front circle 1/- and balcony 9d. Locke's policy of cine-variety continued until 1916, when from 3 April there was a change to stage plays. The next year entertainment reverted to variety revues until the Empire ended its short life as a theatre on 31 August 1918, with a variety entertainment entitled *Mr & Mrs John Bull at Home*.

The Empire began its 44 years of life as a cinema on 2 September 1918, with the Star Exclusive Picture Attraction, *The Heart of A Lion*, together with a supporting programme including the latest Topical Gazette with music by the augmented orchestra.

The theatre was taken over in July 1928 from Garston Theatre and Empire Pictures Ltd, by the JF Woods cinema circuit, from that time known as Bedford Cinemas (1928) Ltd. Sound films began on 16 June 1930, with *The Gold Diggers of Broadway* featuring Nancy Welford and Godfrey Tearle, the theatre having been equipped with Western Electric sound system. Under the same ownership until the early-1960s, the Empire screened the leading films of the major circuits, ABC, GB, Rank, at later dates, normally for 3 days only, with daily matinees and continuous evening performances. CinemaScope began at the Empire on 17 January 1955 with *The Command* starring Guy Madison.

Possibly due to declining audiences, a change to mainly double feature programmes, in June 1961, became the policy until closure, with evening performances only from September. A gradual change to bingo began in August 1962 with sessions on Sundays only. This was soon increased to 3 evenings weekly on Friday, Saturday and Sunday, before the complete change was effected after the last film performance on 8 December 1962, with *Jailhouse Rock* starring Elvis Presley, and *The Fastest Gun Alive*.

The Empire Bingo and Social Club (Garston) Ltd, in which Bedford Cinemas retained an interest, ran the bingo operation until 1986, when it was taken over by Andrew Sale of J & A Entertainments, Kirkby. Since then, considerable refurbishment has taken place, including tables and chairs in the stalls replacing cinema seats and a licensed bar below the stage. But at the upper levels, the original architectural features, including the boxes, remain. Now, over 90 years after the opening as a live theatre, the Empire is a unique location for bingo.

1916
Garrick
Westminster Road, Kirkdale

With a capacity of 1,500, including a large balcony, this was Liverpool's largest cinema in 1916. A long building with elevations to Westminster Road and Foley Street, the main entrance was at the head of several steps at the junction of the two roads. Above, was an iron and glass verandah which extended for a short distance along the right-hand-side of the building. Above the verandah, the upper part of the building had a facing of light painted plaster and included several windows at first floor level, the lower part was of ordinary brick.

The first proprietors were the W Gordon cinema circuit, West Derby Road, who opened the Garrick on, or about, 7 January 1916, the date of the first Cinematographe licence. The Garrick was an early location of talking pictures, which began on 8 April 1929, presented in addition to the normal programme by the sound-on-disc system. The following year Western Electric sound system was installed for sound-on-film, which commenced on 26 May 1930 with *The Desert Song* featuring John Boles.

The Garrick was among the Gordon circuit cinemas which were leased in May 1933 to ABC's subsidiary, the Regent Circuit, London, before purchase by the company in December of that year. Their period of ownership was extremely short, for in May 1934 the new proprietors were the Liverpool-based Regent Enterprise Ltd. The cinema was taken over in March 1938 by the country's largest independent circuit, Southan Morris Associated Cinemas Ltd, London, and it remained under their control until October 1954, when the last proprietors were the Newcastle-based Essoldo circuit. With strong competition from numerous local cinemas, especially those of ABC and GB, the Garrick presented a mixed selection of later run films for 3 days only, at continuous evening performances, and, until October 1954 there were matinees daily. Due to steeply declining attendances during the latter part of the 1950s, the Garrick was among several cinema closures in 1959. Its 43 years as a cinema ended on 14 March 1959, with the double feature *Lust for Gold* starring Glenn Ford, and *To the Ends of the Earth* featuring Dick Powell. The building was later demolished to make way for new housing.

1916
Scala Super-Cinema
Lime Street, Liverpool city centre

This was the second cinema opened by Sol Levy, the dominant personality of the Midland film business during its early years. Following the opening of the Scala, Birmingham, in 1914, Levy formed the company Scala (Liverpool) Ltd. In 1915 construction began on the new theatre in Lime Street, to the plans of architect JS Bramwell. On completion, due to its artistic design and expensive furnishings, the description of the directorate as 'The SuperCinema of the Mersey City' was considered to be well justified.

Although a rather small building, erected between the Futurist cinema and another property, it was given an arresting appearance, having a tall, three-storeyed frontage of white terracotta, which at the upper level featured five groups of first and second floor windows, surmounted in the centre by a stone panel bearing the name, Scala. Above a prominent coping, at the highest part of the frontage was a balcony with an iron balustrade and columns supporting a central arch, surmounted by a gable. Above the lower part, a white opaque glass-fronted metal verandah displayed, in the centre of the facia, the words 'super-cinema', illuminated by electric lamps in globular shades.

In the centre of the cinema's frontage, flanked by square columns at the head of a short flight of steps, the main entrance had three pairs of doors to the elegant foyer with mosaic floor, and walls and paybox faced in white marble. At either side were entrances to the 400-seat stalls, consisting of a central block, separated from the short rows at the side by a gangway. Behind square marble columns at each side of the foyer, a white marble staircase led up to the luxurious first floor lounge. A continuation of the staircases led to the rear of the 220-seat balcony, and straight side extensions to the exits at the front of the auditorium.

The original, Egyptian-style decorations had large murals on the walls and the proscenium and stage were flanked by appropriate lamp standards. The high, straight ceiling was decorated towards the front by panelled recesses and over the balcony, by a large oval dome. The effect was enhanced by electric lamps within bowl-shaded fittings suspended from the ceiling. The projection room was equipped with Simplex machines under the control of J Hunt.

The Scala celebrated its opening on 31 January 1916 with a collection on behalf of the widows and orphans of sailors and soldiers, which raised £70. The well known firm of JD Walker World Films Ltd contributed ten guineas, whilst the cinema's directorate gave a similar amount. The performance, continuous from 2pm to 10.30pm, featured Aubrey Smith in *John Glayde's Honour*, supported by the exclusive comedy *Chip Off The Old Block*, with Maurice Costello's son aged ten, as well as the *Scala Gazette* of exclusive local events, and the latest news. All such entertainment was accompanied by the Scala Grand Symphony Orchestra under the direction of Harry Freeman. This accorded with Sol Levy's policy of full orchestral accompaniment and the complete exclusion of live acts. The admission prices were 6d, and 1/6, but seats in the balcony, described as tubs, were at the then unheard of price of 2/-, to encourage high class patrons. This charge was the idea of the first general manager, Vivian van Damm, who in later years became well known in the theatrical world at London's Windmill Theatre.

In less than 5 years the Scala came under the same ownership as the Futurist, with the formation in October 1920 of the new company Futurist (Liverpool) Ltd, both sharing virtually the same directors, with Sol Levy's younger brother Alfred as joint managing director. A similar policy of operation was announced, delivering the same standard of service. Until the late-1920s, full orchestral accompaniment to silent films was by excellent orchestras, the most notable, from November 1923, being that of Jules Gaillard, the violin virtuoso.

Although the Scala, concurrently with the Futurist, presented, for the first time in Liverpool, talking pictures by Lee de Forest Phono films during the week beginning 29 November 1926, it was the first to introduce with-sound films as a permanent attraction by the RCA Photophone system, on 8 July 1929, when the feature film was *Lucky Boy*, starring George Jessell, the American vaudeville entertainer. This was shown at separate performances, four times daily at: 2pm, 4.10pm, 6.30pm and 8.40pm, to which admission was 1/3 in the stalls and 2/4 in the balcony. Although seats could be pre-booked at 1/10 and 3/6, long queues nevertheless extended to Bolton Street at the rear of the building.

Sketch of the Scala from 1916.
Opposite. Scala, 1931.

From the early-1930s, as in the case of the Futurist, first runs of most leading films were lost to the major circuits, and adding to this disadvantage, in 1941 the Scala was also closed due to bomb damage. It reopened after about 6 weeks on 17 June with *The Bank Detective* starring WC Fields and *San Francisco Docks*. For years bookings were of second runs of the circuit releases, off-circuit films and in 1954-55, X certificate French films. These ended on 26 March 1955 with *Unmarried Mothers*, and *Adventure in Berlin*.

The Scala had then been leased to the Twentieth Century-Fox Film Corporation as a second venue to the Futurist for the first runs in the city of CinemaScope films with stereophonic sound. The balcony sides were removed to provide sight lines to the large screen, in front of which the festoon curtain extended over the full width of the auditorium and front stall exits, around which wall speakers provided stereo-phonic effect. The Scala reopened on 10 April 1955, when a sequence of Twentieth Century-Fox CinemaScope films began with *Carmen Jones*, with Dorothy Dandridge and Harry Belafonte.

Before the end of the 1950s, too few of the company release films for their two adjoining cinemas were available. The Futurist, having the larger seating capacity, continued to present them, whilst from April 1959, the Scala screened a mixed selection of films reverting back to the pre1954 policy. This continued into 1960, when the Scala was taken over by Gala International, who styled it as Merseyside's Continental Theatre and opened on 15 May 1960 with *Sins of Youth* and *Travelling Light*, a continental X certificate double feature, which attracted over 30,000 patrons during the first 4 of a 6 week run until 25 June. Gala withdrew on 30 June 1962. The Scala's description as a continental theatre ended that day, but the Scala continued to be a popular venue for adult films and was well patronised, especially in the afternoon performances from 1pm. There was then a return to later runs of the circuit release films and off circuit bookings. Of necessity this policy was continued from 3 September 1967, when the Scala became an ABC cinema, having been acquired by EMI (Electrical and Musical Industries). On withdrawing from the Scala, Gala International leased the Clayton Square News Theatre as Liverpool's continental film theatre.

ABC/EMI took control of the cinema from 3 July 1967, the smallest of the company's three cinemas on Lime Street. The change of ownership resulted in the modernisation of the frontage, the lower part of which had a small mosaic pattern. The canopy was replaced by a full width lettering display panel, illuminated internally, and the three pairs of doors had full length metal framed doors. Dispensing with the former architectural features, the plaster-faced frontage was relieved by a line of windows on each of the three storeys. In the centre, a square illuminated sign displayed 'ABC Scala EMI'.

EMI operated the three Lime Street cinemas for a further 15 years. However, despite being owned by a major circuit, the Scala was still at a disadvantage with regard to film bookings, being the smallest. With considerably reduced attendances, the decision was taken to convert the largest of the three, the ABC (Forum,) to three screens, and to close the Scala and Futurist. Five weeks after the closure of the latter, only 200 patrons attended the last performance at the Scala, on 24 August 1982 for *Firefox*, starring Clint Eastwood.

The building was on a 75-year lease from 1918, with 10 years to run and only a peppercorn rent to be paid, but despite attempts to find a buyer or lessee, it was not used until acquisition by Kimberley Inn (NorthWest) Ltd in March 1987. After a £50,000 conversion scheme including a dance floor and licensed bar in the former stalls area, and a 1920s Art Deco cocktail bar on the first floor, it opened as the Hippodrome, styled as one of the city's brightest drinking and dining venues. This venture terminated in 1992, and the building was not used until reopening as the Baraka nightclub in the autumn of 1997, which closed after 18 months. The building remains unused.

1916
Swan Picturedrome • Swan Cinema
Mill Lane, Old Swan

The Swan Cinema, 1979.

The *Kinematograph and Lantern Weekly* stated that this cinema would be ready for opening in April 1916; this is the only apparent reference to the opening. The white stone frontage, with recessed divisions, surmounted centrally by a broad, Eastern-style dome, conveyed an impression of oriental splendour. The curved central section included the main entrance and the upper level at either side featured a square tower. The 950-seat, stadium-type auditorium faced a 35'-wide proscenium and 8'6" deep stage. Two dressing rooms were provided for live entertainment.

During its 40 years as a cinema, the Swan was run by several independent owners and lessees. The managing director of the first proprietor, Kirkdale Picture House Ltd, was Councillor John Walker, who 6 years previously had opened the Moulton Picture Palace in Everton. At the time of opening, the two nightly performances and daily matinee were accompanied an orchestra. A notable attraction the following year, for 3 days commencing 31 December 1917, was *The Dumb Girl of Portici*. Accompanied by orchestral music, it was reputed to be the most superb contemporary production, starring the incomparable ballerina, Anna Pavlova, with an all-star cast including the entire Russian Ballet, as shown before Her Majesty, Queen Mary and the royal family.

The proprietors in 1923 were Swan Cinemas Ltd who, in 1925, presented pictures and variety, which was the main format until the arrival of the talkies by Western Electric sound system, on 17 February 1930 with *King of the Khyber Rifles* featuring Victor McLaglen and Myrna Loy. Performances were at 2.30pm, 6.30pm and 8.50pm, at 6d, 9d, 1/- and 1/3.

In the mid-1930s, under the ownership of Oakhill Picture House Ltd as the Swan Cinema, it was run by Regent Enterprise Ltd, as lessees who, by that time, controlled a 12-cinema circuit in the Liverpool area. The last proprietors, Radam Entertainments Ltd (formerly referred to in connection with the Doric and Roscommon cinemas), took over c1947, continuing the policy of matinee daily and continuous evening performances, with admission prices at 9d to 1/9.

After being named the New Swan in January 1953, it only survived for a further 3½ years. With decreasing attendances against circuit opposition, it was the second cinema closure of the 1950s, the last show being on 22 July 1956 – *I Believe in You* and *The Raging Tide*. The hall was used for bingo, but later became a private club known as The Swan.

1916
Mere Lane Picture House
Mere Lane / Breckfield Road North, Anfield

The cinema was situated in a well-populated area, at the corner of Mere Lane and Breckfield Road North, with elevations to both roads and a main entrance at the head of a flight of steps on the corner. A substantial metal and glass verandah with the cinema name on the facia spanned the entire frontage.

With accommodation for an audience of 1,050, including the balcony, it was an above average sized hall at that time, and early advertisements described it as a super-cinema. The rectangular auditorium had a balcony at the rear, above which the ceiling was at a higher level. The side walls were decorated by panels, with three curtained windows below the carved cornice. The trade press stated that the hall was attractive and up-to-date in every respect, and designed on most artistic lines.

The cinema was opened on 4 November 1916 by the W Gordon circuit, proprietors of the nearby Homer cinema and the Garrick, Kirkdale. Roland Edge, manager of the former, was appointed manager of the Mere Lane. The opening film was William Fox's *Infidelity*, supported by short films with music by a small orchestra. Admission prices were from four and a half pence to 1/-. Orchestral accompaniment to the silent films continued until 1930, when Western Electric sound system was installed.

In May 1933, the Mere Lane, together with others of the Gordon circuit, was taken over by the Regent circuit, a subsidiary of ABC Ltd. Only 2 years later they came under the control of the Liverpool-based Regent Enterprise circuit, which incidentally had no connection with the London Regent circuit. With the addition of the Gordon's circuit cinemas, Regent Enterprise then controlled ten cinemas in the Liverpool area, but in March 1938, these were taken over by the large circuit of W Southan Morris. The last change of ownership of this group of cinemas was to the Essoldo circuit in October 1954. CinemaScope was installed and Twentieth Century-Fox releases began on 18 July 1955, with *Garden of Evil* starring Gary Cooper and Susan Heyward.

With the exception of the Fox releases, the Mere Lane normally played second runs in the district. However, surviving until 1963, the cinema outlasted its principal opposition, the Gaumont in Anfield, the final performance being on 14 September 1963 with *Barabbas* starring Anthony Quinn.

The hall was converted to a bingo hall by the Top Flight Leisure Group, then became a snooker hall and finally, in 1992, a sports centre. This was the last Liverpool cinema opened during World War 1.

Mere Lane Picture House, 1975.

1920
Corona Cinema
College Road, Great Crosby

Building began in 1914, but due to the outbreak of the Great War, it was not completed until 1920. The site, then known as the Marsh Fields, had long been an entertainment venue. Lord George Sanger brought his travelling circus in the1890s and the land was also used by troupes of pierrots and for fairs. To Liverpool architects Fraser & Ainley's plans, the building was constructed by R Costain & Sons of Crosby on a main road site, opposite the Alexandra Hall and public library. The imposing frontage was mainly of white glazed faience, relieved by brick at the sides. The central section included the three tall windows of the first floor lounge, each surmounted by a curved stonework feature, and below the coping a large panel displayed the name in large, gold painted letters.

There was no canopy, the spacious interior waiting rooms obviating the need for outside queues. In addition to the large circle waiting room, a covered extension along the entire left-hand-side of the building was provided for stalls patrons. In the centre of the frontage, three separate entrances gave access to the foyer, from which a short flight of steps in the centre led to the rear stalls. At either side, patrons ascended a staircase to the lounge or balcony, which was unusual in that it had a straight front, instead of the normal curve, and extended over the stalls to nearly half the auditorium length. It contained 324 of the 1,100 seats.

The interior was described as being neo-Grecian, with a bronze head over the proscenium. The walls had large panels above a dark dado relieved by horizontal flutes. Behind the orchestra pit was quite a large stage, often in use during the 1920s, across which was drawn a dark curtain, relieved only by a light-patterned border. Although from 1928 it was a GB cinema, the Corona was originally built for a small company whose directors were J Johnson and H Hughes. At that time the company had fairly extensive holdings among Liverpool places of entertainment, including the Magnet in Wavertree and the Empress in Tuebrook, opened by Hughes as a new cinema in 1915.

The Grand Opening of the Corona took place on 21 May 1920 in the presence of Councillor William J Jackson, chairman of Great Crosby UDC, as well as other local dignitaries. The film programme, of which no details are available, was accompanied by a quintet, the management announcing that music was to be a regular feature. Every seat was bookable for the performances at 2.30pm, 6.45pm and 8.45pm and originally films were changed daily. Unfortunately, the Corona did not receive great public support, and was gradually given over to complete concert party shows. In fact, in 1923, under the management of WJ McAree, it was advertised as *The Fashionable Rendezvous,* with a change of programme every Monday, Wednesday and Friday and performances at 8pm, and Saturday shows twice-nightly at 6.30pm and 8.40pm. Admission prices were: pit 9d, pit stalls 1/3, orchestra stalls and balcony 1/7.

Towards the end of 1923, 3 hours of entertainment was being offered with a programme of first class films followed by a first rate concert party. Within a short time, films with orchestral accompaniment formed the bulk of the entertainment, and from March 1928, when The Corona became a GB cinema under the ownership of Denman Picture Houses Ltd, synopses were handed to the musicians in an effort to ensure that the music was as appropriate as possible. The Corona was the first local cinema to be equipped for sound, commencing a 6 day showing on Monday 31 March 1930 of *The Great Gabbo,* featuring Eric von Stroheim and Betty Compson and full supporting programme including *Gaumont Sound News,* which was to be a regular item. It was renowned as the Talkie House with an Orchestra.

The Corona was also the first in the district to be equipped for CinemaScope, which opened 5 December 1954 with *The Black Shield of Falworth* starring Tony Curtis, a GB circuit release in accordance with the CMA film booking policy of first suburban run. At this time, afternoon performances were normally only on Monday and Wednesday with Saturday continuous, a policy in operation since September 1953, designed to reduce running costs, a caution necessary due to falling admissions. The advantage of first run films was lost when the Rank Organisation opened the New Gaumont in Bootle in January 1956. Probably due to this, and the fact that the company also controlled the more modern Odeon in Crosby, the Corona had the unfortunate distinction of being the first post-war closure in north Liverpool, closing on 1 December 1956 with a continuous performance from 2pm of *The Proud and Profane,* featuring William Holden and Deborah Kerr, supported by *Zanzabunited Kingdoma.* The building was demolished in 1957 and the site later redeveloped with shops.

1920
Royal Cinema
Breck Road, Anfield

The building was originally a live theatre named the Theatre Royal, opened on 24 December 1888 by Thomas Montgomery, who the previous year had opened the Westminster Music Hall. It was reported in the *Liverpool Review* of 29 December 1888, that this cosy, middle class establishment had seating for about 1000 people. The street level pit and stalls had about 650 seats and the dress circle, balcony and boxes were all on one floor. With several exits, hydrants etc, the cinema was felt to be safe in the event of fire. The architect and builder was W Redman, and decoration was by Goodall & Co. Special mention was made of the fibrous plaster mouldings adorning the dress circle, boxes and proscenium.

The opening night began with the National Anthem, after which the chorus joined in a military march by JB Richardson, the theatre's musical director. James English, the general manager, concluded the opening ceremony with a short speech and Arthur Rousby's company then performed the Balfe opera, *The Bohemian Girl.* The next week saw performances of *Maritana* and *Figaro.*

Later a capable stock company was engaged for the performance of notable plays, after which came visits from touring companies. There was a complete change of entertainment on 3 August 1891, when the house reopened as the Theatre Royal Palace of Varieties. This continued until c1906, when it reverted to up-to-date drama played by a stock company, with popular twice-nightly performances. This was reintroduced by Matthew Montgomery, son of the founder, Thomas Montgomery, and the former was commended for this type of entertainment. According to a reliable source, prior to the opening in 1913 of the Cabbage Hall cinema in the same district, Cabbage Hall had been the theatre's affectionate nickname, and in 1891, following its opening as the Palace of Varieties, Liverpool comedian Robb Wilton was among the first artists to appear, making his stage debut.

The Royal was a well known, legitimate theatre, staging plays for almost 15 years until 1920, when it was acquired by the Gordon cinema circuit. At a cost of about £11,000 a transformation took place in the conversion to a 1,100 seat super-cinema. The marbled walls of the spacious entrance also featured oak panelling. Mackereth & Holland of Dale Street were responsible for the electric lighting and the furniture was supplied by Beeby & Windebank of Birmingham. The decorations were carried out by John Tanner & Sons, whilst the builders were Roberts & Sloss of Liverpool and Prestatyn.

Advertised as Liverpool's latest luxury cinema, the Royal was opened on the afternoon of Thursday 11 November 1920, with a free show to the guests of the directorate. Such guests were received by W Gordon, managing director, and R Duncan French, secretary, accompanied by the new manager, HA Hall, who, for about 10 years, had been dispatch clerk for film renters, Weisker Bros. There was a collection for St Dunstan Hostel, after which a performance, with orchestral accompaniment to the supporting short films, led appropriately to the exclusive attraction *The Bramble Bush* starring Corinne Griffiths, described as a tense, modern, human drama. The cinema was open to the public in the evening with continuous performance from 6.40pm to 10.40pm, when admission prices were: stalls 6d and 9d, balcony 1/3. Thereafter the cinema also had a matinee at 3pm, Monday to Saturday.

Thus began the 45-year history of the Royal as a cinema under four successive companies. The first change came in May 1933, when it was among the Gordon circuit cinemas leased by the Regent Circuit Ltd, London, an ABC subsidiary. Their short period as lessees ended in May 1934, when the new proprietors were the Liverpool-based Regent Enterprise circuit, who had 12 cinemas in the area. In March 1938 the circuit was acquired by the country's largest independent exhibitor, Southan Morris Associated Cinemas Ltd. The last proprietors were the Newcastle-based Essoldo circuit, by whom the Southan Morris cinemas was taken over in October 1954.

CinemaScope, began on 12 May 1955, with *The Black Shield of Falworth* starring Tony Curtis. With subsequent runs, normally for 3 days only of the circuit release films, the Royal survived for nearly 10 more years. As Anfield's only remaining cinema, it closed on 16 January 1965 with *Robin and the Seven Hoods* starring Frank Sinatra and *The Bugs Bunny Show No3*.

The Royal was reopened by the Top Flight Leisure Group, as a bingo and social club, extending the building's history as a leisure location to over 100 years. Like many bingo halls, it finally closed, the closure in March 1997 coinciding with the opening of the Mecca new hall in the district.

1920
Stella Picture House
Seaforth Road, Seaforth

Built at a cost of £36,000, the Stella was in a well populated district on a site at the highest point of Seaforth Road between the railway station and the Palladium cinema. The architect, George E Tonge, FRIBA, Lord Street, Southport, had vast experience in picture theatres, numbering about 15 at that time and he excelled himself in the planning of the Stella. It was described in the local press as, without exaggeration, a super-cinema, with seating accommodation for an audience of 1,200 including about 350 in the horseshoe-shaped circle.

The impressive frontage of white glazed stone was an excellent example of the classic style of architecture, with an abundance of carved designs and panels. At the head of a flight of white marble steps the wide main entrance was flanked on either side by a pair of fluted columns, between which the space was allocated for poster advertising with a panel above. The columns extended above first floor level, supporting a narrow entablature below the architrave, carved frieze and cornice, above which was an oblong area featuring carved stonework, and at either

Seaforth Road, showing Stella Picture House.

The Stella Picture House, 1920s.

side, panels directly above the columns. The windows of the first floor lounge were central between the pairs of columns, and at the right-hand-side of the frontage, the white stone facing extended via two splayed walls up to the brick construction of the auditorium elevation, incorporating three windows at ground and first floor levels. Above the main entrance steps, the slightly curved canopy displayed the name in white opaque glass. Interestingly, the name of the district was boarded over during the war in case of invasion.

External lighting consisted of fittings suspended from metal brackets directly above the columns and from globe-shaped fittings at either end of the canopy, whilst lamps on the soffit illuminated the steps. The wide main entrance was lit by a row of electric lamps above a line of glass-panelled doors, set at an angle, allowing space for the paybox to the right, with a small bay window set in the white-tiled wall.

For the convenience of patrons queuing outside, a glass verandah was provided along the right-hand-side of the building. Beyond the main entrance, the wide foyer with attractive grey marble floor, led to the stalls entrances at either side. The seating was arranged in two sections, providing a centre gangway and one along either side. In the middle of the foyer, the foot of the highly polished teak staircase was flanked by square pillars, on which were mounted cone-shaped, coloured glass light fittings. The foyer was lit by indirect light from glass-shaded fittings suspended from the ceiling. A short flight of stairs divided to the left and right up to the first floor landing and lounge and, at either side, doors at the end of a short passage gave entry near to the circle front. The steeply raked, horseshoe-shaped circle, with a similar arrangement of seating to that of the stalls, merged into two curved bays next to the proscenium where, beyond a few single seats, exit doors enabled the auditorium to be emptied in a couple of minutes at the rear, whilst patrons for the next performance were entering at the front. From the rear of the circle, two further exits gave direct access to street level.

Internal decorations were most artistic, executed in fibrous plaster in grey and gold. Flanked by panels, a large gold star bearing the cinema name occupied a central position above the proscenium, which was adorned by a gold-trimmed pelmet and curtain of red plush in front of the plain light screen curtain. This was replaced by a gold-coloured festoon curtain in the mid-1930s. Along the side walls, full length pilasters extended up to the classic green and gold frieze, and from the cornice, carved gold painted ribs spanned the high, steeply arched ceiling. Between the ribs, bowl-shaped light fittings provided principal illumination, suspended by chains. From the side walls, subsidiary lighting was from groups of three shaded lamps, of which the central red lamps cast light on the gangways during performances.

The seating consisted of red plush tip-up seats, with greater than normal space between the rows. Stated to be fireproof, the operating room was approached by a separate stairway, and equipped with a safety shutter, which could be operated from outside or inside, making the risk of a fire spreading practically non existent. Two of the latest type of Simplex projectors with film rewinding were installed. Other rooms were added to include a boardroom and manager's office, the entire scheme being very modern. It was noted that the directors of the Seaforth Stella Picture House Ltd, were all local gentlemen, namely Councillor H Blundell, MBE (chairman), T Foulds, W Ashworth, S Hibbard, W Costigan, John Davies and H Kennedy, (secretary).

Under the management of JB Hothersall, formerly at the Wigan Playhouse, the Grand Opening took place on the evening of Saturday 4 December 1920, when bookings surpassed expectations. With separate performances at 6.30pm and 8.30pm, musical accompaniment to the programme of pictures was provided by the orchestra, directed by Frank Creswell. *Children of Banishment,* featuring Mitchell Lewis, was shown, with a comedy, *Nymphs and Nuisances.* The great cinema actress, Ethel Clayton, played the leading role in *More Deadly than the Male*, a powerful Paramount Artkraft masterpiece. Prices were: front circle 1/6, rear circle 1/3, stalls 1/- and pit stalls 8d. Seats could be pre-booked for 3d extra at the box office which was open from 10.30am. Silent films with orchestral accompaniment continued until the installation of RCA Photophone sound system. The first talkie, the Warner Bros picture *The Gamblers* starring HB Warner and Lois Wilson, was shown on 28 April 1930, with three performances daily at 3pm, 6.30pm and 8.30pm.

Facing strong competition from the cinemas of ABC and GB, nearby in Bootle, film bookings consisted mainly of later runs of the leading films, and supporting programmes including the *Pathé Gazette*. A similar policy continued after the takeover in 1943 by Bedford Cinemas (1928) Ltd. During the years of peak cinema attendances in the late-1940s there was some increase in the hours of opening, with continuous performances from 2pm. From the autumn of 1955, there was a reduction to performances continuous from 5.30pm. The almost proscenium-width screen, installed late in 1954, was used for the showing at a reduced height of the first CinemaScope film, the Warner Bros picture *The Command* starring Guy Madison, which began on 10 January 1955.

Around 1955 the position of the Stella, with regard to film booking, became more difficult due to increased competition from the three cinemas in the area, controlled by the ABC, GB and Essoldo. The Essoldo had taken over the Coliseum, Litherland in October 1954; the Regal, Litherland became an ABC cinema in July 1955, and in January 1956 the Rank Organisation replaced the old Broadway, Bootle with the newly-built Gaumont. Bookings at the Stella were therefore virtually restricted to second runs within a limited area. A similar disadvantage was felt by the nearby Palladium, although the Stella was the first to close, the last show being on Saturday 5 July 1958, with the double feature *If I'm Lucky* starring Perry Como and *Plunder Road* starring Gene Raymond.

For a short time, from May 1959, it was used as a roller skating rink, then a firm of printers applied to take it over, but the council successfully opposed this and a public enquiry went in their favour. It was demolished in May 1964 and the site was redeveloped as the Stella shopping precinct, as it remains to date.

1920
Regent Picture House
Liverpool Road, Crosby

The Regent Picture House, 1926.

Situated on a main road, in a good residential district, about 7 miles to the north of Liverpool. In his plans for this cinema, architect A Ernest Shennan, who was later to design several of Liverpool's largest super-cinemas, provided for the first café lounge in a Liverpool suburban cinema. The lower part of the frontage was of stone, whilst the dark brick of the first floor was relieved by carved stonework above the windows. The full width metal and glass verandah displayed the name on the deep facia in large letters of white opaque glass, and accommodation for queuing patrons was provided by a glass-covered area along the right-hand-side of the building. In front of the auditorium elevation, considerable space having been allocated for the foyers on the ground floor and the first floor café lounge, a large flat roof extended between the frontage and the projection suite from which there was access.

The central main entrance with two supporting stone columns had a splayed frontage and a two-sided paybox of dark panelled wood and glass. On either side, at the rear of the paybox, a pair of glass-panelled doors led into the attractive circular foyer with, around the walls, columns with bases and capitals supporting an elegantly carved cornice, with a column in the centre. From here, two pairs of swing doors at the left and right led into the rectangular-shaped stalls waiting room, with oak-panelling up to about three quarters of the height. Glass-panelled doors led directly to the two stalls gangways at either side of the centre block of seats, flanked by short rows extending up to the side walls with spaces for access to the exits.

The capacity of the stalls was 825 and for front stalls patrons, further exits were provided at the head of short stairways, at either side of the proscenium. Flanked by square marble columns, the proscenium was adorned by red plush curtains with an elaborate gold lace pattern. The lower part of the walls, to just below balcony height, was panelled in dark oak, and above a plain surface, a row of pilasters flanked a line of red-curtained windows. Above the carved cornice, ribs of carved plaster spanned the very high curved ceiling, from which the main auditorium lighting was from electric lamps within large, buff-coloured shades. From the sides of the foyer, the first floor café lounge was reached via a white marble staircase with a dark wooden dado. A continuation of the stairs led to the rear of the curved-fronted, 250-seat balcony, with a stepped floor, which extended over the rear stalls, with a similar seating arrangement. The expensive red-plush seats were complemented by a luxurious red and blue carpet which also covered the area between the rows, making footsteps virtually inaudible. The principal directors of the original proprietors, the Crosby Picture House Ltd, Bryce and Phillip Hanmer, in later years formed a substantial Liverpool cinema circuit.

The Grand Opening of the Regent, under the management of H McCarthy, was on Saturday 11 December 1920 at 3pm, the entire proceeds being donated to the St Dunstan Hostel for blind soldiers and sailors. Opening with the Regent Grand Orchestra, under the direction of TE Sharrock, playing selections from Rossini's famous overture to *William Tell*, short films were then presented entitled *Granger Marvels of the Universe*, with latest news in *Topical Budget* and also a comedy, *Lost, A Bridegroom*. The feature film was the Walterdaw production *The Isle of Conquest*, starring Norma Talmadge.

The evening performance was continuous from 5.45pm to 10.30pm, with admission prices at: stalls 9d and 1/3, balcony 2/-, then the highest at a Liverpool surburban cinema. Subsequent performances consisted of a matinee Monday to Saturday at 3pm, continuous evening from 6.30pm and separate performances at 6.30pm and 8.40pm on Saturdays, bookable in advance (necessary in the 1930s to be certain of obtaining a seat).

After the installation of Western Electric sound system, the first talkie at the Regent was on Monday 21 April 1930, *Under the Greenwood Tree*, a Wardour British film featuring Marguerite Allan and John Batten. Due to its high standard of comfort, the Regent was for many years the best attended cinema in the north of Liverpool, including Waterloo, Seaforth and Litherland, with little opposition until the opening in 1939 of the new Plaza, Crosby. The nearest cinema was the GB-owned Corona in Crosby. Film bookings at the Regent were notably those of MGM,

Warner Bros/First National and Paramount, and the UK-produced films of British International Pictures, with supporting programmes including the latest *Pathé Gazette*. This arrangement was continued after November 1935 by the new proprietors, ABC Ltd, who discontinued advance booking for Saturday evenings in favour of a continuous evening performance. During the period of peak cinema attendances in November 1946, the opening hours increased, with continuous performances throughout the day, except Sunday from 5pm. The café, so long appreciated by patrons, had by that time closed.

In line with most cinemas, the Regent, in 1955, was equipped for CinemaScope, although minus stereophonic sound. The new-style proscenium, with a rise and fall festoon curtain, allowed for the installation of the widest possible screen, approximately 30'. The first CinemaScope film, the Warner Bros colour musical *Lucky Me* starring Doris Day, began on Sunday 23 January 1955. To mark the new projection system, a gala performance on the following evening at 8pm was attended by Crosby's Mayor and Mayoress. Subsequent CinemaScope films included some Twentieth Century-Fox releases, of which there was a concurrency with the Essoldo, Litherland.

From 4 March 1957, matinee performances were restricted to Saturdays and school holidays. From October 1965, with admissions continuing to decline, there was another reduction to one evening performance, Monday to Friday, a policy which continued for just over 3 years until closure.

The Regent was taken over by Mecca Ltd in 1968, for conversion to a bingo and social club, and closed as a cinema on 30 November with *Barbarella* starring Jane Fonda. The stalls seats and the raked floor were replaced by tables and chairs on straight sections of flooring at descending levels to the front, with a bar on the right-hand-side, whilst the seats in the balcony remained in use. The bingo operated for a little over 25 years, for several years under different control, until closure in 1994, when extensive alterations were carried out for use as a sports centre under the direction of a local college.

1921
Coliseum Picture House • Essoldo
Linacre Road, Litherland

The Essoldo, as a bingo hall, c1963.

In a slightly later stage of construction than the Regent in Crosby, the design of this cinema, also by EA Shennan, was practically identical. The main difference was of size, the Coliseum having a considerably larger auditorium with a seating capacity of approximately 1,400 and claimed by the proprietors to be Liverpool's largest cinema. The two storey, red brick frontage was relieved by stonework of the upper part, extending along either side of the flat-roofed elevation, which projected forward from the auditorium to provide space for the main entrance, foyers, and first floor café lounge. Extending right across the frontage, in the centre of the facia, a metal and stained glass verandah displayed the name in white opaque glass.

The main entrance, with two central columns, had a paybox at either side, beyond which two pairs of glass-panelled doors led into the circular foyer, like the Regent Crosby but without the columns, although similarly leading via two doors into a rectangular waiting room. From this area, further glass-panelled doors led directly onto the gangways separating the central block from the short rows at either side. Spaces about halfway along provided access to the side exits, whilst further exits at either side of the proscenium were sited at the head of a short flight of steps. From the foyer, a white marble staircase at each side led up to landings with doors to the spacious, well furnished café lounge. From the landings, a flight of steps led to the rear of the curved fronted, 300-seat balcony, set back from the stage in the long auditorium, arranged in a similar way to the stalls. Above a plain surface, the upper side walls featured a line of curtained windows between pilasters which extended up to the carved cornice, from which ribs of carved plasterwork spanned the very high, curved ceiling, panelled at either side of the central ventilation grilles. The cinema had fine oak panelling and marble enrichment along the stairs, whilst the seating in the theatre was well designed and beautifully upholstered in blue and red plush, with corresponding handsome Wilton carpets.

For the Grand Opening on the Monday afternoon of 28 February 1921, the management issued a large number of free invitations to local residents. The spacious building was crowded, with every part of the building thrown open for inspection. Every feature gave the utmost satisfaction. At 2.30pm, the chairman of the Coliseum Litherland Ltd, welcomed the guests from the stage, stating that it was the directors' intention to make the Coliseum a first class entertainment venue, and that, with the support of the local residents, they intended to exhibit the finest pictures obtainable. The two films were accompanied by the orchestra, under the direction of HG Curtis, and during the screening of *The Toilers*, the title song was sung by the cinema tenor, J Wolstenholme. In support, a five-reel comedy featured May Allison.

The public opening was in the evening, when a non-stop 3 hour programme began at 7.30pm to which the popular prices were: circle 1/3, stalls 9d and front stalls 6d. On Saturdays, performances were continuous from 6pm to 10.40pm and matinees daily at 2.45pm at only 4d, 6d and 1/-. Despite the anticipated success of the enterprise, the Coliseum was not, in the long term, among the better attended of the district cinemas. In 1928, the position with regard to the availability of the leading films worsened, following the takeover of the nearby Broadway, Bootle by GB. In 1932 there was further circuit competition when the Gainsborough, Bootle became an ABC cinema. First runs in the district were then restricted to those films not booked by the major circuits, and during the 1930s these included British comedies such as Lucan and MacShane's *Old Mother Riley* series.

Throughout the 1920s, the café opened from 6pm to 10pm, offering various moderately-priced refreshments but the operation ceased in May 1929 for some months due to fire damage. The Coliseum was closed in 1931 for redecoration, reopening on 25 May of that year, still showing silent films, the last cinema in the district to do so. A Western Electric sound system was installed for the first talkie on 25 June 1931, *Call of the Flesh*, featuring Ramon Navarro, with prices lower than at the time of opening, at only balcony 1/- and stalls 4d, 6d and 8d.

The Coliseum was leased in 1933 to the expanding, Liverpool-based Regent Enterprises circuit. In March 1938 Southan Morris Associated Cinemas, London, took over the cinemas of the lessee company. Although now run by a considerably larger company, the booking situation did not improve until after the destruction of the Broadway, Bootle during an air raid in May 1941. GB circuit release films and later many of those released on the Odeon circuit then became available to Southan Morris. With improved attendances from June 1945, opening hours increased, with continuous performances from 2pm and children's club matinees introduced by manager, Ronald Hunt. A considerable time before the Essoldo circuit became the cinema's last proprietors admissions were declining. The Coliseum was one of 23 Merseyside cinemas of Southan Morris, which passed to the ownership of Essoldo, and the first of the group to take that name.

Under Captain Mark Sheckman and district supervisor, AJ Slade, at a cost of £20,000, the building was externally and internally redecorated, with new seating and carpets. CinemaScope was installed to screen a 40'-wide picture with stereophonic sound, incorporating 30 speakers, 18 of which were positioned around the auditorium. An arrangement with Twentieth Century-Fox, who copyrighted the system in 1953, secured the first run in the district of their CinemaScope films, beginning on 8 November 1954 with *The Robe* at 2.40pm, 5.40pm and 8.40pm daily. Attendances improved temporarily, but increased circuit opposition came in 1955 when ABC acquired the Regal, Litherland, followed by the opening of the New Gaumont, Bootle, replacing the old Broadway, in January 1956, which, by the end of the 1950s had taken over the showing of Twentieth Century-Fox CinemaScope films.

In the early-1960s, admissions again declined with a mixed film booking policy at evening performances only. Bingo was introduced on Sunday and Thursday evenings and the last films were shown on Saturday 14 September 1963: *Secret of the Incas* starring Charlton Heston and *The Guns of Fort Petticoat*, with Audie Murphy. Top Flight Leisure Ltd took over and converted the hall for bingo. Chairs and tables replaced the stalls seats and a licensed bar was added. The balcony was sectioned off by a suspended ceiling.

Reverting to its former name, the Coliseum continued as a bingo and social club until September 1983, during which a serious fire damaged the auditorium and roof. The building then stood empty, and in a continually deteriorating condition was demolished in 1990. New houses were eventually built on the site in 1997.

1922
Beresford Cinema
Park Road, Dingle

*The Beresford Cinema
photographed in 1946.*

In 1922 this was the final addition to the cinemas of the Halliwell Hughes cinema circuit, prior to their takeover by Denman Picture Houses Ltd, thereby becoming a GB cinema in March 1928. Erected on the site of a furniture repository which had been destroyed by fire, the mainly stone-faced building was lengthways to Beresford Road at the junction with Park Road. A single-storied, flat-roofed elevation formed the main entrance at the corner. This area, with flooring of black and white tiles, was divided by two square columns, and the doors gave access to the waiting room with crush rails. To the left, a staircase led up to the balcony, whilst doors led to the rear of the stalls where a centre block of seats was divided at either side from the short side rows by a gangway. Total capacity was 1,047, including 250 in the balcony.

The lower part of the walls had a green tiled dado, the upper part being panelled. The only indication of the opening date is the first cinematograph licence of 26 January 1922. Although a GB cinema in 1928, the Beresford's strongest competition in that area of south Liverpool was from the company's recently opened Rialto on Upper Parliament Street, which was given first or second runs in Liverpool of their release films. They appeared at the Beresford soon afterwards for 3 or 6 days until 1937, when the company opened the New Gaumont, also on Park Road, providing even stronger competition. This resulted in a mixed film booking policy of later showings, including ABC circuit releases for 3 days only, and low admission prices which, even during the 1950s, ranged only from 1/- to 1/6.

Due to its poor situation, the Beresford was among the company's (then CMA) first closures of the 1950s. The final programme was on 25 September 1956 with *Seminole Uprising,* starring George Montgomery, and *Not So Dusty*. The building was later demolished for road widening.

1922
Gainsborough
Knowsley Road, Bootle

The Gainsborough Cinema, c1920.

Bootle's fifth cinema and the last to be opened in the district before the outbreak of war in 1939. It was named after the celebrated painter, Thomas Gainsborough (1727-1788). At the time of the opening it was stated that, were the artist able to visit the borough, two things about the latest picture theatre would no doubt have impressed him very favourably. Firstly, the structure, like the artist's works, was one of grace and refinement. Secondly, the dominant colour in the auditorium was blue, reminiscent of the gloriously brilliant colour, which, applied by the artist, created the famous picture, the *Blue Boy,* and earned for him an imperishable name in the annals of British art.

The frontage, mainly of white glazed stone, was relieved by red brick and featured a line of small windows at first floor level, with circular windows directly above, and a stone architectural feature in the centre. Above the lower part of the frontage was a central full-width canopy, with opaque glass facia featuring the cinema's name. At the head of a short flight of steps, two separate arched entrances gave access via two pairs of doors to the large rectangular foyer. Immediately beyond the doors, a two sided paybox was provided for the speedy admission of patrons. The

The Gainsborough as a bingo hall in 1961.

flooring was of large black and white tiles, and up to near ceiling height, the walls were veneered in rose wood. In the centre, opposite the entrances, two pairs of doors led to the rear stalls, whilst at the extreme left and right were stairways to the rear of the circle, which extended over the stalls to nearly half the length of the auditorium, providing seating for nearly 300 of the 1,300 total capacity.

At the time of opening, the Gainsborough was perceived to be the finest cinema in the suburbs, a new cinema with new ideas. Performances were in the expert hands of the managing director, Walter C Scott, and orchestra leader, Dr James Lyons, who had many notable compositions to his credit and was to provide a unique musical setting to the best of the world's films.

The opening programme was on Saturday 18 May 1922, at 8pm, when the entire proceeds were donated to the Mayor of Bootle's Unemployed Fund. The luxurious auditorium was filled by an admiring audience who gave the Mayor, Alderman JH Johnston, and WC Scott a cordial reception. Following their speeches, a long and varied programme was enhanced by orchestral selections, under the direction of Dr Lyons, which deservedly earned enthusiastic applause.

On Monday 20 May, for 3 days, at 3pm and 8pm, DW Griffith's masterpiece *The Love Flower*, with Carol Dempster and Richard Barthelmess, was supported by a programme of topical, educational and humorous films. Admission prices were then 6d, 9d, 1/- and 1/3, reduced to 4d, 6d, 9d and 1/- at the matinee performances.

The orchestra was retained longer than at most cinemas, sound not being installed until the showing of *Under the Greenwood Tree*, starring Marguerite Allen and John Batten, plus the comedy *All Riot on the Western Front*, on 25 August 1930, with a matinee at 2.30pm and evening performances at 6.30pm and 8.40pm.

The Gainsborough was taken over by ABC Ltd in June 1931, resulting in the booking of ABC circuit releases concurrently with the Commodore, Bankhall, a new cinema recently acquired by the company. Despite strong opposition from the Broadway, Bootle, quite close to the Gainsborough, it continued to be quite well attended until the early-1950s. By the mid-1950s admissions were falling, although CinemaScope was installed, opening on 3 January 1955 with *The Command*, starring Guy Madison. ABC then provided its own opposition with the acquisition of the more modern Regal, Litherland, less than a mile away, with concurrent showings of films from 25 July 1955. Later, the Gainsborough lost even more patronage when Rank's new theatre, the Gaumont, Bootle, opened in January 1956.

In its last 2 years as a cinema, the Gainsborough normally opened, with the exception of Saturdays, in the evenings only, until closure on 12 November 1960, with *The Bellboy*, featuring Jerry Lewis, and *Tarzan the Magnificent*.

The building was then acquired by Mecca Ltd and converted into a bingo hall, the stalls area being considerably altered, with the seats removed and replaced by rows of tables and chairs. The space under the balcony was sectioned off by arched glass panels and entrances, for use as a licensed bar.

Bingo at the Gainsborough was successful for many years, but its decline in popularity during the late-1980s and the opening of a purpose-built bingo hall in Bootle, resulted in its closure. For many years a 'For Sale' sign was on the frontage. More recently, there is a 'Sale Agreed' notice, the building having been acquired for an extension of the adjacent car showrooms.

1922
Trocadero • Gaumont
Camden Street, Liverpool city centre

Then the largest of Liverpool's city centre cinemas, the Trocadero was opened by an associate company of Provincial Cinematograph Theatres Ltd, about 12 months prior to the takeover by Savoy Cinemas Ltd, London (of the Prince of Wales cinema), which was opened by PCT in 1912. The company representation in the city centre situation was thereby maintained, and in May 1927 was reinforced by acquiring a controlling interest in the Trocadero, after 5 years of management. This proved to be for a short period only, for in February 1929, although PCT, with 96 cinemas countrywide, was successful and expanding, it was nevertheless taken over by GB. The Trocadero was among the many later additions to that circuit, formed in March 1928.

The Trocadero was built by Bevis Ltd of Portsmouth, to the plans of Liverpool architects Taliesin Rees, FRIBA & Holt, who took full advantage of the site. The practically square-shaped building had a wide, imposing frontage of white glazed stone. Although less elaborate than many earlier entertainment venues, it presented an attractive appearance. A narrow metal and glass verandah, minus facia, extended the full width, with illumination from a line of torch-style, shaded light fittings along the edge. At the extreme right was the main entrance, whilst two exits from the foyer were provided near the centre. A row of small, first floor, stone-framed windows, was surmounted by panels, the largest in the centre displaying the name. Above a substantial coping, stonework panels relieved the highest part of the frontage, which included a short tower and dome at each end. Two pairs of doors in the main entrance led into the large rectangular foyer, decorated by marble-patterned wall panels with wickerwork settees, chairs and potted palms and trees spaced around. Opposite the entrance, at the rear of the paybox, a marble staircase with metal balustrade led up to a luxurious mezzanine lounge. From here patrons had a view of the screen

and could hear the music, due to a unique feature, which provided an extension of the steeply raked circle beyond the rear wall of the auditorium and above the lounge.

Overlooking the stalls floor, was a row of pillars with a metal balustrade between. The 831 stalls seats were arranged in three blocks with four gangways, making the total width 100'. Being virtually square, the plan represented a considerable departure from the rectangle of earlier practice. Curving round to the front of the hall, the circle occupied a large portion of the total area, with 516 seats similarly arranged to those in the stalls. On this floor an extra exit was provided on either side at the front. This was in the form of a long curve between the sides of the circle, which was divided by pilasters into three separate areas, including the unique feature of a miniature stage at either side. Upon these were picturesque scenes by the Playhouse Theatre's artist, illuminated during intervals. Whilst it is not possible to determine the duration of this novelty, it probably ended before the end of the 1920s, as later photographs show the areas above the stage adorned by a curtain and pelmet, matching those of the centre. A concave screen was declared to be scientifically correct with the main advantage being an undistorted stereoscopic effect and an entire absence of eye strain for the audience. Projection was originally from behind the screen, where a stage, 30' wide and 40' deep, allowed the possibility of theatrical productions. A relatively large orchestra pit, used only for musical accompaniment to silent films, was used almost to the end of the 1920s.

The internal decoration was most attractive, in light colours, with the walls of the lower floor carried out by horizontal flutes terminating at the cornice above the exit doors. At circle level, between pilasters with capitals supporting a deep cornice, the walls were decorated by panels below windows covered by dark curtains and pelmets. From the cornice, the ceiling was spanned by ribs of carved plaster, with circular ventilator grilles between. The principal illumination was indirect, light from electric lamps being directed upwards from within large bowl-shaped shades suspended from the ceiling. Secondary gas lighting was from wall mounted shaded fittings.

Although the city was then generously catered for with regard to cinemas, it was acknowledged that the Trocadero was a super-cinema, embracing all that was new and progressive and offering the best pictures, accompanied by carefully selected music by the orchestra of hand-picked musicians.

The Grand Opening was on 13 April 1922 with, on the new concave screen, the super production by William Fox of *The Queen of Sheba*, starring Betty Blythe in the title role and Fritz Leiber as King Solomon. Performances were continuous throughout the day from 2pm to 10.30pm, in accordance with future policy. Admission prices were 1/-, 1/9 and 2/4, with each seat said to be a luxuriously comfortable armchair. Up to the end of the 1920s, the proprietors adhered to the original policy of music forming an important added attraction, the Grand Orchestra of Clyde Lewis being one of the first.

From the mid-1920s, for almost 2 years, there was Harold Gee and his All British Orchestra, but the Trocadero also became the first Liverpool cinema to present organ interludes. These began on 10 October 1927, when the mighty Wurlitzer was played by its greatest exponent, Sydney Gustard, the well known London broadcasting organist. Another famous organist to visit the Trocadero was Reginald Foort. Organ and orchestral interludes continued until near the end of the silent era, which ended with the installation of Western Electric sound system for the opening of the talkies on 26 August 1929, with the musical *Showboat* starring Laura la Plante and Joseph Schildkraut, with supporting programme including *British Movietone News*.

Silent films with orchestral accompaniment returned for one week from 23 June 1930, during the installation of a new Western Electric sound system, but was poorly attended. By this time, the Trocadero had been taken over from Provincial Cinematograph Theatres by GB, a later addition to the large circuit formed in March 1928. Continuing as a first run city cinema with the circuit release films, it was for many years one of the better attended.

In 1950 the cinema was renamed the Gaumont in accordance with the policy of CMA, a company formed in June 1948, which brought under one control the cinemas of the GB and Odeon circuits. The company was the first to install CinemaScope with magnetic stereophonic sound in Liverpool, starting at the Odeon on 10 January 1954 with *The Robe*. The Gaumont was similarly equipped for the opening on 31 January of *How to Marry A Millionaire* with Betty Grable and Marilyn Monroe. CinemaScope was a considerable draw at both cinemas until other city cinemas also presented this attraction. Following the aforementioned opening presentations, no other Twentieth Century-Fox CinemaScope films were shown at CMA theatres for about 5 years.

Due to a dispute between producer and exhibitor, TCF leased the Futurist, and in 1955, the Scala, Lime Street, for first run of their releases. The closure of the Odeon for conversion into twin cinemas between 30 June 1968 and 21 March 1969 provided a welcome boost for the Gaumont, which played the leading circuit release films to larger audiences. The Odeon's reopening resulted in the Gaumont's decline, with bookings restricted to the less attractive films and those which had been played at the Odeon. The position worsened when Odeons 3 and 4 opened on 23 December 1973, practically dispensing with the need for an additional large single-screen cinema.

The Gaumont remained open for a further 4 months, the final performance being on 4 May 1974 with a minor X certificate programme, *Sex of their Bodies* and *Love Hungry Girls*. The building was unused for several years, until acquired about 1979 by Golden Leisure Ltd for conversion to snooker rooms, which closed in the 1990s. In a deteriorating condition, it was demolished in the summer of 1996.

1922
Graphic Cinema • Cosy Cinema
Boaler Street, Kensington

The cinema building as a meat warehouse, 1970s.

Erected in 1922, at a cost of £15,000, this was a small, square building with two, almost equal length frontages, and a small entrance at the right-hand corner. The construction was mainly of dark brick relieved by stone above the entrance, with vertical sections extending above first floor level along the Boaler Street frontage. The overall capacity was 630 including a small balcony. During 36 years as a cinema it was run by several independent owners and lessees, the first of which, Graphic Cinema (Liverpool) Ltd, named it accordingly and announced the opening on 12 May 1922. They advertised it as the last word in cinema luxury, the most comfortable and best ventilated hall in the district. The programme, including the feature film *Idols of Clay*, was accompanied by live music, and seats for the opening shows at 7pm and 8.50pm were bookable. The cinema was closed in 1927 and offered for sale by auction on 16 March.

The new proprietors, Baines & Purley Ltd, 146 Dale Street, announced the grand reopening on 16 May 1927 with a presentation of *The Shining Adventure* starring Percy Marmont and Mabel Ballin, the first showing in Liverpool. Admission to the matinee at 2.30pm and continuous evening show from 6.30pm to 10.45pm, was: 4d and 6d in the stalls, 9d and 1/- in the balcony.

Under the control of lessees Regent Enterprise Ltd, in 1932 the cinema was renamed the Cosy, and in 1935 it was run by the proprietors, Cosy Picture House (Liverpool) Ltd. At this time, performances were continuous in the evening, with prices from 4d to 9d. The last proprietors, Bateman Enterprises Ltd, took over about 1942. Based at the Hippodrome Cinema, Ellesmere Port, it was an associate company of Capitol (Edge Hill) Ltd, whose managing director was WJ Speakman. In competition with numerous independent and circuit cinemas, the booking policy included many leading films at later dates for 3 days only. However, the cinema was the first in the area to close, the final performances being on 4 January 1958 with *Zarak* starring Victor Mature, and *Cha, Cha, Cha, Boom*. The building was converted into a storage depot for meat products by ER Hughes Ltd, retail store proprietors, and remains in this use to date.

1922
Grosvenor Picture House
Stanley Road, Kirkdale

This purpose-built cinema was erected on a squarish site about 2 miles to the north of the city. After nearly 75 years the building has changed little on the outside, with the exceptions of the considerable alteration of the main entrance and removal of the verandah with deep facia which extended full width. Over the entrance, the red brick is still relieved by three arched stonework features surmounting three pairs of small first floor windows and, at the highest point, the name is carved in stone within a long panel.

During its years as a cinema, three separate entrances, each with a pair of glass-panelled doors, led into the wide, shallow foyer with the paybox in the centre next to the rear wall. At the extreme left and right, short corridors led to the sides of the squarish, stadium-type, 1,040-seat auditorium. The rear ten rows were stepped and, of these, the back three under the projection room were supported by columns and separated by a crossover gangway. In the style of many older cinemas, the side walls and arched ceiling were decorated by panels, and from the pilasters along the side walls, ribs of carved plasterwork extended across the ceiling.

The Grosvenor as a bingo hall, 1976.

The Grosvenor was the last addition to the W Gordon circuit which opened it on 14 August 1922, advertised as Liverpool's most up-to-date cinema. The celebrated Minarets Jazz Band, advertised as 'Something New, Something Novel; Something Attractive', accompanied the great film success Persuasive Peggy, starring Peggy Hyland, with supporting programme of comedies and the latest news, with admission from 5d to 9d. From May 1933, together with the other cinemas of the Gordon circuit, the Grosvenor was run by the Regent Circuit Ltd, London, a subsidiary of ABC as lessees, then acquired by the Liverpool-based Regent Enterprise circuit, proprietors until March 1938. The circuit was then taken over by Southan Morris who ran it for 16 years against competition from numerous circuit and independent cinemas in this well populated area.

Under the ownership of Essoldo from October 1954, CinemaScope began on 2 May 1955 with *Demetrius and the Gladiators,* starring Victor Mature. The difficult position with regard to bookings was improved by the fact that Twentieth Century-Fox CinemaScope films were not generally booked by the major circuits. The Grosvenor survived for 8 more years, during which the leading opposition cinemas stayed open. Like other Essoldos, after closure it was converted into a bingo hall by the Top Flight Leisure Group.

The last film programme was on 31 August 1963 when *Warrior Empress,* featuring Kerwin Matthews, supported by *The Wackiest Ship in the Army* starring Jack Lemmon, were shown. After closing as a bingo hall in 1995, the building was acquired by Coyne Bros, wedding and funeral directors who carried out external refurbishment and repainting. The original architectural features were retained in addition to appropriate internal reconstruction.

1922
Victory Picture House
Walton Road, Walton

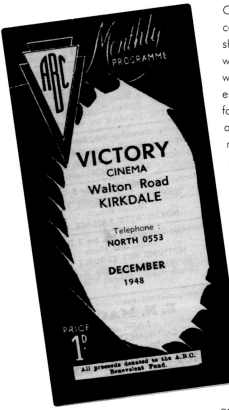

On a busy main road site about 3 miles from the city, the Victory had frontages to Walton Road and Luton Grove, connected by a curved corner incorporating the main entrance. Front stalls access was by a small door at the end of the shorter elevation to Luton Grove, where there was quite a large waiting room. Both frontages were mainly of red brick, with, from first floor level, a light coloured plaster facing on the corner, and broad stonework surrounds of the many large windows. Queueing space was provided by a substantial metal and glass verandah along both frontages. The corner main entrance, divided by two columns, had a central paybox flanked on either side by a pair of glass-panelled doors to a small foyer, with entrances to the rear stalls which extended straight back from the corner, and the intervening space between this and the frontages used for various rooms. From the left of the main entrance a double door led onto an enclosed white marble stairway to the first floor waiting room and side entrances to the balcony, and on a higher level, a long corridor gave access to the rear.

The balcony accommodated 330, of the 1,130 capacity, in two sections, with centre and side gangways and two short rows of seats sectioned off by a wooden partition at the right-hand-side behind the rear crossover gangway, referred to by some as the 'Jury Box'. The auditorium was most unusual, as it was not symmetrical. The proscenium was to the left of centre with a much longer splayed wall on the right-hand-side, where the balcony curved round further than on the left. The centre gangway had narrow columns at each side, supporting the front of the balcony, which was in line with the centre of the proscenium, resulting in a greater proportion of seats on the right-hand-side.

Decoration of the lower walls was by horizontal flutes, whilst on the splayed walls flanking the proscenium, short pilasters extended up to the carved cornice with panels in the intervening spaces; a style of decoration repeated on the side walls above the balcony. The screen was set quite high in the rather narrow proscenium and a picture approximately 17' by 13' was shown at a distance of 80' from the projection box to which there was a door on the right of the circle entrance corridor. The proprietors, the Victory Picture House Co appointed as resident and booking manager, Austin Durrans, who had 15 years' service in the industry and was later to open three super-cinemas.

For the Grand Opening on Wednesday 4 October 1922 at 2pm, the feature film was DW Griffith's 1915 epic, *The Birth of A Nation,* featuring Henry B Walthall and Lillian Gish, with music by the popular Martinique and his orchestra. For this and subsequent days there was a continuous evening performance from 6.30pm, and two separate performances on Saturdays, with seats bookable in advance. On a main road, convenient for several tramcar routes, up to 1925 the cinema was well attended, helped by the popularity of Martinique, then George Dawson, styled as the musical director of the renowned Victory Orchestra.

The orchestra as an attraction ceased with the installation of Western Electric sound system. The Victory announced the Grand Opening of the talkies on Monday 3 February 1930. For this there was a special attraction, *The Broadway Melody,* starring Anita Page, Charles King and Bessie Love, showing at three performances daily at 2.30pm, 6.30pm and 8.30pm, with advance booking reinstated for Saturdays evenings. Although sound films attracted more people, the improvement was curtailed when the company opened the Astoria, a new super-cinema on the opposite side of Walton Road, 5 months later. This provided even stronger competition in an area already housing a great many cinemas, and although both were taken over by ABC in the mid-1930s, the Astoria had the advantage of the more attractive films. In the immediate post-war years, when there was a temporary shortage of new American films, the Victory screened the greater number of reissues, and even these were concurrent with ABC's other cinema in the district, the Coliseum, Walton.

In 1955 a new screen was fitted, the maximum width within the 30' proscenium, films being advertised as on the panoramic screen, which was later used for CinemaScope at a reduced height starting on 3 October 1955 with a late run of *Seven Brides for Seven Brothers.* By the end of the 1950s, all but the Astoria had closed in Walton, thus increasing the availability of films. But the Victory's audiences continued to decline, resulting in closure on 29 July 1961. The last show was an unusual combination of films: *Rip Van Winkle* with Jamie Uys, plus *Son of Ali Baba* with Tony Curtis and Piper Laurie. The building was demolished and the site redeveloped with a row of small shops.

1922
Walton Vale Picture House
Walton Vale

Erected on a busy main road in the Walton Vale shopping area, in a similar situation to that of the Victory, but at the opposite end of the district, about 4½ miles from the city, near the Cheshire Lines Warbreck railway station. The length of the building was adjacent to Walton Vale, to which there was a long, mainly red brick frontage, relieved by stonework above the main entrance at the far left, where three tall window groupings were surmounted by a gable. From here a verandah extended along about half of the frontage, beyond which were large poster boards. The main entrance had two pairs of glass-panelled doors to a small foyer with paybox on the left, beyond which a white marble stairway with metal balustrade led to a small landing with entrances to the rear of the quite steeply-raked balcony, which extended over the stalls to about half the length of the squarish shaped auditorium.

The 300-seat balcony was divided into three sections with four gangways. A separate foyer to the right of the main entrance gave access to the 850-seat stalls in two sections, with centre and side gangways, but patrons of the front seats, or pit as it was known, entered at the extreme right of the frontage. The lower part of the auditorium walls was covered by a dark wooden dado, whilst above were large panels between curtained windows. The shallow-arched proscenium was adorned by curtains and a slightly curved, dark brown pelmet with gold trimmings. The orchestra pit was separated by a brass rail and suspended curtain. The hall was lit by electric bulbs within 6 large, buff-coloured shades and small red-shaded wall fittings.

The Walton Vale was always independently owned by the Walton Vale Picture House Co Ltd, whose managing director, J Leslie Greene, was a well known cinema proprietor in Bootle. Following 8 successful years at the Sun Hall, in March 1922 he headed a syndicate which gained control of the Metropole Theatre. The first cinematograph licence was issued on on 2 November 1922, followed by a brief mention in the local press that *The Prodigal Judge* was showing at this recently opened, magnificent cinema. Performances consisted of a matinee at 2.30pm and a continuous evening performance at 6.30pm, with seats from 6d to 1/2. In 1930, talkies and the latest Western Electric sound system replaced the orchestra, opening on 12 May with *The Hollywood Revue,* a spectacular musical introducing 26 well known artistes, at two separate performances of 6.30pm and 8.40pm.

Without nearby competition from the major circuits, the cinema was very well attended until the early-1950s, showing later runs of the circuit releases with mainly single features, including *British Movietone News*. Falling audiences in the 1950s resulted in evening only performances and mainly double features. CinemaScope began on 18 August 1955 with *Rough Company* featuring Glenn Ford and Barbara Stanwyck, but in the case of independent cinemas like the Walton Vale, the installation of CinemaScope, at a considerable cost, mainly served to increase the number of films available for booking, people still preferring the circuit cinemas, where they were shown at earlier dates. The closure of the Walton Vale in 1959 took place only a few months before the closing of its nearest rival, the Aintree Palace. The last feature film was *The Key,* starring William Holden and Sophia Loren, on 31 January 1959. The building was demolished to make way for a supermarket and several shops.

1922
Coliseum Cinema
City Road, Walton

On a site not far from the Everton FC ground, the building was constructed lengthways to City Road, providing a long frontage of mainly red brick with some stonework. Between the taller extreme ends of this elevation, the centre section was surmounted by a stonework architectural feature bearing the name. At the right-hand-side, above the main entrance, windows of the first and second floors were grouped in two, tall, stone-framed surrounds, above which was a coping, gable, and glass verandah extended along about three quarters of the frontage and along the rear of the building. Two pairs of glass-panelled doors in the entrance led to a small vestibule with a paybox on either side and doors to a long waiting room, whose walls had wood panelling on their lower part, with full height pilasters from which prominent ribs spanned the curved ceiling. Parallel with this was the front stalls waiting room below the centre of the auditorium. The centre and rear stalls could be reached by stairs to the immediate right of the vestibule doors, leading to a landing with doors to the left-hand-side of the stadium-type auditorium.

Seating for 978 was arranged in two blocks with centre and side gangways on a floor which had a much steeper than usual rake, the rear being at first floor level above the waiting rooms, descending to the front of the auditorium at street level. The side walls were decorated by a dark dado, panels and pilasters, extending up to the cornice from which carved plaster ribs spanned the curved ceiling. The projection room, over the rear crossover gangway, 80' from the screen, allowed a picture 16' by 12'. Above the screen, flush with the ceiling, was a deep, dark brown pelmet with gold trimmings. Matching drapes flanked a light-coloured screen curtain. The orchestra pit was sectioned off by a curtain suspended from a brass rail.

Advertised as the most novel and beautiful cinema in the suburbs, the Grand Opening was at 2.30pm on 7 December 1922, when the feature film, starring Edith Roberts, was *The Firecat*, with the comedy *The Show with Larry Semon*. A continuous evening performance followed at 6.30pm and admission prices were 6d, 9d and 1/-.

The original proprietors, Coliseum (Walton) Ltd, ran the cinema for about 5 years, after which it was taken over by the expanding Regent Enterprise circuit, who introduced the talkies, installing Western Electric Sound System mid-1930. In 1936 there was a final change of proprietor when the Coliseum became an ABC cinema, one of three in Walton, the Astoria and the Victory also having been acquired by the company at about the same time.

For many years the Coliseum was well attended by family audiences, despite opposition from the Bedford, a GB cinema, as well as the fact that ABC policy was to book all the leading films to the Astoria, leaving the less popular attractions, and from the late-1940s many reissues, to be shown concurrently at the Coliseum and the Victory. At this time there was a change of newsreel from Universal, of which the copies were shared with the Queen in Walton, to an unshared copy of *Pathé News*.

Little more than a year before closure, the front of the auditorium was revamped by the construction of an attractive, floodlit proscenium, to provide an appropriate setting for the new CinemaScope screen, on which *Bad Day at Black Rock,* featuring Spencer Tracy, began on 3 October 1955. Despite this, admissions continued to fall. On 1 December 1956 *Ramsbottom Rides Again,* starring Arthur Askey, with *Bobby Ware is Missing,* formed the last programme at the Coliseum. The building was subsequently acquired by Everton FC to become their supporters' club, involving the removal of the verandah, and of course the painting blue of the red brick exterior to accord with the team colours.

1922
Lyceum Cinema • Lyceum Talkie Theatre
St Mary's Road, Garston

The Lyceum, 1938.

This was the last of eight Liverpool cinemas opened in 1922, when the silent film was at the height of its popularity. The location, about 4 miles south of the city centre, was midway between the Grassendale and Garston railway stations. The frontage being to St Mary's Road, and the auditorium parallel to the railway line, necessitated that the auditorium should be constructed at an angle extending to the right of the frontage. The site area was limited and irregularly shaped.

Although described as a medium-sized house, it had a tall, attractive frontage, with white stone facing in horizontal recessed divisions, including four vertical sections extending up to the coping, forming three areas incorporating windows at first and second floor levels, the former with metal balustrades and carved stonework surrounds. Above the coping, in the centre, was a large panel displaying the name. The lower part was surmounted by a full width coping, below which were several metal light fittings, and similar, larger fittings were suspended from brackets to light up the upper levels. Recessed in the central main entrance, a wall to the left of the doors held a film category board, and from this area was access to the small foyer with paybox immediately on the right, with doors to the rear stalls. On the left, the staircase terminated on a landing with doors to the curved fronted balcony supported along the front by pillars. The narrow, 700-seat auditorium had a proscenium of only about 17'.

Advertised as the most luxurious picture house in Liverpool's districts, the Lyceum opened on 11 December 1922 with *Hands Off,* featuring the famous cowboy star, Tom Mix, supported by a full programme of news, comedy and dramatic pictures. Admissions were at popular prices from 6d to 1/-.

Despite considerable initial success, increasing competition meant that by the end of the 1920s, the cinema was being run at a loss and, although every effort was made by the proprietors, the loss became even greater. In 1925 William James Grace became the managing director of the new company, Empress Cinemas (Liverpool) Ltd, which took over the cinema and improved its fortunes. The name, Empress, was chosen because Grace had been the manager of the Empress at Tuebrook, owned by his father-in-law, T Halliwell Hughes. Hughes became a shareholder following the sale of his cinema circuit to Denman Picture Houses in 1928, and in 1929 purchased the Lyceum.

The cinema was then in a very run down state but, bringing with him 10 years' experience of cinema entertainment across the country, Grace was convinced that, by thorough overhaul and reorganisation, the Lyceum could be transformed into one of Liverpool's most popular picture theatres. Realising that the day of the silent film was passing, soon to be made obsolete by the talking picture for a new kind of audience, a spectacular transformation took place by redecoration and modernisation executed by Walter Hughes, brother of Halliwell, who became the chief operator, with his brother-in-law, George Chapman, a painter and decorator.

The capacity was increased to 750, including the 220 seats in the circle. In co-operation with the engineers of the RCA Photophone company, whose talkie apparatus had been selected, the theatre's acoustics were improved; sound projection at the Lyceum was generally admitted to be among the best in Liverpool. The success of these improvements was revealed after reopening as the Lyceum Talkie Theatre, when it was almost invariably well attended and also profitable, despite the extremely popular prices of 6d to 1/-. The weekday performances were continuous from 6.30pm, with two separate performances on Saturdays and Bank Holidays, when all seats were bookable at no extra charge. There was a matinee on Monday, Wednesday and Thursday, and a special children's show on Saturday. Film bookings were stated to be the best available on general release, and Grace paid particular attention to British pictures whenever possible, all supported by one or two comedies, an interest film and newsreel. Details of each show were made available in a monthly programme. The Lyceum's popularity was enhanced by the sale of cigarettes, chocolate and other refreshments throughout the house, served by neatly uniformed staff.

Grace relinquished control of the Lyceum in 1939, to take up the position of manager of the new Abbey cinema, Wavertree. The Lyceum was then leased to Leslie Blond, who later formed a small circuit of Merseyside cinemas. His period of 20 years in control extended through the difficult times of the 1950s until the termination of the lease in 1959. The final programme, presented on 10 October of that year, was the double feature: *Never Steal Anything Small,* with James Cagney, and *No Name on the Bullet,* with Audie Murphy. The building was sold for commercial use, and now has an almost unrecognisable exterior, the former architectural features having been plastered over. The property was last used as a tyre depot for Autotyres Services, but currently remains for sale.

1923

Casino Cinema

Prescot Road, Kensington

Then the largest of Liverpool's cinemas, the Casino was constructed on the main road at the junction with Beech Street. It was the enterprise of the Kitchen brothers, one of whom, Robert, took over the position of manager, becoming co-owners with Mrs H Hampson. The wide, square-shaped building was constructed of red brick and white glazed terracotta, the latter being used as a facing for the lower part, forming horizontal, full-width bands above and below the line of first floor windows with terracotta surrounds. Above the coping the cinema's name was displayed, and at either side there were sections of metal balustrade between short, square, terracotta-faced pillars enclosing the flat roof at third floor level. Surmounted by a full-width, streamer-type posterboard advertising the current film, the lower part of the frontage included the central main entrance, flanked on either side by large, film advertising boards. At the extreme ends was a small shop. No canopy was fitted, but queueing patrons were adequately catered for internally with spacious waiting areas, even though the large auditorium, including balcony, accommodated 1,659.

Described as the last word in cinemas, adding greatly to the amenities of the populous neighbourhood, the Grand Opening took place on Bank Holiday 4 August 1923, with everything as regards comfort and programmes to satisfy even the most fastidious. There was a continuous performance from 2pm to 10.30pm of five films: *Lights of New York* (Drama), *The Married Flapper* (Comedy), *Peace and Quiet*, *Radio Hours*, *White and Yellow* and also *Pathé Gazette*. An attraction was the musical accompaniment by the eight-piece orchestra, under the direction of Frank Stokes, the former musical director of the Liverpool Royal Hippodrome. He conducted on the opening day, after which Bertram Cawthorne took over as leader. Admission prices, among the lowest at that time, ranged from only 3d to 1/-, and the original proprietors were pioneers of the 3d matinee, including a full stage show with some of the big names of music hall.

The Casino was among the few Liverpool cinemas to present Lee De Forest Phonofilms Talking Pictures, shown during the week beginning Monday 24 October 1927, following successful runs at the city's Futurist and Scale cinemas. The silent *War Hawks*, an epic of the British flying forces at war, was supported by sound-on-film shorts, *The Stocking*, with 'The Three Rascals', John, Henry and Blossom of wireless fame, Roxy La Rocca, a harpist and Hall Jones in *Swizzles*.

The Casino was taken over in March 1928 by the GTC, becoming a GB cinema. In July of that year the company announced that £518,000 was to be spent on alterations and improvements, including a new 80' by 20' stage and eight dressing rooms behind the 60'-wide proscenium. With improved sight lines in the stalls, the scheme was intended to develop the entertainment policy of cine-variety. In October 1928 the Casino acquired a new orchestra of ten players, and a new manager, WJ McAree from the Bedford, Walton, believed to be the first managerial promotion by GB since their takeover. The policy of live entertainment as a regular attraction was soon to be replaced by the talkies. The Casino was equipped with Western Electric sound system for the opening of the talkies on 5 September 1929, with *Sonny Boy* played by Master Davey Lee with Betty Bronson and Edward Everett Horton and supporting programme including Frankie Darro in *Circus Kid*, as well as *British Movietone News* and the Casino orchestra, a feature retained until early-1930. In accordance with future policy there was a continuous performance from 6.15pm, with admission prices at: 6d, 9d and 1/3, and a matinee at 2.30pm at the reduced prices of 4d, 6d and 9d.

The Casino screened first suburban runs of the GB circuit release films, which from early-1930 were often concurrently shown at the Plaza, Allerton. In 1937 a similar booking policy operated at the New Gaumont, Princes Park, but it was not until 1946 that the regular concurrency of screening dates was applied to the three cinemas. All three were equipped for CinemaScope at about the same time and opened simultaneously on 6 December 1954, with *The Black Shield of Falworth*. Admissions decreased during the cinema's last 6 years, due to television and bingo. Continuous performances throughout the day were kept until the last show, on 30 December 1961: *The Queen's Guards* starring Raymond Massey and *The Judas Goat*. The Casino was then converted into a Top Rank bingo club, operating from 1962 to 1997. The building was demolished in 2001.

1923
Victoria Cinema • Essoldo
Cherry Lane, Anfield

The interior of the Victoria Cinema, 1923.

A group of Liverpool businessmen formed a company in December 1922, with a capital of £20,000, known as the Victoria Super-Cinema (Liverpool) Ltd, whose chairman, John Henry Liptrott, was a general merchant, the other five directors including Arthur John Kelly of Williams and Kelly, Liverpool, the cinema's architects. It was formed for the purpose of acquiring a piece of land, at the junction of Queens Drive and Cherry Lane, to build a large, stadium-type hall with a seating capacity of 1,378.

The building was completed by November 1923, and was said to present an artistic, attractive and imposing appearance on the very important site. The length of the hall, adjacent to the road, provided a long, although not very tall, frontage which, except for the higher section above the two entrances, extended only up to the lowest part of the roof. The mainly red brick frontage was relieved by sections of short balusters, surmounted by a shallow gable. There were small shops on either side of the entrance and a glass-covered verandah along the entire length. Beyond the main doors, the commodious, well appointed lounge led into the right-hand-side of the auditorium at the front, centre and rear, where the seating was arranged in two sections, with centre and side gangways.

Above a dark dado the walls had plain, rough-cast surfaces, relieved below the four curtained windows on either side by a light, multi-coloured area. The upper part was adorned between the windows by a deep, curved cornice. The curved arch of the proscenium, flush with the ceiling, and the two side sections, included carved plasterwork and across the screen hung a gold curtain with a deep red border. The ceiling incorporated large, eye-catching panels, the centre one of these including two circular recesses and those at the side, rectangular ventilation grilles. Lighting was mainly by several electric bulbs within eight elegant circular shades, hung from the ceiling by long chains. Secondary lighting in the gangways was from small, metal-shaded fittings, also from the ceiling.

The first cinematograph licence was granted on 20 November 1923 but the first advertised film was not until 13 December, when *The Ruling Passion* was shown, starring George Arliss, accompanied by orchestral items under the direction of TA Morgan. Initially attendances were disappointing, and a loss of £1,300 during the first year was improved to a small profit in 1927. By this time an additional attraction was a Jazz Night on Tuesdays and Fridays and a special musical programme on Saturdays by an augmented orchestra. This may have accounted for the increase in numbers, since in 1925 the district had an additional cinema, the Clubmoor.

In 1930, following the installation of sound equipment at the nearby rival cinemas, the Victoria was equipped with BTH sound system for its first talkie on 5 May 1930: *King of the Khyber Rifles,* with Victor McLaglen and Myrna Loy. After being run by a lessee company, Regent Enterprise Ltd, from 1932 to 1938, the Victoria was among the cinemas acquired by the Southan Morris circuit, which in turn were absorbed by the Essoldo circuit. The following year CinemaScope was installed, presentations starting on 14 March 1955 with *The Robe.*

Surviving for a further 8 years, the Essoldo was the last cinema in the district when it closed on 31 August 1963. For the last 3 days there was a double feature: *Rob Roy* starring Richard Todd and *Moon Pilot*. The Essoldo was one of the cinemas acquired by the Top Flight Leisure group for use as a bingo hall. In more recent years, bingo was continued by another company until a recent change to a double glazing factory. The building is still sound but its verandah has been removed and the auditorium has a lower, panelled ceiling below the original, from which the lights remain suspended.

1925
Olympia Theatre • Olympia Super-Cinema
West Derby Road, Tuebrook

After 20 years presenting practically every form of live entertainment, the Olympia became a super-cinema in 1925. In recent times it has been described as an Edwardian jewel which must be conserved, but the fact that the building still survives, with the benefit of considerable refurbishment, is due solely to the popularity of bingo, for more than 20 years from 1964. This magnificent theatre's architect was Frank Matcham, one of the great designers of British theatres. In 1925 he was associated with Scottish-born architect, Thomas W Lamb, in the redevelopment of the cinema of London Empire Theatre, Leicester Square. The striking four storey frontage, designed in the free Italian Renaissance-style, was of red pressed bricks with stone dressings with a long splayed section at either side of the straight centre. The arched entrances were surmounted by a steeply-roofed glass canopy with the theatre's name in

The Olympia, 1920s.

white opaque glass on the facia. Directly above, the construction was of white stone with columns supporting an entablature in front of the main first and second floor windows. Above the coping a half circular glass sunray design was surmounted by a massive tower, supporting a mechanical revolving sign. At this level, the splayed sections included a long stonework panel also bearing the name, with small minarets at either side.

The auditorium of Britain's then largest variety theatre was a masterpiece of exquisitely-carved plasterwork in cream, blue, red and gold. The stalls had 16 rows of comfortable tip-up seats, and a purpose-built cinematograph room at the rear. Also at the rear, were ten private boxes in addition to the two at the sides of the stage, of Indian-style with scarlet plush drapes. Side elevations on the dress and upper circle levels featured Indian panelling in the areas divided by ornamental pilasters, upon which stood full length elephantine figures supporting trusses carrying the ceiling. Adorning the huge, magnificent proscenium, the tableau curtains were also of Indian design, being of brilliant Oriental scarlet plush, enriched by wide, embossed, upright bands, and further ornamented at the base and sides by borders of appliqué design in deeper shades of scarlet and gold finished with a 3' deep silk fringe. Surmounting the tableau curtains, the proscenium valance was magnificently draped and embellished by appliqué designs in gold and silver, with a deeper scarlet plush on a brocaded background. The proscenium opening was fitted with a double asbestos fireproof curtain, which could be lowered from the flies, stage, or stage door. The stage, second in size only to that of London Drury Lane Theatre, incorporated a novel hydraulic feature. At the pull of a lever, the 42' diameter arena collapsed, folded up into sections and disappeared in 20 seconds. It was replaced in less than one minute, with the aid of electricity, by a lake for aquatic displays containing 80,000 gallons of water.

Since the circus was also to be among the attractions, a solid brick and concrete pit was constructed below the stage to house the lions' cages and accommodate the other animals. In the auditorium the first dozen or so rows of seats were removable, to make way for the sawdust ring. The auditorium was so vast it could seat 3,750 in the stalls, dress circle, upper circle, gallery and boxes.

The architect provided waiting rooms for all patrons and no fewer than 36 exits. However, the problem soon arose of how to get people into, rather than out of, the theatre. Nevertheless, the Olympia opened successfully on Easter Monday, 24 April 1905. Performances were at 6.50pm and 9pm, showing the spectacular equestrian revue *Tally Ho!* direct from the London Hippodrome, starring the famous George Formby senior, running for 4 weeks with pictures on the Bioscope as an added attraction. Stated to be as low as the standard of the performance was high, private boxes to seat four were 5/- and 7/6, arena stalls 1/6, orchestra stalls 1/- (all numbered and bookable in advance without extra charge), grand circle 6d, balcony 4d and gallery 2d (3d on Mondays, Saturdays and holidays).

During 20 years as a theatre, the Olympia staged circuses, water pageants, opera, ballet, music hall, pantomimes, films and boxing with exhibition bouts including the great Jack Johnson. Here, Liverpool theatre-goers first heard Wagner's *The Ring* and Puccini's *Girl of the Golden West*. Sarah Bernhardt gave her last Liverpool performance at the Olympia. Among other famous artistes were: Seymour Hicks, Ethel Levey, Lawrence Irving, Albert Chevalier, Wilkie Bard and George Robey. A change from live entertainment was presented between 24 April and 20 May 1916, when the Olympia became a cinema for a special presentation of DW Griffith's *The Birth of A Nation*, accompanied by the 36-piece symphony orchestra. The 3 hour long performances began at 2.15pm and 7.15pm, with prices ranging from 6d in the gallery to 2/- in the stalls.

During the early-1920s, in an attempt to improve attendances, Moss Empires appointed one of their most astute managers, Pierre Cohen, to take charge. Unfortunately, the Olympia still did not become viable as a theatre and in 1925 was sold to Savoy Cinemas Ltd, associated with ABC and the latest organisation to commence big scale cinema operations. The last performances as a theatre were given on Saturday 7 March 1925, when the British National Opera Company presented *Faust* at 2pm and *Tannhauser* at 7pm.

The Olympia was then closed for 3 weeks for conversion to a super-cinema, with a reduced capacity of 3,400, in a rearrangement of the sight lines to the new screen. Described as among the best in the country, it was set 30' from the first row of the stalls. The latest Ross projectors were installed for silent films, accompanied by the 24-piece orchestra under C Kottaun, later of the Oxford Theatre. The auditorium was redecorated to the designs of Clarence Elder, of the Cosmos Studios in Glasgow, who rejected the normal monochrome walls and ceilings, producing a vari-coloured setting sun effect.

Pierre Cohen was retained as manager by the new proprietors, who stated that use would be made of the stage facilities for acted prologues. The Olympia super-cinema opened on 30 March 1925, when the inaugural attraction was *The Thief of Baghdad*, starring Douglas Fairbanks senior, supported by *A Society Knockout* with Jack Dempsey, and The Grand National. Other special events included live entertainment by the celebrated operatic star, Frank Mullings. To the continuous performance from 2.30pm to 10.30 pm, admission prices were: back stalls 1/6, grand circle and stalls 1/-, upper circle 6d and balcony 4d.

Nearly 4 years later, the Olympia reached peak success as a cinema, being the first in Liverpool, and only the fourth outside London to be equipped for the permanent exhibition of sound films. The first of these, *The Singing Fool* starring Al Jolson, opened on 11 January 1929 for 7 weeks until 30 March. Performances were separate at 2pm,

4pm, 6pm and 8pm and prices were from 6d to 3/6. For the first time, the enormous seating capacity was insufficient to cope with the crowds who rushed to see the film. With no advance booking, queues were so long that people at the end were out of sight of the theatre!

Early in 1930 the Olympia came under the control of ABC Ltd, together with the Prince of Wales cinema in the city centre, these being the first of the company cinemas in the Liverpool area. Although normally presenting the same feature film, during the early-1930s variety acts were a regular added attraction at the Olympia. In addition to opening the new Forum, Lime Street, in 1931, ABC added to the circuit in the Liverpool area, and by the end of the decade controlled numerous suburban cinemas. They ultimately closed the Olympia, possibly by reason of unviability due to excessive size.

The last programme, on 25 March 1939, featured *Stablemates* with Wallace Beery and Mickey Rooney and *Girl School*. The building was used as a naval depot during World War II, and in March 1948 it was acquired by Mecca Ltd, who converted it into the Locarno ballroom, which opened in 1949. A small, semi-circular bandstand was built against the rear wall of the stage, with the stalls area becoming the ballroom floor. The projection room under the main balcony was demolished and a glass-fronted room on the main balcony was used to house spotlights and electrical control equipment.

The ballroom was open for 15 years, after which the interior was again extensively altered for the opening in August 1964 as a luxury bingo casino, with the decorations restored to their former glory. Bingo ceased in August 1982 due to decreasing attendances and the building put up for sale. For 4^1/$_2$ years Mecca sought a buyer, but with none forthcoming and the £60,000 per annum cost of maintaining the disused property, they were prompted to reopen with bingo. Great efforts were made to bring the building back for this purpose, whilst preserving its unique character. £150,000 was spent on skilful repairs to the elaborate internal plasterwork, including the famous elephant heads. New bingo equipment was installed, and since only the stalls and first floor balcony were to be used, the upper levels were curtained off to contain the heating system. The reopening on 5 April 1987 was for a limited time due to a fall in population after redevelopment.

Ownership then passed from Mecca Ltd to Silver Leisure Ltd, proprietors of the adjoining Grafton Room dance hall. However, the Olympia lay unused for a further 7 years, then was reopened by Silver Leisure on Easter Monday, 24 April 2000. This date exactly coincided with the Easter Monday of 1905, when the theatre first opened, at 8.30pm, for shows including a compère, DJ, dancing girls and supporting acts headed by Voulez Vous (Abba tribute band) and comedian, Stan Boardman. Cabaret, preceded by the opening of the restaurant at 7pm and licensed bar until 2am, is presented every Saturday evening with occasional American wrestling. And so this Edwardian jewel has been conserved and remains in the new millennium, Liverpool's only surviving theatre of that era.

1925
Clubmoor Picture House
Townsend Lane, Clubmoor

During the early-1920s, the Victoria was the only cinema within a mile radius of a council housing estate. To the plans of Liverpool architects Pritchard and Lewis, a building was constructed by Monahan and Brown of St Anne's Street. The length of the building, being adjacent to Townsend Avenue, provided a longish frontage of dark, rough-cast brick, relieved by terracotta. No canopy was fitted, adequate internal provision having been provided for waiting patrons. A press report stated that passing through the handsome glass-panelled doors past the booking office where the latest devices for facilitating quick entrance had been installed, were spacious waiting rooms with Gothic-style lighting. Rooms had been built large enough to accommodate as many patrons as the main hall.

Next to the right-hand-side was access to the front, centre and rear of the stadium-type auditorium, with about 1000 all tip-up seats and no forms at the front. With a floor gradient of 1:8, it was claimed to be the only Liverpool cinema where patrons were able to see over the heads of those in front. There was an 8' deep stage, and two dressing rooms for occasional variety. In addition to the orchestra of the finest musicians, there was a piano which cost 250 guineas. The operating box, described as the finest in the city, was equipped with Simplex projectors. These were fitted with lenses by the well known Taylor Hobson company, providing a clear and flickerless picture, the theme of which could be accentuated by a three colour lighting system.

The auditorium was painted in mauve, amber and gold in a unique scheme consisting of a lower plain surface, surmounted by short pilasters. Between the pilasters were murals depicting landscapes viewed through stone archways. To eliminate the glare then associated with electric lamps, the main lighting was from opaque glass shaded fittings hanging from the curved ceiling, and during performances, the gangways were lit from wall-bracketed light fittings.

Mr Prendergast, the general manager of proprietors, New Clubmoor Picture House Ltd, stated that the company's aim was to provide consistently good entertainment, with maximum comfort and efficiency, at minimum cost. These policies were to be found in operation on the opening day, Saturday 31 October 1925. The programme consisted of a double feature, rarely seen at that time: *Argentine Love*, starring Bebe Daniels and Ricardo Cortez and *Empty Hands*, featuring Jack Holt and Norma Shearer. The admission prices were low: 6d and 1/- to the continuous evening performance from 6.30pm and 2pm matinee. The policy of double feature programmes was regularly maintained during the latter half of the 1920s, and before the installation of Western Electric sound system in 1929, the cinema was controlled by the same company as the New Premier Cinema, Old Swan. These cinemas were among the first in the Liverpool suburbs to show sound films, which began concurrently on 19 August 1929 with *The Doctor Secret* starring Ruth Chatterton and HB Warner. Separate performances were at 2.30pm, 6.30pm and 8.30pm, with no increase in admission prices,

The Clubmoor building as a supermarket, c1960.

but on this occasion seats could be booked in advance for 1/6. From this time and for many years, the same films, sometimes concurrently, were shown at both cinemas, booked at the hall by CO Davies. There was occasional variety, when admission prices were 6d to 1/6.

Whether or not connected with the air raids during World War II remains unclear, but the Clubmoor cinema was closed from 8 May until 25 August 1941. The grand reopening was with *North-West Mounted Police,* starring Gary Cooper. Whereas at the beginning of the sound film era in 1929 the cinema had been in quite a favourable position with regard to bookings, this could not be maintained during the 1930s due to the increase in the number of suburban cinemas operated by the major circuits, ABC and GB. The relatively successful period of the late-1940s was followed by dwindling attendances in the 1950s, when performances were normally in the evenings only. The bookings continued to consist mainly of later showings of circuit releases, for 3 days only, and although a wide screen for CinemaScope was installed, the first of these films was not until 12 May 1955, when *The Command,* with Guy Madison, was the Warner Brothers' first CinemaScope film.

The Clubmoor survived for just over 5 more years, the final programme, on 2 July 1960, was the Twentieth Century-Fox CinemaScope picture, *The Story on Page One,* starring Rita Hayworth, and *A Gun in his Hand.* After use as a discount store, it became a supermarket and remains in this use to date.

1925
Popular Picture House
Netherfield Road, Everton

In 1925 there were objections to the building of this cinema by members of the Methodist Mission, when they discovered that it was to be sited immediately adjacent to their hall. The land rose steeply from Netherfield Road and, after the objections had been overcome, the resulting construction was a building of considerable height at the front, reducing to a single storey at the rear. The tall frontage was almost entirely of red brick, relieved by a small amount of stonework which formed a semi-circular design above the four central first floor windows. There was no canopy and the main entrance for patrons of the centre and rear stalls was through two pairs of glass-panelled doors leading into a squarish, medium-sized foyer, with the paybox opposite. This area represented all the ground floor space at the front of the building to which the public had access. At either side, a stairway with several turns led up to the very large waiting room under the rear half of the auditorium with several supporting pillars. At the opposite side in the centre, a short flight of steps with doors at the head gave access to the centre of the hall, with a crossover gangway between the two sections of seats. A continuation of the main stairway led up to two entrance doors at the rear.

At the time of opening, this was Liverpool's largest stadium-type cinema, having 1,500 seats in the long auditorium, arranged in two sections with central and side gangways. The curved ceiling had plaster ribs between the line of pilasters along the side walls, between which panels relieved the intervening spaces above a dark wood dado. A stage and two dressing rooms were provided for the variety acts which were a regular feature pre-1930. The Popular's first cinematograph licence was granted on 21 December 1925 to the Netherfield Picture House Ltd, the only indication of the opening date. However, records indicate that for most, if not all of the first 7 years, the cinema was run by lessees, the Regent Enterprise circuit. It was under their control that the Popular made the change to the talkies with Western Electric sound system, opening on 13 March 1930 with *Broadway Melody*, starring Bessie Love and Charles King.

The cinema was an early addition to the ABC circuit c1932, serving local working class audiences with prices ranging from only 5d to 9d, increasing in the early-1950s to only 1/- and 1/6. It was one of the company's less profitable situations. Bookings were mainly later runs of ABC circuit releases, with double features and *Pathé News*, shown concurrently with the company's other local cinema, the Gem. Between straight walls, the arched proscenium was wide enough for the installation of wide screen and CinemaScope in 1955, but with a similar film booking policy, it did little to improve the attendances and it continued to open in the evenings only.

The Popular was among the first of the ABC cinemas to close, the last show being on 8 December 1956 with *Mad at the World,* featuring Frank Lovejoy and *Women without Men*. The building was not subsequently used, and was badly vandalised during the years before demolition in the early-1970s.

1926
Cameo Cinema
Webster Road, Wavertree

The Cameo Cinema, 1958.

With the exception of the main entrance on the left-hand-side of the frontage, the architectural features of the original building, a chapel, remained. The earliest available photograph, in 1945, shows a short flight of steps divided into two sections by metal railings, up to the main entrance with two pairs of glass-panelled doors, and at either side, small still frames. Above this was a plain canopy supported by narrow columns, with 'Cameo' engraved on the soffit at the front and sides. Beyond the doors, a small foyer gave access to either side at the front of the 690-seat, stadium-type auditorium, whilst the back of the building housed the projection box and other rooms including the manager's office. The original proprietors, Bedford Cinemas Ltd, 19 Sweeting Street, Liverpool, whose managing director was picture pioneer, John F Wood, were granted the first cinematograph licence on 4 March 1926. On or about that date the cinema opened with the name, New Cameo Picture House.

In March 1928 it was among the company's cinemas to be taken over by the GTC, in the amalgamation of circuits under the control of GB. The cinema was closed by the early-1930s, with a Grand Reopening by GB on 25 October 1937. There was a matinee at 2.30pm and a continuous evening performance from 6.20pm of the feature film, *Elephant Boy,* starring Sabu, at the low admission prices of 5d to 9d. The Cameo being one of the company's smaller suburban cinemas, the mixed selection of film bookings included circuit and other release films for 3 days only, following runs at the more prestigious cinemas. The policy of mainly double features was continued from June 1948 by CMA, the amalgamation of the Odeon and GB circuits.

After a fairly uneventful history, the Cameo was the subject of front page news on Saturday 19 March 1949, due to the murder of manager, Leonard Thomas, and his assistant, John Catterall, by a gunman who entered the office and snatched the takings, a paltry sum of little more than £50. The shootings occurred at about 9.30pm, soon after the audience had settled down after the start of the feature film *Bond Street*.

In the mid-1950s, despite the rather narrow 23' proscenium, CinemaScope films commenced on 28 October 1955 with the Warner Bros colour musical *Lucky Me*, starring Doris Day. At this time admission prices were: 10d and 1/6. Simultaneously with the Rivoli, Aigburth, the two smallest CMA cinemas in the Liverpool area closed on 5 January 1957. The final programme was the double feature *Calcutta*, starring Alan Ladd and Frankie Howerd in *The Runaway Bus*. The building was unused for many years, the windows and doors bricked up. Demolition enabled the site to be used for housing.

1926
Burlington Cinema
Vauxhall Road, North Liverpool

Despite its lowly situation, close to a canal and the north Liverpool docks and warehouses, the Burlington, or 'Burly' as it was called locally, was considered to be rather posh. It boasted glass-panelled doors, a foyer with large circular paybox and glass front, adorned with gold lettering. Admission prices were 7d and 10d for the centre and rear seats. The entrance to the 4d front stalls was around the corner by the canal, so that patrons could go directly to their seats and avoid clattering down the steps. The seats were of plain wood whilst those further back were slightly more comfortable with skimpy padding.

This quite large cinema had a fan-shaped auditorium with 1,100 seats, and was erected lengthways to Vauxhall Road, the side elevation to Burlington Street and the main entrance at the corner. The proprietors, Burlington Cinema Co, of 60-62 Christian Street, were granted a cinematograph licence on 26 July 1926. They ran the cinema until 1931, when a lease was taken by Percy Whiteley, a showman who had been thrust into the business at the age of 14, having a concession at New Brighton Tower Grounds, whilst his father had picture houses at Leigh, Pendleton and Salford. Whiteley was responsible for the installation of Western Electric sound system for the showing of the first talkies at the Burlington. This included the smash hits of 1930: *All Quiet on the Western Front* and *Song of My Heart*, starring the Irish tenor John MacCormack, for which a special showing was requested by the local church, this being a strongly Roman Catholic area. Whiteley agreed, only on condition that the priests played down their counselling that cinema-going was sinful during Lent!

With the exception of special attractions, business was slow at first, before the factory and soap-works hands were lured in to see and hear the new stars of the talkie screen. On Saturday afternoons, hundreds of children were held in suspense by popular serials such as *Flash Gordon*. With numerous other cinemas in the area, competition for patrons was intense, and Whiteley accompanied other independent exhibitors, to trade shows at the Lime Street cinemas 4 days weekly, vying with each other to book the latest offerings from the major producers at the earliest possible date. At that time the hire fee was £10 to run a big film for 3 days, £7.10 for a B movie, and the supporting programme £2 for a two reel comedy, and £1 for a cartoon.

The Burlington lease expired in 1937 and was not renewed by Whiteley. It was then taken up by Stanley Grimshaw, managing director of Byron Picture Houses Ltd, who the previous year had taken over the Prince of Wales in the city from ABC Ltd. At around this time, the sound system at the Burlington was changed to RCA and prices reduced to between only 2d and 6d.

Although nearing the end of its days as a cinema, there was another change of lessee in 1939, to Phillip M Hanmer, managing director of the Regent Enterprise circuit, under whose control the Burlington was run until closure in 1941. Requisitioned for the war effort, it was never again used as a cinema. Pulled down after the war, the site became part of the Tate & Lyle complex.

1926
Gem
Vescock Street, Everton

This was one of the first three cinemas of the newly-formed Regent Enterprise circuit, whose managing director was Phillip M Hanmer. Just outside the city boundary, between Scotland Road and the north Liverpool docks, it was the latest addition in an area which then had numerous cinemas.

A long frontage next to the road was covered by painted plaster lacking any notable features. At the extreme left was the main entrance at the head of a flight of steps, and beyond the paybox, on the right, two pairs of glass-panelled doors into the long foyer. This was practically the full width of the building with, on the right, three entrances to the rear crossover gangway of the large, squarish, stadium-type auditorium which seated 1,350 in three sections across, including four gangways. The decorative style was that of many older cinemas, with pilasters and panels on the side walls above a dark dado, with carved decorative ribs spanning the curved ceiling, from which lights were suspended from glass-shaded fittings. Although of average width, the extent of the proscenium was limited by the long flanking walls.

The Grand Opening was on 19 August 1926, beginning with a matinee at 2.30pm, then a continuous evening performance from 6.30pm to 10.30pm. The feature film, *Merry Wives of Gotham* starring Marion Davies, was supported by Wilfred Lytell in *The Man who Paid*. Admission prices were 3d to 9d and there was to be a children's matinee every Saturday at 2.30pm. The Gem was a lower status cinema, which in 1935 increased the representation in Liverpool of the expanding ABC Ltd. As in the case of their other acquisition in that area, the Popular, Netherfield Road, the booking policy was mainly of last runs on the circuit of the company release films, for 3 days only, other dates being allocated to off circuit bookings. But, with low admission prices of 3d to 9d at daily matinees and continuous evening performances, the Gem enjoyed steady local patronage for many years.

Following the period of high admissions in the late-1940s, there was a drift of patrons away from cinemas like the Gem towards those offering higher standards of comfort. CinemaScope had provided a boost to attendances for nearly 2 years. Belatedly installed, it began on 29 September 1955 with the colour western, *Bad Day at Black Rock* starring Spencer Tracy.

In its remaining short time as a cinema, admissions fell at performances normally continuous in the evening only, and prices stayed low at 1/- and 1/6. Among the first of ABC's closures in Liverpool, the last show was on 8 February 1958, with the double feature *The Vicious Circle* starring John Mills and *The Wayward Girl*. The building was sold to St Sylvester's Church and converted for use as a parochial club.

1926
Regent
Prescot Road, Old Swan

The Regent was originally independently owned by former funeral directors, the Wilkinsons, who, during the early-1920s took over the Warwick Picturedrome in Windsor Street. In 1926 Robert Wilkinson formed the Regent Cinema Co, and the construction work was completed by October of that year. Although the 1,140-seat auditorium was of the single floor, stadium-type, the three storey frontage of white, glazed terracotta relieved by red brick was impressive. The prominent central section housed the main entrance, whilst above, the first and second floor windows were grouped within three vertical panels, surmounted by a pedimented gable below the straight apex.

Records indicate that the Regent was opened in October 1926, but the first press advertisement is that of 1 November, when the feature film was *Don Q*, starring Douglas Fairbanks senior, with a matinee at 2.45pm and continuous evening performance from 6.40pm. The Regent was among Liverpool's additions to the ABC circuit in June 1935, but for a limited time only, until 7 May 1938, then closing with the film *I'll Be Yours*, featuring Madeleine Carroll and Francis Lederer. The company presence in this district was then continued from 9 May by the new super-cinema of the same name, built on an adjacent site. Over 60 years later, the old Regent building, after many years as Casino Car Sales, is now a supermarket. The New Regent, which replaced the cinema in 1938, was demolished nearly 35 years ago.

1927
West Derby Picture House • West Derby Plaza
Almonds Green, West Derby

The West Derby Picture House Co, with a capital of £10,000, was registered in August 1926 for the purpose of acquiring a site in Almonds Green, for the construction of a modern cinema. The directorate comprised of: William Charles Cuff, a solicitor; chairman of directors, Alfred Adams, also the director of Clubmoor Picture House Co, Alexander McLaren, managing director of Belle Vale Orchards, Dawson Radcliffe, retired purser, and Horatio Kenton, garage proprietor. During the previous 3 to 4 years, marked changes had taken place in and around the once secluded old village, which had been replaced by the huge and much needed Liverpool housing scheme which provided 5000 dwellings. The chosen site was a few yards from the West Derby electric-tram terminus, and a short distance from Muirhead Avenue. Also, there was no other cinema within a one mile radius.

The local press reported that work on the imposing structure began on 14 October 1926, and was completed in 10 months under the supervision of GR Wright, Bridge Road, Litherland. The architectural work, both external and internal, by Lionel AG Pritchard, ARIBA, 57 Moorfields, Liverpool, was greatly admired and considered to be an ornament to West Derby. The front of the building, with central main entrance, was mainly of rustic brick, relieved at first floor level by an area of pale cream terracotta around a central group of windows. A prominent coping spanned the frontage.

It was claimed that every possible device to ensure the comfort of the patrons had been incorporated in the stadium-type, 939-seat auditorium. The very latest tip-up seats were fitted in beautifully upholstered grey velour. For hygiene reasons these were fixed to a flooring of a patent composition instead of the usual wood, and with a gradient of 1:8, it was claimed that an uninterrupted view of the screen was possible from every seat. The novel, cleverly conceived lighting produced a pleasant, soft glow on each side of the auditorium in the cornice.

There were numerous acceptances of the directors' invitation to the inaugural performance at 3pm on Saturday 30 July 1927, when for this and the evening performance at 6.30pm, a special programme was shown: The King of the Turf (drama), Blue Ribbon (comedy), Speed (educational) and Pathé Pictorial and Gazette. The directors, aware that first class music was an essential component of any performance, stated that no discordant note would be sounded in the new cinema. With Thomas Hornsby as conductor, the Neapolitan orchestra comprised experts in their profession. A Bluthner grand piano and Mustel organ were supplied by Jas Smith & Son, Lord Street, Liverpool, indicating the high class of music played. Orchestral accompaniment to silent films continued for over 3 years, the cinema being among the last to change over to the talkies for which BTH sound system was installed, beginning on 13 October 1930, with Paris, starring Jack Buchanan and Irene Bordoni.

By the mid-1930s the strength of existing local competition from the Regal, Norris Green and the Carlton, Tuebrook, increased, when both were taken over by ABC. Although therefore restricted to later showings of the leading films, the West Derby remained a popular local family cinema, with low admission prices from only 7d to 1/- at daily matinee and continuous evening performances, with seats bookable for the separate performances on Saturdays and Bank Holidays.

In 1946, the West Derby was taken over by Cheshire County Cinemas Ltd of Runcorn, who retained it as a family cinema. By about 1950 the matinees had been discontinued, performances being continuous in the evenings only, with admission prices 1/- and 1/9. Installation of CinemaScope was delayed but this was among the few cinemas in the suburbs complete with magnetic stereophonic sound, originated by Twentieth Century Fox. The feature film There's No Business Like Show Business, starring Ethel Merman and Dan Dailey was West Derby's first CinemaScope film, shown on 24 October 1955. From mid-November 1955, known as the West Derby Plaza, the cinema stayed open until 5 January 1960. The last show was The Mouse that Roared, with Peter Sellers, and Juke Box Rhythm. The building was later converted into a supermarket

1927
Rialto
Upper Parliament Street, Toxteth

The Rialto, 1964.

Although for many years a leading GB cinema, the Rialto was originally the enterprise of the company Rialto (Liverpool) Ltd. With a capital of £35,000, they issued a subscription list to prospective shareholders on 8 September 1925, offering 34,000 ordinary shares at £1 each, list closing on or before 15 September 1925. The board of directors consisted of: Hugh Bicket, director of Chester Music Hall, the Savoy, St Helens and Glynn (Chester) Picture Theatres; Douglas A Gordon, director of the Homer Cinema and the Garrick and Grosvenor Picture Theatres Ltd; Josiah Taplin, director of Chester Music Hall and Glynn (Chester) Picture Theatres Ltd; Fred Banks; and Harold Lipson, director of Trocadero (Liverpool) Picture Theatre and Radcliffe Picture Theatres. The estimated cost of the

The Rialto's Venetian interior, 1927.

Rialto, its cafés and 12 ground floor shops, was estimated at £57,000 including the site, which was felt to be ideal. There were over 40,000 homes within a one-mile radius and a rapidly increasing population, being only one mile from the city in a district favoured for residential flats.

The Rialto proved to be a local success. Designed by Liverpool architects Gray and Evans of North John Street, it was erected by William Griffiths and Cromwell of Upper Duke Street. It was not only a cinema/theatre, but in modern parlance could be described as a leisure complex, the first of its kind in the Liverpool area, including a large ballroom, considered the finest in the UK, a large café, a billiard hall and 12 first class shops on the frontages. Linking these, at the corner of Upper Parliament Street and Berkeley Street, the main architectural feature was the wide, curved corner, flanked by dome-topped towers. Here was the main entrance with balcony above, both divided by pairs of white columns matching the white-glazed faience tiling. At either side, above the shops, this was relieved by red brick. A line of doors led into the large foyer which gave access to all the public areas, displaying the most remarkable schemes of decoration ever achieved in modern building.

The auditorium, with 1,200 seats in the stalls and 500 in the balcony, took over the distinction of being the largest in Liverpool. Considerably more adaptable for use as a theatre than the average cinema, it had a stage 18' deep, spacious enough for a whole company of players, with adequate dressing rooms.

On entering the auditorium the effect was described as that of a vast apartment draped in cloth of gold, the keynote being struck by the drop curtain, which under the glow of the footlights gleamed as if beaten out of the precious metal. In harmony of colour, decorated with gigantic spear-like shafts shooting upwards, and great panels in darkly jewelled hues, the side walls were splayed to the front of the balcony. This was an immense single span from wall to wall, beneath which the stalls were indirectly lit from immense, moth-like lanterns. Unsupported by pillars, there was not a single break in the view of screen and stage, from which the acoustics were of such high quality that the slightest sound was perceptible, even on the back row.

Ascending by stairways from the foyer to the first floor, patrons could enter the splendid ballroom set amid scenes of Venice in order to provide a different setting for each dance. There was accommodation for about 500 couples

on a special sprung floor which glistened like a nut-brown lake, bounded by banks of tables. On the same floor, the 60-table café had a decorative scheme and carpet to give an old-world garden effect, with paintings of the beautiful Wye Valley between lattice work frames containing artificial flowers and leaves. In cream and green, with a flower-bedecked balcony, it was appropriately named the Rialto Garden Café, in which patrons could listen to music broadcast from the theatre or the ballroom. The projection unit was about 74' in length, and included a projection room, equipped with Kalee projectors, as well as a rewinding room and generating room.

The Grand Opening of the Rialto was at 6pm on 7 October 1927, by the Lord Mayor of Liverpool, to whose hospital appeal fund the entire proceeds of the theatre and ballroom were donated. The manager was W Peel Smith, formerly of the Trocadero, Camden Street. The opening film was a pre-release run of the PDC production *The Last Frontier,* with a vocal prologue presenting The Southern Melody Quartette. Also on stage was Harold Gee, former musical director at the Trocadero, and his all British orchestra, providing special musical programmes. The supporting programme consisted of the *Topical Budget*, the *Pathé Pictorial* and *Eve's Review*. The non-stop show ran from 6.30pm, but thereafter there was a matinee daily at 2.45pm and a continuous evening performance from 6.30pm, except Saturday, with separate performances at 6.40pm and 8.50pm and seats bookable in advance. In the ballroom there was dancing from 8pm to 1am to Billy Cotton's London 12-man Savannah Band for an admission charge of 5/-, evening dress essential.

The Rialto was independently owned for a short time only, in March 1928 being among the eight Liverpool cinemas acquired by the GTC in the amalgamation of circuits under the GB Picture Corporation. It was the aim of GTC's managing director, Sir Walter Gibbons, to provide the best films, combined with a first class variety programme, for which the Rialto was ideally suited.

The first film with sound at the Rialto was *The Jazz Singer*, featuring Al Jolson, which began on 4 February 1929, with a jazz prologue by the Rialto Dance Band and, on stage, Nora Delany, the popular male impersonator. All Talking films with Western Electric sound system started on 2 September 1929, with *Showboat* starring Laura La Plante and Joseph Schildkraut. By this time, cine-variety had ceased, although the orchestra was retained for a few months at performances, continuous from 2pm to 10.45pm. From this time, bookings were quite regularly concurrent with the Trocadero in the city, but following GB opening the Hippodrome as a cinema in West Derby Road in July 1931, this gradually changed. By the mid-1930s, almost entirely with the Hippodrome, they were soon second run following the Trocadero.

The Rialto continued to be one of the better attended cinemas outside the city centre, and in the less successful years of the early-1950s, it was among the few locations of 3D films. The first of these to open, on 3 August 1953, was the Paramount picture, in Technicolor, *Sangaree*, starring Fernando Lamas and Arlene Dahl, which was viewed wearing coloured glasses to obtain the 3D effect. For this reason the system proved to be only a temporary novelty, and was followed only by *It Came from Outer Space* on 21 February 1954, before the rather longer lasting attraction of CinemaScope, for which the Rialto's wide proscenium, was ideally suited. This began on 21 February 1955 with *Sign of the Pagan,* starring Jeff Chandler and Jack Palance. The regular concurrency of film bookings with the Hippodrome had gradually been phased out, with the exception of leading attractions, made possible by the inclusion of second run Odeon circuit releases. This was a result of the amalgamation in June 1948 of the Odeon and GB circuits under the new company, CMA.

CMA underwent a name change in 1962, to become the Rank Theatre Division, by whom film bookings were allocated either for Rank release to mainly Odeon theatres, or on the National Circuit; less attractive films being reserved for those cinemas considered to be old or inferior. Probably because they were close to the city centre, the Rialto and Hippodrome were chosen to play the National Circuit releases, which were first shown when road-show extended runs were played at the Odeon in the city, the Rank releases then being switched to the Gaumont. The former concurrency of bookings to the Rialto and Hippodrome was then to a great extent resumed. Although presenting a good selection of first or second runs of the latest films, in the 1960s, the large Rialto became unviable.

Surviving for only 2 years under the control of the Rank Theatre Division, the final programme on 29 February 1964 was *The Thrill of It All*, starring Doris Day, and *Silent Raid*. The building was acquired by Swainbanks Ltd for use as an antique furniture store, but after severe fire damage during the Toxteth riots in 1980, it was demolished.

1927
The Woolton
Mason Street, Woolton

With its 75-year history, the Woolton is Liverpool's only remaining independent cinema, and the last virtually intact survivor from the Golden Age of the cinema. Situated about 6 miles to the south-east of the city, in a conservation area on the steeply sloping short Mason Street, between Woolton Street and Church Road. The first announcement concerning the new enterprise appeared in the *Kinematograph Weekly* of 26 August 1926, stating that Liverpool architect, Lionel AG Pritchard, ARIBA, was designing the new cinema. It cost £10,000 and was intended to seat 800, but the actual capacity fell short of this.

In March 1927 the Woolton Picture House Co Ltd announced that the prospectus for the issue of shares would shortly be forthcoming. By that time building had begun, and the magistrates granted a licence on condition that the work was completed within 6 months. The steep site resulted in quite an unusual style of construction in that the single storey frontage was adjacent to the length of the auditorium, which was angled back from right to left. The frontage of dark brick was relieved in the centre immediately above the canopy by a panel of white, glazed terracotta bearing the cinema name. A flight of steps, increasing in number towards the right-hand-side, led up to an entrance at either side of the paybox. This area had a steel and glass canopy, adorned with two shields and splayed back towards the front wall. At the top of the steps an entrance at either side of the paybox was provided to divide the patrons in accordance with the different parts of the auditorium, front, centre and rear stalls, at prices which originally ranged from 6d to 1/-.

Beyond the entrances, doors in the small foyer gave access to the right-hand-side of the stadium-type auditorium, with a seating capacity of 711 on the quite well raked floor, facilitated by the natural slope of the site. To achieve this maximum capacity, the rows of seats were fitted as close together as possible, as also their distance from the front, where the screen was set within the 27'-wide proscenium, in front of a small stage, although there appears to be no proof that it was ever used for live entertainment. Extending over the rear of the auditorium, the projection room was supported by columns, behind which the seats were fitted on an even more steeply raked floor.

There is apparently no official announcement of the opening, as the cinema did not advertise in the local press. At that time it was considered to be a long way from Liverpool, so the proprietors relied upon local advertising, such as posters, or small bills in shops. However, many older residents of the district agree that the cinema opened on 26 December 1927, with a programme of long forgotten silent films. Affixed to the projection box fire doors are the plaques of Mather and Platt, Manchester, dated November 1927, therefore the opening date may well have been 26 December 1927. Sound films, began in the early-1930s, probably by the BTH system, which was definitely being used in the mid-1930s, reducing the seating capacity to 673, the screen having to move forward to make space for the speaker.

By the end of the 1930s, the proprietors were Weller & Stevenson Theatres, based at the Broadway Cinema, Chalfont St Peter. Bucks and Cheshire County Cinemas Ltd took over in the late-1940s. This highly esteemed small cinema circuit was founded in 1922 by RH Godfrey who, with his son as joint managing director, added the Woolton to the circuit, following their takeover of the West Derby Picture House. This coincided with the Woolton's first press advertisement on 23 January 1947, for the film *In Old Chicago*, with Tyrone Power and Alice Faye. At about the same time as they equipped the West Derby Picture House with CinemaScope and magnetic sound, they similarly equipped the Woolton, for the opening of *There No Business Like Show Business* on 31 October 1955, after its showing at West Derby.

The Woolton has led a charmed life, not only having survived the years of generally decreasing cinema admissions, but also twice having narrowly escaped destruction by fire. The more serious of these broke out in the early hours of 22 September 1958, resulting in damage to the stage, curtains, sound equipment and some of the seating. The cinema was closed for 3 months, during which the front of the auditorium was completely restyled, with wall-to-wall curtains in front of the new, larger screen.

In the mid-1980s, reseating reduced the capacity to the present 256 luxurious, broad-backed seats, providing armchair comfort in widely-spaced rows, of the type seen in few cinemas prior to the opening of the multiplexes. Early in 1991 CCC announced that they had decided to sell this small but popular cinema in order to concentrate their efforts on the Regal Twins at Northwich, Cheshire. After concern for some time that this might have meant the end of Liverpool's oldest surviving cinema, it was fortunately saved by the present owner, David Wood, whose grandfather opened the city's first purpose-built cinema, the Bedford, Walton, in 1908. Father and grandfather established the JF Wood cinema circuit, later known as Bedford Cinemas (1928) Ltd, and in the 1930s opened some of Liverpool's finest suburban cinemas.

When Woolton cinema was for sale, David Wood was in the film renting side of the business, and declined an offer of a move to London in order to take over the cinema on 10 January 1992. Despite extensive internal modernisation, it was not until 1995 that the projection room was equipped with a Westrex tower, long-running film system, and a Xenon lamp for screen illumination. Although retaining the Westar projectors and Westrex sound, the Woolton was the last cinema on Merseyside to dispense with the Peerless Magnarcs and the use of two projectors to screen 20-minute reels of film, mounted on 2000' spools. Chief projectionist, David Swindell, with over 30 years service at the cinema, provided the highest standard of presentation. The Woolton continues, as always, to be maintained to a high standard. Normally showing films for family audiences, patrons come from a wide area to sink into the comfortable, plush seats and experience film presentation reminiscent of earlier years.

1928
Plaza • Gaumont • Odeon • Classic • Cannon • ABC
Allerton Road, Liverpool

Described as a handsome addition to the many beautiful picture theatres in the Liverpool area, the Plaza was erected with the frontage to the new wide boulevard section of Allerton Road. The enterprise of the JF Wood cinema circuit of 19 Sweeting Street, Liverpool, it was erected by the building contractors, Rimmer, to the plans of the well known cinema architect, AE Shennan. The upper part of the three storey frontage was of rustic bricks, relieved by carved features in Portland stone, which was also used as a setting for the principal windows of the first and second floor. Between these, the large cinema sign in block letters was illuminated by electric bulbs, whilst below the first floor windows, the frontage was lit by spotlights. The lower part was faced in white Portland stone and the wide central entrance was divided by large columns supporting the entablature. At either side were stonework sections, divided by horizontal flutes.

Three pairs of glass-panelled doors in the main entrance gave access to the unusually large foyer, with a coffered ceiling supported by square fluted columns and flooring of travertine; a hard, white limestone. In the middle was an unusual feature; a large basin, lined with blue mosaic and enclosing a central

The Plaza, 1928.

fountain and pedestal, also of travertine, supporting a statuette. At the rear, doors led to areas from which there was entry to the auditorium at either side of the stalls floor, on which were approximately 900 of the 1,432 total seats, the long foyer encroaching to some extent upon the length of the stalls. On the first floor, above the foyer, the café was decorated in cream and gold, with blue carpet and chairs. Next to the café was the nursery; a neat, soft, carpeted room decorated with pictures of animals and equipped with a rocking-horse and furnished with settees, where mothers could leave their children in the custody of a nurse. Above this area and extending over the rear stalls, the long balcony with curved front terminated at the widest part of the auditorium, beyond which a deep carved rib spanned the curved ceiling up to consoles on the side walls.

With long, splayed walls, the front of the auditorium narrowed markedly to the proscenium set beneath a grilled arch. The splayed section included an exit at either side, and in the centre above a balustraded panel, a balconette was surmounted by an arched area adorned by a dark curtain and pelmet. This area was highlighted by the ceiling decoration in which rows of dark octagonal panels contrasted with the light colour scheme. Lighting was by cone shaped, glass shaded electric fittings suspended from the ceiling. The proscenium had a gold curtain with dark borders, whilst the stage curtain and pelmet were in deep red with gold trimmings. At the rear of the balcony, the most up-to-date operating room was equipped with two Ross projectors.

Although intended to be the latest addition to the cinemas of the JF Wood circuit, in March 1928 the Plaza was among their cinemas taken over in the amalgamation of circuits under the GTC to become a GB cinema. LN Rowley, formerly of the Super Picture House, Birkenhead, as well as working with the Wood circuit for 17 years, was appointed as manager. The Plaza opened on Saturday 31 March 1928, with a continuous performance from 2.30pm to 10.30pm. The feature film was *The Sorrows of Satan*, featuring Adolphe Menjou and Lya de Putti, with musical setting by Delmonte and his Plaza symphony orchestra, said to be a combination of talent unequalled in the north of England. Admission prices were: stalls 1/- and balcony 1/3. After the opening, performances consisted of a matinee at 2.30pm and a continuous evening performance from 6.30pm to 10.30pm. On Saturdays, separate performances were at 6.30pm and 8.45pm, for which all seats were bookable.

The Plaza soon became Liverpool's acknowledged Mecca of Music, for, in addition to that of the orchestra, a Wurlitzer organ was installed, and played in the week beginning 6 August 1928 by its most famous exponent, Reginald Foort. Also on stage at every performance, even the 6d bargain matinee, was The Reginald Foort Trio.

The Plaza was an early venue for sound films, equipped with RCA sound system. The first talkie show was on 23 September 1929, when the 100% dialogue film, *The Valiant,* starred Paul Muni and Marguerite Churchill. In support were *Detectives*, with Karl Dune and George K Arthur and also *British Movietone News*. The arrival of the talkies did not mean the end of the Wurlitzer, and Arthur Crossland was resident organist for many years until 1939. In the post-war years the organ was occasionally used by William Whittle and Harold Thiems, but was removed when the cinema closed in 1971.

With first suburban runs of the GB circuit's release films, the Plaza for many years was among the better attended Liverpool suburban cinemas. The amalgamation of the Gaumont and Odeon circuits under CMA, resulted, as at many individually named cinemas, in the Plaza being renamed the Gaumont in 1950. During the years under this company, CinemaScope was installed starting on 6 December 1954 with *The Black Shield* of *Falworth* starring Tony

Curtis and Janet Leigh. The Rank Theatre division took over in 1962, and the cinema became known as the Odeon. Then, in December 1967, it was taken over by Laurie Marsh's classic group, who retained a similar film booking policy of mainly Rank release films until closure on 10 April 1971 with *A Shot in the Dark* starring Peter Sellers and *The Hills Ran Red*.

It was announced that the cinema was to be demolished to make way for a new shopping centre at ground level and luxury cinema on the first floor. At the extreme right of the cinema entrance was a carpeted stairway leading up to a first floor licensed bar, beyond which were the entrances to the luxurious, carpeted, stadium-type 493-seat auditorium, with full air-conditioning. The projection room was equipped with a Westar 5000 projector, Westrex sound system, and tower, long running, projection system.

The new Classic cinema opened on 11 August 1973, with a continuous performance from 2.30pm of *The Lovers*, starring Richard Beckinsale and Paula Wilcox and *Birds of Prey* with David Jansen. Performances were continuous throughout the day until September 1984, but thereafter were in the evenings only except Saturdays. In this greatly reduced form it was under the control of the Classic circuit until April 1986, when the new proprietors, Cannon cinemas, made the appropriate name change. They continued the policy of normally continuous evening only performances, with the exception of Saturdays and school holidays. After a further 10 years, in June 1996, most of the traditional cinemas were acquired by Richard Branson's Virgin cinemas, purchased by Virgin's former managing director, Barrie Jenkins. A national circuit of 90 cinemas was formed, reinstating the name ABC, and the former triangle sign in the company press advertisements. This has continued into the new millenium as a single screen cinema, now under the control of Odeon.

1929
Ritz
Utting Avenue, Anfield

This was the last of the Liverpool cinemas to open with silent films, and another of those erected to the plans of Lionel AG Prichard. At a cost of £26,000, it was a venture of the Ritz Picture House Co (Liverpool) Ltd, 229, India Buildings, whose directorate included Mr and Mrs RL Kenton (Postmaster) of 33 Utting Avenue, Anfield, and Alfred Adams, who was connected with the Clubmoor Cinema. Situated at the junction of Utting Avenue and Bidston Road, the building was constructed with frontages of rustic brick accented by panels of terracotta, to highlight the diagonal section including the wide main entrance, flanked by columns with capital supporting the entablature. This was surmounted by a metal and glass canopy with deep facia, which displayed the full name, Ritz Super-Cinema, in large, white, block letters. On the front of the canopy, four globe shaded electric fittings, and four spotlights illuminated the upper part of the frontage. This incorporated the three main first floor windows set in carved stonework, above which the highest part terminated in a deep, carved coping. Diagonally in the main entrance, two pairs of glass-panelled doors led into the quite large foyer with terrazzo floor, and here were the stalls entrances and a short stairway to the rear stalls. A separate entrance in Bidston Road was provided for the front seats.

The attractive, stadium-type, 1,100-seat auditorium had a well raked floor, with curtained windows along the side walls, and stunning Egyptian-style murals, predominantly in brown. The proscenium curtain was pale cream and a stage and orchestra pit were used for performances of cine-variety during the first year when silent films were shown.

The Ritz opened on 16 March 1929, with a matinee at 3pm and a continuous evening performance from 6.15pm, to which admission was 3d to 1/-. *The Joker*, *Sailors Don't Care* and *The Betrayal* were screened, accompanied by a full orchestra. Just over a year later, BTH sound system was installed for the opening of the first talkie on 7 April 1930, *Fox Movietone Follies of 1929*, featuring Sue Carol, Lola Lane and an all-star cast.

Although a popular and attractive cinema, from the early-1930s the Ritz faced strong competition, particularly from the major circuits, ABC and GB. The cinema was mainly restricted to later showings of leading films, at daily matinees Monday to Saturday and continuous evening performances. Matinees ceased in the early-1950s. The booking situation improved in 1955, when the Ritz was among the independent cinemas to install CinemaScope and magnetic stereophonic sound, thereby securing first run in the district of Twentieth Century-Fox films in the wide screen format. The first of these opened on 10 January 1955 with *The Robe*, starring Richard Burton and Jean Simmons. For a few months, matinees were resumed, reverting to continuous evenings only for the last 2 years, when plummeting attendances resulted in the Ritz being the first Anfield cinema to close. The final show, on 30 June 1957, was the double bill *The Raid,* starring Van Heflin and Anne Bancroft, and *Bomber Moon* with George Montgomery. Initially acquired by a Mr Ross, a coach tour operator, the premises was for many years the Tasker DIY Store, then, by 1990, the Tasker Sports Superstore, packed with every possible type of sporting equipment and accessory.

1930
Regal
Broadway, Norris Green

In addition to being Liverpool's largest stadium-type cinema, with 1,756 seats, the Regal had the distinction of being the first to be built specifically for the talkies. The location, in the Norris Green shopping centre in the city's largest housing estate, was very favourable; the only cinema in that area of about 7,000 post-war houses. Erected under the supervision of Liverpool architect Kenmure Kinna, ARIBA, work began in June 1929 and was completed in about 7 months. The simple, dignified exterior, complemented the style of the surrounding property.

The 76' frontage of rustic bricks finished with Snowcrete cement, had a Tinos marble facing around the wide main entrance. In the middle, the paybox was flanked on either side by two pairs of swing doors to a vestibule with terrazzo flooring, from which two staircases led to the rear of the auditorium. Three pairs of doors separated the vestibule

from the large waiting room which stretched 40' under the auditorium. From the waiting room, patrons entered the theatre from each side by a short stairway to the sides of the auditorium midway between the stage and the rear. The auditorium was 126' by 76', with all the seating on one floor. To overcome the difficulty of sight lines, it was given a gradient of 1:10 in two raked sections, achieved by stepping the floor at the cross centre line.

Between the rear entrances a recess, 21' by 11', contained four rows of seats, over which was a structure equipped with the latest type of Kalee projector and Western Electric sound system, achieving a picture throw of 146' onto the Western Electric screen, set in a 50'-wide proscenium. Behind this was a 14'-deep stage and a suite of five dressing rooms at the rear, for supplementary variety acts. The stage foot and overhead lighting battens each contained about 24 lamps in four colours, and a spotlight projected onto the stage through an aperture on the right of the proscenium opening.

Decoration of the front of the auditorium was atmospheric, depicting lake and mountain scenery, with four large panels at the stage end described as fine examples of theatre artistry. From the top of the pilasters separating the panel, glowing tongues of flame-coloured lighting shed a luminous hue on the graduated sky-blue ceiling. The top moulding of each pilaster concealed three cornice lamps in reflectors and each panoramic view was lit by eight concealed floodlamps in reflectors. The back of the hall was painted mauve.

Special attention was paid to the lighting; from the main ceiling hung ten distinctive Nacrolaque (non-flame celluloid) shades, and there were 19 wall brackets, 18" in length, with flame-tinted glass panels. The installation of batteries and an electrical charging plant eliminated the use of gas for secondary lighting. Outside, a large electric sign, built up of 2' high gilded block letters spelling the name, was lit by 20, 30-watt lamps.

Under the ownership of HE and WL Hampson, Regal Cinema Co, the Grand Opening was on 27 January 1930, with the record-breaking film *Broadway Melody* starring Anita Page, Bessie Love and Charles King. There was a matinee at 3pm and continuous performances from 6.30pm to 10.45pm, with admission from 6d to 1/-. Huge crowds attended, with hundreds unable to gain admission. Patrons were advised to obtain their seats as early as possible.

Competition increased considerably with the opening of other large super-cinemas, the nearest being the Gaumont Palace, Anfield, in 1931, and the Carlton, Tuebrook. Both had the advantage of first runs in the district of their company release films, resulting in the Regal screening the off circuit bookings, mainly those of GB, following that company's suburban cinemas. Although from the mid-1930s under the ownership of ABC Ltd, a similar booking policy was maintained. But the Regal, with its large catchment area, continued to do well into the early-1950s with continuous performances throughout the day. In 1955 the availability of films increased with the arrival of CinemaScope and a new 40' screen on which *Demetrius and the Gladiators,* featuring Victor Mature and Susan Hayward was shown on 28 March. This was the first of the Twentieth Century-Fox releases in the new format at the Regal.

The Regal closed on 6 August 1955 for a £20,000 facelift, with complete restyling and modernisation of the auditorium and foyer, also installation of the latest seating, furnishings and equipment. The main change was to the rear half of the auditorium, where the flooring was stepped and divided into two sections by a crossover gangway and wooden partitions, whilst the raked front half was similarly separated. Outside, the cinema was repainted, with black and white faience tiles on the lower part. Over the four entrances, a wide lettering display panel, illuminated from within and with side extensions, had the name in block letters above the new still frames. This entire unit projected from the wall, with numerous circular shaded lights underneath. A modern paybox in the waiting room replaced the one in the centre of the frontage.

Due to the restyling of the auditorium, the capacity was reduced by over 500, but still having 1,200 seats and offering far greater comfort for patrons. The Regal was reopened on Monday 10 October 1955 with guest appearance by Billy Liddell, captain of Liverpool FC. There followed a continuous, double feature performance from 2pm to 10.30pm, of *Such Men are Dangerous* starring Kirk Douglas and *Circle of Fear* starring Charles Starrett, with *Pathé News.* The improvements led to increased attendances for a limited time, but, in 1963, low attendances prompted an experiment with bingo on Tuesday and Friday evenings, operated by the ABC bingo division, Alpha Bingo. This proved successful and the following year a change was made to full time bingo. The last picture show was on Saturday 10 October 1964 with *Carry On Spying* and *Who was Maddox?* After about 2 years the hall was taken over by Mecca Ltd, under whose control the Regal Bingo and Social Club still continues.

1930
Capitol
Overton Street, Edge Hill

The fact that the district of Edge Hill, just outside the city area, was poorly served with entertainments, led to a group of local businessmen, in 1929, deciding to develop a site in Overton Street, with the erection of a large super-cinema by a company known as Capitol (Edge Hill) Ltd. As the overall dimensions of the site were 95' by 95', some ingenuity was required by the architect, AE Shennan, FRIBA, to plan an auditorium with dimensions of 106' by 81'. This was achieved by its diagonal setting to the street. Next to this, the long, stone and brick facade had a taller centre section accentuated by four tall arched windows and three trough letter signs, one horizontal and two vertical, each reading Capitol. They were built of 3' letters, illuminated by about 250, 30-watt lamps.

Economic use of space masked the irregularities of the angular setting of the auditorium, without compromising safety, comfort or convenience; the number of exits generously exceeding local authority requirements. The main waiting room, under the auditorium, with its comfortable furniture wood block floor, and large Axminster carpets, had space for several hundred people.

At the extreme right of the frontage, the main entrance led into a large foyer, with staircases to the first floor lounge for balcony patrons, similarly furnished to that of the lower floor, but also with a kitchen for the preparation of light refreshments between performances. The auditorium at its greatest width was 81' clear span by 106', seating 1,045 people, whilst the balcony, 53' by 81', had 540 seats. The latter had been designed on the American principle, having entrances at three different levels. The balcony front was unusual, having two straight sections from the side walls, linked by a curved centre.

The modern decor featured large, plain surfaces in brilliant tones of yellow, flame and rich green. The ceiling was painted in yellows varying from primrose to a full Naples, with each geometrical face treated in a different tone. The

upper portion of the walls was finished in tones from fawn to warm yellow, with pilasters of a deeper shade enriched with gold and bronze, whilst below, the dado was treated with texture paint forming an inter-lacing pattern. The cubist proscenium was fawn enriched with gold, the opening having curtains and a pelmet. The gold curtains had appliquéd ornaments in brilliant green, whilst the green velvet pelmet had gold appliqué. A float on the stage and a batten fixed behind the curtain, lit up a battery of coloured screen lights. The auditorium was illuminated from the main ceiling by V-shaped, six-sided fittings about 36' across, containing 300-watt lamps. Twelve similar, but smaller fittings hung from the ceiling under the balcony. The operating suite was cantilevered out at the rear of the balcony and the projection room was equipped with twin Kalee machines on Western Electric bases, with a picture throw of 95'.

The local press of 1 February 1930 announced that the cinema would be open to the public in the evening with two performances: 6.30pm and 8.30pm. The feature film for that evening only was *King of the Khyber Rifles* starring Victor McLaglen and Myrna Loy. On Monday 3 February, *Broadway Melody* was to be shown for 6 days, with a matinee daily at 3pm and seats bookable for the evening performances at 6.30 and 8.40pm.

Although one of the larger suburban cinemas, independent ownership meant that the Capitol soon faced strong competition from the large circuits, as well as from the independently-owned Majestic, which mainly screened second run films after the city cinemas. The Capitol was therefore always restricted to a mixed selection of film bookings, including those of ABC and GB release and off circuit films at later dates for 3 days only.

In the early-1950s attendances fell and from 1952 performances were in the evenings only. The Capitol had the doubtful distinction of being the last to install CinemaScope, starting on 4 December 1958, with *Sign of the Pagan* starring Jeff Chandler. From the early-1940s the cinema was run by the WJ Speakman circuit, whose managing director (of that name) was a well known figure among Liverpool exhibitors, being also the managing director of four associated companies, and also chairman of the North-Western branch of the Cinematograph Exhibitors Association.

Just over 4 months before closure, cine-bingo was introduced on Sunday evenings, with one feature film and a bingo session. Briefly, Wednesdays were also given over to this, but soon discontinued before closure on 2 December 1961 with *Portrait in Black*, starring Lana Turner and Chartroose Caboose. The building was first acquired by Clement Freeman Ltd, for use as a warehouse, but later it was an Ambassador Lanes Bowling Alley. By the late-1960s ten-pin bowling had lost popularity and the building was closed and later demolished.

1930
Astoria • ABC
Walton Road, Walton

The Astoria, 1930s.

The trade press reported that no one viewing this handsome theatre would suspect that it was originally designed as a ballroom, billiard hall and café rendezvous. Such plans were prepared by Gray & Evans, of North John Street, Liverpool, who also redrew the designs when the directors decided to depart from their original idea in favour of a super-cinema. The proprietors were Astoria Entertainments (Liverpool) Ltd, whose directors were JA Appleton (chairman); J Iles (vice chairman); AE Fortman, and DB Davies, whilst A Ellison of Bryce Hanmer & Co was the secretary.

Situated in a main traffic thoroughfare, and commanding an important position at the forking of Walton Road, the facade was principally of white glazed faience relieved above the canopy by tall, red brick sections, which flanked an arched central section in glazed faience, incorporating the larger first and second floor windows, whilst above this was carved the cinema name. The frontage was wider than the auditorium, being splayed at the left to provide various rooms, and along the entire length was a canopy edged with white opaque glass sections, with central panels bearing the words, 'Astoria Super Sound'. The central main entrance had two pairs of glass-panelled doors inset, flanked on either side by a separate entrance with one pair of doors leading to the wide foyer with paybox adjacent to the opposite wall and stalls entrances on either side. These led onto quite a wide crossover

gangway, from which the seating was separated by a high glass-panelled partition. On this floor, 870 seats were installed in two sections with centre and side gangways.

The first floor lounge was reached by a stairway with a metal balustrade at either side of the foyer, and from the lounge a continuation of the stairways led up to the rear circle entrances in the centre. Doors at either side of the lounge led to a corridor, with at either end, the entrances to the front circle seats, separated by a crossover gangway. The 516-seat circle extended 46' over the stalls. The curved front, in textured plaster to a fan-shaped design, connected with the splayed walls flanking the 35' proscenium with side gangways, giving access to the front exits.

The auditorium was a blaze of light and colour with fibrous plaster detailing. The proscenium was reminiscent of the Mexican Astec period with mouldings in strong primary colours. Plain surfaces of the proscenium were green with frame and mouldings bronzed, relieved with wine colours. Large modelled plaster heads, glazed in shades of copper, projected from the panels in a frame of red and gold on the flanking walls of the proscenium, which also incorporated glass-shaded light fittings within gold bordered panels. Above the proscenium was a hand-tinted vase with trailing flowers in soft natural colours.

The 31'-wide by 11'-deep stage, was sufficiently large for live entertainment and dressing rooms were close by. Along the side walls at the front of the auditorium were curtained windows between pilasters, with panels beneath incorporating a square design in soft blue and buff tints, whilst the pilasters were in green and wine with plaster chevroned caps relieved with black. The main ceiling was divided into bays with moulded beams, between which were circular ventilating grilles. From this hung lamps within massive, hand-tinted, Nacrolaque silk shades, four over the front of the theatre and another four over the circle. The large projection suite, entirely cut off from the rest of the building, was situated near the roof of the frontage, extending to a length of 56'. Kalee projectors were installed and, at approximately 100' from the screen, a picture size of 22' by 16' was obtained, with sound by Western Electric. The all tip-up seats were covered in wine-coloured velvet and a rose-pink, thick pile carpet covered the floors.

The Astoria's first manager, Austin Durrans, had been connected with films and theatres since 1907, when he began his career at the Paddington Palace. After 5 years in charge of the nearby Victory cinema, Walton Road, under the same ownership as the Astoria, Durrans was transferred for the Grand Opening which took place on 21 July 1930. Press advertisements styled it as Liverpool's 'Ultra Modern Talkie Theatre' and 'Liverpool's Wonder Cinema'. The feature film was the one in which French music hall singer, Maurice Chevalier, made his Hollywood debut in Paramount's first musical, *Innocents of Paris*, with *British Movietone News* and a cartoon. The performances began with a 2.30pm matinee, followed by a continuous show from 6.30pm, with popular prices of 6d to 1/3.

Although in competition with numerous other local cinemas, the Astoria was infinitely superior to its competitors and alone justified the description of a super-cinema. Its success, by the mid-1930s, was probably the reason for the ABC circuit adding it to their growing number of Liverpool suburban cinemas. The takeover from Astoria Entertainments Ltd also included the Victory Cinema; probably a condition of gaining control of the Astoria.

In subsequent years the cinema continued to be very well attended and from the early-1940s performances were continuous throughout the day. With regard to film bookings, the Astoria enjoyed the most favourable situation of ABC's suburban cinemas, screening first suburban runs of the company circuit release films and those of Rank A circuit (Odeon) release, which replaced the less attractive of the ABC schedule. Not surprisingly, the Astoria was the first in Walton to present CinemaScope, but due to the sides of the circle and the flanking splayed walls of the proscenium, the picture width could only be increased to a maximum 30'. The new format used normal standard 35mm film and optical sound. The Warner Bros picture, *The Command,* with Guy Madison, introduced the new system on 9 December 1954.

In accordance with company policy, the cinema was renamed the ABC from 15 December 1963, by which time all Walton's other cinemas had closed, leaving only the ABC Commodore, Bankhall, and the Princess, Kirkdale, an Essoldo cinema, in that area to the north of the city. By the end of 1968, these too were closed, leaving the ABC unopposed for its last 6 years. Continuous performances were retained until January 1970, when there was a reduction to continuous evenings and matinees on Monday, Wednesday and Saturday. Six months later evenings were reduced to one performance only.

The cinema continued without change for another 4 years, when the proprietors, EMI, unsuccessfully attempted to sell or lease the building, due to dwindling audiences. It closed on 23 February 1974, with Bruce Lee in *Enter the Dragon* and *Cleopatra Jones*. The building lay unused and vandalised for the next 10 years, until a Liverpool businessman took it over and converted the stalls into a luxurious cabaret with licensed bars, opened in 1984 as the Astoria Social Club. The unused circle, stripped of its seats, was separated by a suspended ceiling. The club remained open for several years up to the end of the 1980s. After a period of closure, it was reopened c1990 as the Astoria Bingo Club. Due to the opening of a purpose-built bingo hall nearby, the Astoria closed in 2001, and no plans for future use are known.

1930
Carlton
Moss Lane, Orrell Park

The Carlton interior and exterior, 1930s.

The trade press of October 1930 described the Carlton as a very satisfying example of suburban picture theatre design. It occupied an island site in the centre of a large residential district within easy reach of the LMS Orrell Park station and an important shopping thoroughfare. Williams & Kelly of Liverpool were the architects for the proprietors, Orrell Park Picture House Ltd, and the promoter, Ernest Spencer of Walton, was responsible for carrying out the general contracting work, in association with Walter Spencer of Aintree. The Carlton was erected with frontages to two roads, the long, main one being to Victoria Drive, which was extended adjacent to Moss Lane, incorporating the main entrance. Set back from this elevation was the auditorium at an angle to the main road. The plan provided for 10' wide passages at each side and a carpark at the rear. The frontages were of white, glazed faience and rustic brick, the former being used for the main entrance and to relieve the brickwork of the upper part, where high above the entrance was a neon sign of the cinema's name. Three pairs of doors, inset into the main entrance, led into the vestibule, from which a similar set of doors gave access to two comfortable, spacious waiting rooms, running parallel and separated by a partitioning wall with archways.

The Tudor-style decoration was of rough textured plaster lined into blocks in a Bath stone colour. The terrazzo floors had decorative central motifs within inlaid ebonite borders, and both rooms were furnished with settees. Near the doors to the circle waiting room, a long, enclosed staircase led up to the rear of the auditorium, whilst from the adjacent stalls waiting room, short flights of stairs had outlets to the lower floor in the centre and at either side.

The lofty, airy auditorium was felt to be unique, not being of the usual type with seating beneath an overhanging balcony. From the proscenium the stalls floor, with a rake of one in ten, extended 80' to the balcony front, and had 870 seats including several rows in two sections between this and the crossover gangway. Above the waiting rooms, the balcony, about 4' above the rear stalls, had 580 seats on a stepped floor to the rear, where even the back row was only 10′ 6″ above the stage level. At the Carlton even the tallest person would have no cause for complaint, for there was sufficient room between each row for a person to pass without disturbing those already seated.

As in the waiting rooms, the decoration was carried out in rough texture plaster and plastic paint, with the walls divided into bays by fibrous plaster piers on which rested grilles representing sunbursts, illuminated by concealed lighting. Side walls had a line of windows adorned by curtains and pelmets, below which panels were treated with textured plaster in a fan-shaped design. The ceiling was divided into bays with moulded beams and circular ventilating grilles between, with three large centre domes with bays finished in warm firelight shades and mouldings in bronze and green. From the moulded beams hung eight elegantly shaded lights, providing the main illumination, whilst the side gangways had lamps within small circular shades.

The 38′-wide proscenium was flanked by decoratively-lit grilles and the arch was surmounted by a large sunburst design. An 8′-deep stage was provided, with dressing rooms behind to enable the presentation of live entertainment. At the rear of the auditorium the operating box was 125′ from the 23′ by 17′6″ screen, onto which the picture was shown by two Kalee projectors with Western Electric sound equipment. Advertised as having 'City standards of comfort and entertainment at suburban prices', tickets cost from 6d to 1/3.

The local press announced the first public show on 1 September 1930, at 6.30pm. Thereafter, there was a daily matinee at 3pm, and continuous from 6.30pm, with Saturdays and holidays twice-nightly at 6.30pm and 8.40pm. The feature film for the opening, also Tuesday and Wednesday, was *The Cohens and Kellys in Scotland*, starring Charlie Murray and George Sidney, a popular 1930s comedy team. Although independently owned throughout its 44 years as a cinema, due to its excellent planning and high standard of comfort, for many years the Carlton kept quite a large regular patronage. They had a film booking policy of screening the leading attractions of the ABC and GB circuits following their suburban cinemas. Performances were twice-nightly with single features, but from the mid-1950s matinees ended and mainly double features were shown continuous in the evenings.

Early in 1955 a wide screen, nearly the width of the proscenium, 32′ by 17′, was installed for normal format films, CinemaScope having to be shown at a smaller height with the top masking lowered accordingly. The first film to be shown in CinemaScope was *The Robe*, on 7 February for 6 days. Later in 1955, performances were continuous in the evenings only. There was a reduction to one evening performance in June 1966, a policy which continued until closure on 2 February 1974, with *The Mackintosh Man*, featuring Paul Newman, after which it was converted into a bingo hall by the Coral Leisure Group.

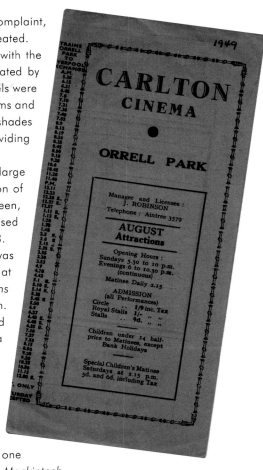

1930

Commodore
Stanley Road, Bankhall

Towards the end of 1930s, the Commodore was the latest addition to the city's super-cinemas, and with a total of 1,906 seats, it had the greatest capacity. At a cost of about £50,000, it was designed by Gray & Evans, specialists in cinema construction, who claimed to have provided Liverpool's north end with a refined, quality theatre, on a par with the finest in the city. Situated on a main tram and bus route and within 100 yards of Bankhall railway station, few cinemas were better served with transport facilities. The impressive facade was principally of white glazed faience varied by areas of brick, the former being used entirely in the wide main entrance hall, where a line of doors led into the spacious foyer with three double doors to the rear of the stalls, in which 1,306 seats were arranged in three sections across the hall.

Due to the offset arrangement of the seats and the steeply-raked floor, an uninterrupted view of the screen was possible from all parts. A feeling of space was created by the fact that the balcony extended only a short distance over the rear stalls. At the right-hand-side of the main entrance a wide staircase led to the first floor waiting room, from which corridors at either side gave access to the front of the balcony at the sides of the auditorium, whilst a

continuation of the stairs led to the rear. The 600 semi-tub seats, as in the stalls, were upholstered in wine-coloured velvet on matching Wilton carpet.

A striking feature of the Commodore was the screen, the largest in Liverpool and the first wide screen in Lancashire, with a picture size of 34' by 22' in the massive 54'-wide proscenium. This also provided an excellent setting for live entertainment, for which dressing rooms were provided backstage. The stage curtains were embellished in russet brown and gold, harmonising with the rest of the decor, the design reaching its height in the great proscenium arch. Above the front stall exits were balconettes topped by multi-coloured light fittings and decorative grilles within the pylon-style design of the splayed walls.

The main colours used for the decoration of the walls, which were lightly moulded in plastic paint with heavier ornamentations in plaster at the upper extremities, were peach and green, with flame and crimson picked out here and there with silver and bronze. Skilful use was made of coloured lighting to lend atmosphere. The principal lighting was provided by electric lamps within massive octagonal glass shades suspended from the curved ceiling.

The Commodore was originally equipped for sound-on-disc films, with Western Electric sound system for films with a sound track projected by Kalee machines, situated at a distance of 120' from the screen. The latest electrical equipment for the stage included a battery of 60, 100-watt footlights in three colours, and an overhead lighting float with similar output, all controlled through liquid dimmers.

Although an ABC cinema for most of its 38 years, the Commodore was opened by the independent company, Regent Enterprise Ltd, a small circuit which then controlled several Liverpool suburban cinemas. The Commodore opened on Monday 22 December 1930, with a matinee at 2.30pm, followed by a continuous evening performance from 6.30pm. The feature film was *Disraeli,* with George Arliss, with supporting programme including a Mickey Mouse cartoon and *Universal News.* The films were shown for 3 days, and following a special Christmas programme, continuous from 6pm to 10pm; John Boles as the Red Shadow in *The Desert Song* was shown on Friday

(Boxing Day) and Saturday. Admission prices were: 1/- and 1/6 in the balcony; 6d and 9d in the stalls, children at 4d, 6d and 8d, and further reductions at the daily matinee at 2.15pm.

After about a year, the cinema was acquired by ABC, which was expanding in Liverpool, and the policy was to show first or second suburban runs of the company release films, concurrently with the Gainsborough, Bootle, taken over by ABC at about the same time. Supporting programmes included *Pathé Gazette*, renamed *Pathé News* in the late-1940s. Despite the convenient situation for public transport, there was the disadvantage of this being on the fringe of a built up area; a large expanse between Bankhall and Kirkdale occupied by railways, and in the opposite direction, Bootle was quite well served with cinemas.

From wartime, continuous performances throughout the day were retained until the late-1950s and then reduced to continuous evenings and matinees on Monday and Thursday with a children's matinee on Saturday. The new wide screen system of CinemaScope was shown to maximum advantage at the Commodore, which due to its size was not equipped for stereophonic sound. The first film to be shown in the new format was *The Command* starring Guy Madison, on 6 January 1955.

By the end of 1965, due to falling attendances, there was only one evening performance except on Saturdays and Sundays. ABC gave preference to the ABC Walton, so the Commodore continued to screen many less appealing bookings and reruns, until near the end of 1968. Then Mecca negotiated a takeover of the building with the proprietors, then EMI, for conversion into a bingo hall. Its last evening as a cinema, 30 November 1968, saw a meagre audience for the insignificant double feature – *How to Seduce a Playboy* and *Virgin Youth*.

The Commodore was a bingo hall until January 1982, then, after being empty for about a year, it was acquired by Coyne Bros funeral directors. As well as appropriate internal alterations, the main entrance was converted into a reception area. In 1993 Coyne Bros withdrew the building, later making it into a car parts depot – Commodore Car Sales. This short term venture ended in 1995, since when the property has remained in a deteriorating condition.

1931
Princess
Selwyn Street, Kirkdale

The Princess, 1930s.

Built on a triangular site at the junction of Selwyn Street and Brewster Street, to the plans of G Stanley Lewis, ARIBA, the Princess was described as an excellent example of the modern type of suburban cinema. An unusual feature was the construction of three main frontages, which were treated architecturally in definite relation to each other to give the building a balanced appearance. The rustic brick elevations had artificial stone facings. The architect was initially restricted by the site's limitations and its proximity to a railway tunnel by Kirkdale railway station, necessitating the foundations being laid well below street level.

The two main frontages were adjacent to the two roads, connected at the junction by a short curved elevation. The frontages included, at either side, an exit from the front stalls and a main entrance at the rear, widest part of the building, each with separate canopy above, leading to two waiting rooms. These were separated by a partitioning wall, from which patrons entered the balcony and stalls by short flights of stairs. The balcony, with a stepped floor, being above the waiting rooms, did not extend over the stalls. The total 1,460 capacity was divided into almost two equal parts: the stalls with 760 seats and balcony with 700. Seats were upholstered in rose-coloured plush and double seats were fitted in an alcove at the rear of the balcony.

The auditorium was triangular to fit into the site, increasing in width to the rear from the 28' proscenium, which spanned the entire width at the front. The decoration was in the plain, modern, 1930s-style and included original lighting effects with an abundance of colour. The ceiling was divided into five longitudinal sections, the intervening recesses gradually widening to the rear. These originated from a semi-circular lighting fixture near the proscenium to form a fan ensemble. Decorations between the longitudinal ribs served a definite purpose in the illumination, being in rich colour waves graduating from brilliant red at the ends, to yellow in the centre, with ornamental ventilating grilles.

The concealed lamps were fitted with specially made reflectors focused onto mirrors, which deflected the rays onto the flat open ceiling spaces. The plain, light-coloured surfaces of the side walls were relieved by a dark dado, and windows with dark curtains and pelmets midway between the dado and the ceiling. This converged into a double arch between each wall panel, and the point where the arches met was relieved with wall shades in green tinted glass, whilst further lights were concealed behind the long, leaded glass panels in the pilasters. One hundred lamps were fitted in a decorative channel around the proscenium, from which light was trained on the massive grilles around the opening. Stage fittings included one overhead and one foot batten, each with 36,150-watt lamps in blue, red and amber. Exterior lighting consisted of four powerful floodlights playing on the front of the building. Spotlights were fitted on the four small verandahs over the entrances, and at night, the front elevation was given a very distinctive appearance by a series of white, neon, 3' high letters spelling the name.

Walturdaw Cinema Supply Co provided the operating equipment, which included two Ernemann Number 3 projectors, with a throw of 130' to the 28' by 20' Westone screen, with proportional masking system to provide for sound-on-disc or film, Western Electric Sound System being installed for the latter.

The cinema was opened by an independent company, the Princess (Kirkdale) Liverpool Ltd, who announced the Grand Opening on Monday 11 May 1931 with *Loose Ends,* featuring Owen Wares and Edna Best, and supporting short films. There was a matinee at 2.30pm and evening continuous from 6.30pm with popular prices from 6d to 1/3. Although then the latest of Liverpool's suburban cinemas, the Princess, being independently owned, faced strong competition from the large circuits, GB and ABC. Bookings included many GB releases at later showing dates, and single feature programmes normally shown at the matinee and continuous evening performances.

From the early-1940s until the takeover by the Essoldo circuit in 1958, bookings were arranged by North Western Cinemas Ltd, Central Office, Kensington Cinema Liverpool. When CinemaScope was installed in 1955, the 28' proscenium provided little extra picture width. The new system began on 4 April with *Rose Marie,* starring Howard Keel and Anne Blythe. The availability of films was increased with the Twentieth Century-Fox releases which were not then shown at the circuit cinemas. The policy of evenings only performances, introduced in the early-1950s, was continued under the ownership of Essoldo but with a change to mainly double features from 1958 for the last 8 years. With falling audiences the cinema closed on Tuesdays from February 1966, and occasionally offered wrestling on Thursday evenings. However, the final closure was on 22 October 1966, with *Our Man Flint* starring James Coburn and *The Day Mars Invaded Earth.* The hall was converted for use as a bingo club, and remained in this use until early-2000, when the bingo was relocated to a nearby, purpose-built hall.

1931
Forum • ABC • Cannon • ABC
Lime Street, Liverpool city centre

The site of the Forum was previously occupied by several small shops, and at the widest part of the area was The American Bar Hotel, one of the oldest landmarks in Liverpool's licensing history. It was originally the Oxford Music Hall when sing-songs were a feature of public houses, and the long reigning Sam Haigh Minstrels in the St James' Hall brought much patronage. In 1930 plans for the extension of the American Bar were cancelled when ABC was given the go ahead for a super-cinema extending from the top of Elliott Street to the Palais de Luxe.

The £200,000 picture theatre was designed by William R Glen of FRIAS, with Ernest A Shennan FRIBA, acting as resident architect. In a site just 150' by 75', a 2000-seat auditorium was provided, with a café and two large waiting rooms, avoiding queues in the street at this busy junction. The interior provided plenty of room for large crowds to come and go and traffic noise was minimised by ensuring that no entrances or exits led directly into any part of the auditorium.

The huge facade was faced with Portland stone, with the wide main entrance at the curved corner surmounted by a 100'-long bronze canopy, lit by 300 lights. Paved with Tinos and white marble, the entrance, with four pairs of doors, led into the foyer with a paybox at either side and two pairs of doors to the rear stalls opposite. At the far right, a staircase to the basement waiting room continued up to the first floor waiting room. Above, on the second floor, was a café with 40 tables, and opposite the entrance two pairs of doors led into the circle, with a short flight of stairs to the centre of the crossover gangway, dividing the front and rear circle seats.

The 2000 capacity was possible due to the large proportion of seats in the 750-seat circle. This extended over the stalls virtually to the front of the auditorium, with side extensions to the front circle exits, and a front which curved

to the splayed walls flanking the proscenium. These featured balconettes, above which mirrored glass fountains were lit by concealed lighting and surmounted by a canopy, whilst above the proscenium were the massive grilles of the organ chamber. The three manual Compton console was mounted on an elevator in the organ-well rising in the centre to the level of the 37' stage.

With the exception of the large central fitting, lighting was indirect with a generally amber tone, the four colour lighting effects by the Holophone system being confined to the stage and the proscenium. The huge ornament in the centre of the ceiling symbolised a sunburst in a halcyon blue and white sky, shedding a cheerfully warm tone on the walls of deep honey, above the dado of deep golden brown, fading upwards to warm ivory at the cornice level. To heighten the effect, around the cornices was a series of electric lamps. Under the balcony additional height was obtained by means of a barrelled ceiling, lit by a trough cornice and decorated with ornamental air extraction grilles. The same method was adopted over the rear of the circle, but here the 20' by 14' domed ceiling provided space for the apertures of the operating box. The projection equipment consisted of Ross machines and Western Electric sound system, with a throw to the screen of 146'.

Completion of the work had to be rushed in time for the opening; late in April 1931 the interior was still filled with scaffolding. Finally 3,500 yards of Wilton carpet was laid, upon which 2000 luxurious seats were fitted. To enable the theatre to open on time, a final spurt was made, necessitating almost day and night working by the hundreds of local workmen.

The Grand Opening of the Forum by the Lord Mayor of Liverpool, Alderman Edwin Thompson, was on Saturday 16 May 1931. A large audience responded to invitations from ABC Ltd to the inaugural performance. The striking design and decorations were much appreciated, as was Reginald Foort, the well known broadcasting organist from the Regal, Marble Arch, who displayed his powers and those of the Compton organ. The feature film was the amusing British International Picture bedroom farce, *Almost A Honeymoon*, with Clifford Mollison and Dodo Watts, which provided a rigorous test of the projection and sound apparatus. Specially mentioned in this respect was a film of Liverpool featuring the voice of the Lord Mayor, the perfect reproduction of which was loudly applauded. Affordable prices ranged from 9d to 3/- for evening performances, the stalls being at 2/4, with reductions for the matinees.

Fifty employees worked under manager, EE Lundy, formerly at the Olympia, and his assistant N Fleming. For many years, although against strong competition from 1934 with the opening of the Paramount, the Forum was popular with first runs of ABC release films. Supporting programmes included *Pathé Gazette*, and organ interludes in the early-1930s by Nelson Elms and later by Cyril Busfield, at continuous performances throughout the day.

In 1953, 3D pictures were the first device introduced by film producers to halt declining admissions due to television. The first showing was at the Forum on 18 October 1953 with *House of Wax* starring Vincent Price. Special glasses, handed to patrons on entry, gave an illusion of depth, but 3D proved to be a passing novelty. In 1954 CinemaScope was the new attraction, but, though a large cinema, the Forum had a comparatively narrow proscenium, so was not suited. As a result, the top masking had to be lowered, allowing only a 12' picture height. The first CinemaScope film was *The Command* with Guy Madison, which ran for 2 weeks from 13 June 1954. The main opposition came from the Odeon, formerly Paramount, and the Futurist, both having the advantage of stereophonic sound with CinemaScope, and in 1958 and 1960 respectively were equipped for Todd A0 for the opening of *South Pacific* and *Oklahoma!*. The Forum, renamed the ABC from February 1964, continued with a single-screen until 15 May 1982, closing with *Kentucky Fried Movie* and *The Other Cinderella*.

Work began immediately on the £350,000 conversion to a triple-screen cinema, ABC 1, 2 and 3, with seating of 683, 272 and 217 respectively. The circle area became cinema 1, with a new projection room containing a Phillips DP, 70mm and 35mm projector and cakestand system, enabling films over four hours long to be shown without rewinding. The equipment included Dolby stereo sound, transferred from the Futurist. The problem of screen width was overcome by the installation of a new wide screen and curtain forward of the proscenium and splayed walls. The stalls area was split to form cinemas 2 and 3, with a combined projection room at the rear. Due to its Art Deco interior and listed status, the alterations had to be made without spoiling the essential architectural features.

On the day prior to the Gala Opening, Tuesday 24 August 1982, the public was invited to view the cinemas between noon and 8pm. Over 5000 passed through whilst Thorn-EMI's specially-produced trailer, *The Cinema Strikes Back*, was screened. The title was the company's campaign slogan, designed to win back former cinemagoers. More than 1000 seats were donated for the Gala celebration on 25 August through Merseyside's leading newspaper, the *Liverpool Echo*, the remainder filled by other members of the public and invited guests. The feature film in all three cinemas was *Star Trek – The Wrath of Khan*.

The triple was officially opened to the public on 26 August 1982 with *Star Trek* in 70mm, with dolby stereo sound in cinema 1, whilst *Pink Floyd – The Wall* and *Grease 2* were screened in cinemas 2 and 3 respectively. The ABC cinemas, controlled by Thorn-EMI, were taken over in January 1987 by Cannon cinemas, and the ABC in Liverpool then became Cannon 1, 2 and 3, the name being retained after acquisition in 1992 by MGM. In 1995 Richard Branson's Virgin group acquired the MGM chain of 165 cinemas, including the Liverpool cinema, one of 90 traditional halls. A year later, these were bought from Virgin by MGM's former managing director, Barrie Jenkins, who reinstated the old ABC name and triangle logo.

But the cinema continued to be unviable, losing custom to the out-of-town multi-screen cinemas and also the five-screen Liverpool Odeon, which had the advantage of first runs of the most successful films. In the autumn of 1997, the company announced that the building was for sale. A short term experiment by a lessee with foreign arthouse films on the number 3 screen, from November to December in 1997, proved unsuccessful, and closure was on 29 January 1998.

The closure of the 67-year-old Art Deco building marked the end of film entertainment on Lime Street, lamented during the last week on the illuminated, front-of-house readograph. The notable film for the final performance was *Casablanca*, starring Humphrey Bogart and Ingrid Bergman, which had its first run in Liverpool in August 1943, when the cinema was known as the Forum. Fans formed a long queue for the tickets at only £1, filling to capacity the 680-seat screen 1 for the occasion, which began with a tribute from manager, Julie Pilkington, to past and present members of staff.

Now, in 2002, the building remains boarded up, but with recent information that the owners, Northridge Developments, have applied for a Grade II listing for the building. In consultation with English Heritage and Liverpool Vision, the new plans of David Gilkes (architects David Kirkby) are designed to comply with the requirements of the Grade II listing, whilst providing a new lease of life for the building with a ground floor restaurant and casino on the third floor, retaining the Art Deco interior. Externally, some of the stone panels are to be removed and replaced by the restaurant windows, with shops along the Lime Street frontage.

1931
Royal Hippodrome Theatre • Hippodrome Cinema
West Derby Road, Tuebrook

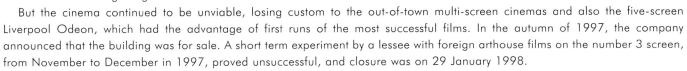

This large, former variety theatre was reopened as a cinema in 1931, after nearly 30 years of live entertainment. It was the first of 14 similarly named halls opened within a period of four years from 1902, by the northern variety entrepreneur, Thomas Barrasford, who challenged the supremacy of the Moss and Stoll Empire theatres. The West Derby Road site, near to Brunswick Street, had been occupied since 1876 by Hengler Grand Cirque. The closure on 9 February 1901 marked the end of a brilliant chapter in the history of the circus in Liverpool. The property remained unoccupied for some months until Thomas Barrasford acquired it on behalf of a syndicate, the Liverpool Hippodrome Co Ltd, of which he was managing director.

With the exception of portions of the four main walls, the building was demolished for the construction of the Royal Hippodrome theatre. The architect, Bertie Crewe, a man of considerable experience in theatre design and music halls in the style of Louis XV, was also the architect of the later Barrasford Hippodromes. The frontage, adjacent to West Derby Road, consisted of the main entrance between a bank on the left and shops on the right. This was linked to the principal elevation, set back from the road by a single storied gabled

elevation. The mosaic floor, the pride and joy of the former circus proprietor, Albert Hengler, was preserved at his request.

Over the main entrance was a glass and iron canopy, supported by iron columns extending to the pavement edge. The name was carved over this in a semi-circular stonework feature, with the royal coat of arms at the highest point of this elevation. Set back from the road, the main elevation incorporated five tall, first floor windows within stone arches, and above, a line of small, square windows surmounted by a stone balustrade along the apex with vases spaced along. The theatre, then amongst the largest in the provinces, was constructed of concrete and iron, the floors resting on iron supports on the cantilever system. The building could accommodate about 4,000 people, with 3,500 seats in the stalls, circle, upper circle and two boxes at either side of the stage.

The auditorium was described as prettily ornate in cream and grey picked out with gold. The ceiling, from which hung handsome electric pendants, was beautifully painted by the London artist, Sicard, in a style emblematical of Music and the Arts. The marble proscenium base was surrounded by an arch in yellow, red and gold, surmounted by five paintings depicting the Five Senses. Adjoining were two attractive paintings of Arcadian beauty by the same artist. The stage, 90' wide, 40' deep and with a height to the flies of 27'5", was fitted with a fireproof curtain. It was claimed that from any part of the auditorium the line of vision was uninterrupted. Although the secondary lighting was gas, the theatre was mostly lit by electricity, which was also used for the latest novelty, animated pictures, shown by a projector housed in a steel, fireproof chamber at the rear of the circle. The plans also included teetotal refreshments.

The Grand Opening of the Royal Hippodrome was on 4 August 1902, with a policy of twice-nightly performances at 7pm and 9pm and rock bottom prices of 2d to 1/-, of which Thomas Barrasford was a pioneer. The opening marked an epoch in Liverpool music hall history. The enormous interest in the event was illustrated by the long queues waiting for admission. After the playing of the National Anthem by the large orchestra conducted by Mr E Walker, the variety show, with ten acts, was headed by the expensively engaged acrobats, the Six Sisters Dainaff.

Barrasford's spirited enterprise and excellent catering were a great success, the Hippodrome providing such powerful competition to Moss & Stoll's Empire Theatre in the city, that rivals decided on building an even larger theatre, the Olympia, on West Derby Road, which, it transpired, failed to approach the success of the Hippodrome.

After the death of Thomas Barrasford in 1910, control of the company passed to South of England, Hippodromes Ltd in accordance with his prior arrangement with their managing director, Walter de Frece. His circuit, plus the larger Barrasford halls, including the Liverpool Hippodrome in 1914, made up the eighteen properties which were then known as the Variety Theatres Controlling Company. Walter de Frece, husband of Vesta Tilley, the famous music hall artist, was knighted for his services to British entertainment in 1919, after which he resigned as managing director to enter politics. He was succeeded by Charles Gulliver, who had replaced Sir Walter Gibbons as head of the London Theatres of Variety.

The Hippodrome then became one of the Gulliver circuit theatres until March 1928, in a £5m countrywide deal, which included the Liverpool Rialto and many other Merseyside cinemas. The Hippodrome's new proprietors were GTC, under whose control it later became a GB cinema. Variety continued for a further 3 years, the final performance being on Saturday 20 June 1931, when there were tears and sighs and standing-room only as the crowds came for the last time to admire their favourites at the end of an era. Heading the bill was Harry Champion with his rollicking choruses, and Vesta Tilley singing *Waiting at the Church* supported by a cast of contemporary artists. The enthusiastic support for this final show gave the impression that variety could have lasted for another 30 years, but, being owned by a cinema circuit, and sound films having become popular, the change to a cinema was complete, and no further live performances were seen at the Hippodrome. The theatre was closed for one month for the conversion, which resulted in a considerable reduction in the seating capacity to 2,100, due to increased spacing between the rows of the stalls and circle seats.

The gallery seating remained unchanged for occasional use, if necessary, and built on the roof and above this floor, a projection room about 18' square was constructed. A British Acoustics sound system was installed, and due to the steep angle of projection, the Kalee machines were set at an angle of 26 degrees. For the opening on 20 July 1931, the feature film was the first Liverpool showing of *Dracula* starring Bela Lugosi, supported by, *We Dine at Seven,* with Herbert Mundin. According with future policy, admission prices ranged from 5d to 1/3.

The Hippodrome survived as a cinema for nearly 40 years, despite dwindling audiences from the mid-1950s and the disadvantages of excessive size, huge capacity and high running costs. Although by the summer of 1967 no cinemas remained in close competition, admissions fell further when many local residents left the area due to a major redevelopment scheme, including the widening of West Derby Road. In these circumstances, the proprietors, the Rank Organisation, closed the Hippodrome on 16 May 1970. The final feature film was *Winning,* starring Paul Newman, with *The Pipeliners*. The building lay derelict and unused until demolition in 1984.

1931
Metropole
Stanley Road, Bootle

At about the time the Royal Hippodrome was converted into a cinema in 1931, similar work was proceeding at the Metropole, which was undergoing major alteration for the screening of sound films, in this case, of cine-variety, which only survived for a few years before reverting back to live entertainment. Built in 1911, the theatre was the enterprise of the Pennington Estate Co, whose managing director, Harry Pennington, realised the need for a first class theatre in the centre of Bootle, the location of their 20-year-old Muncaster Theatre having deteriorated due to the erection of warehouses and timber yards. On the tramcar routes and within 5 minutes' walk of the Marsh Lane station on the Lancashire and Yorkshire Railway, the Metropole was designed in the Renaissance-style by Havelock Sutton & Sons, the well known Dale Street theatre architects.

The building had an ornate five storey, 80'-wide facade in brick and stone, the latter being used to form an attractive setting for the many windows, the central balcony at second floor level and panel above bearing the theatre's name. Across almost the entire frontage was an ornamental verandah of iron and wire woven glass, with lead-light glazing and a metal centrepiece of intricate design with holders for the torch-style electric lamps. The upper part was illuminated by shaded lamps suspended from metal brackets.

The central main entrance was in the form of two wide archways, each with two pairs of mahogany, glass-panelled doors leading to the entrance hall with mosaic flooring and green tiled dado. From this area two wide staircases led to the mezzanine floor which contained the circle refreshment buffet, the gentlemen's cloakrooms, and staircases descending to the stalls. At a higher level, entrance to the dress circle was by two wide folding doors in the well furnished lounge, in which were the ladies cloakrooms. The most remarkable feature of the 1,850-seat auditorium (including the boxes, each with 12 seats at either side of the stage) was that by shrewd design, the circles were very close to the stage. It was expected therefore, that patrons would appreciate the closeness to the stage, both from the point of view of hearing as well as seeing the performance. The Metropole was the first English theatre to be built on this principle and due to the fact that the stalls seats were not fitted directly behind those of the row in front, it was justifiably claimed that an uninterrupted view could be obtained from practically every seat in the auditorium.

Described as artistic throughout, the decorative treatment of the ceiling, the circle front and the 36' by 30' proscenium opening were in fibrous plaster in heavy relief, finished in white. The rich crimson walls, velvet seat coverings and carpets, formed a pleasant contrast, giving a touch of warmth and comfort to the auditorium. An important feature of the new theatre was the 75' by 27' stage, which was entirely cut off from the rest of the building by substantial walls and a fireproof curtain and which provided space for large scale productions.

The Grand Opening of this new Pennington Estate Co enterprise was an important event. Held on Monday 20 February 1911, it was attended by the Mayor and Mayoress of Bootle, Councillor and Mrs JR Barbour, plus several hundred guests. Stanley Road was lit by the brilliant arc lamps on the tall facade adorned by festoons of flags, as a throng of people congregated to witness the arrival of the mayor and mayoress. They were entertained by musical selections from the orchestra, conducted by Tom Shaw. Then came the opening ceremony, and after speeches by the Mayor and Pennington, the former declared the theatre open and activated the electrically-operated drop scene with painted view of the Grand Canal, Venice, which rose to reveal the spacious, illuminated stage.

The opening attraction was Andie Caine's production of *Little Red Riding Hood*. Chosen by Pennington to strike a popular note for the occasion, the pantomime was described as a vivacious entertainment full of melody, mirth and mimicry in nine elaborate scenes. A special feature was that the 12-seat boxes could be booked for 30/-, the charge for a single seat being 3/-. Admission to other parts of the house was: orchestra stalls 2/6, dress circle 2/- upper circle 1/6, pit 9d, gallery 4d and 6d. The theatre enjoyed remarkable success from the time of opening and starting with a change to Shakespeare the following week, the Metropole soon became established as a legitimate theatre, presenting comical dramatic and musical plays and musical comedies at once-nightly performances.

The theatre's prosperity and popularity was increasing when, in 1922, Harry Pennington, JP and Councillor, found that his public and social activities and the strain of business, were becoming too taxing. It was then announced that the theatre had been acquired by a small local syndicate with Arthur Smith, proprietor of the *Bootle Times*, as chairman and J Leslie Greene, former lessee of the Sun Hall cinema as managing director. In addition to being a director of the Southport Palladium, the Hope Hall cinema, Liverpool, and the Kingsway cinema, Hoylake, Greene was also chairman of the Liverpool branch of the Cinematograph Exhibitors Association. The old regime ended on Saturday 25 March 1922 with the Renef American company of actors, vocalists and dancers and their presentation of the musical version of *Uncle Tom's Cabin*.

The new company, the Bootle Metropole Syndicate, spent several thousand pounds on improvements, of which about £2,000 was on new, dark mahogany stalls seats with bronze standards and old rose plush upholstery. The orchestra stalls had a rich, dark blue Wilton carpet and other parts cork linoleum, whilst dark stained wooden screens surrounded the rear and sides of the stalls to prevent draughts. Stalls patrons no longer had to climb stairs, access having been provided in the main entrance hall which had a cream and green tiled floor harmonising with the dado. The walls of the auditorium and the circle and gallery fronts, were renovated, and the dado around the stalls was painted a rich brown. The ceilings of the soffit of the circles were painted cream and the entire main ceiling and gold paintwork were restored. Matching curtains of rich old rose velour added to the charming oriental effect.

The company's aim was that the Metropole should continue to be a first class house of entertainment, providing plays, operas, musical comedies and other productions by first rate companies, at popular prices. The opening attraction on Easter Monday 17 April 1922, was the famous musical comedy *Tonight's the Night,* presented by George G Sharpe's company, as played at the Gaiety Theatre, London for over 2 years. From the mid-1920s until 1931 there was a change to twice-nightly revue and variety entertainment at 6.40pm and 8.50pm. Facing strong competition from sound films, being shown at many local cinemas, the company closed the theatre on 27 June 1931 for extensive internal alterations for the new entertainment policy of cine-variety. A new upper circle was constructed and fitted with tip-up seats, which also replaced the gallery benches. The seating was reduced by 400 to make space for the projection room which was fitted with Western Electric sound system. As at other theatres converted for showing films from the highest floor level, this was achieved only by a very steep angle of projection to a rather small, squarish screen, angled back accordingly to the stage.

For the Grand Reopening on August Bank Holiday, Monday 3 August 1931, the Metropole presented the first of the new programmes of *Star Pictures and Star Variety*, with a matinee at 2.30pm and continuous performance from 6.30pm. On the screen, *The Lottery Bride* starred the famous American actress and singer, Jeanette MacDonald, and on the stage the latest continental entertainment *La Grande Revuette et Cie*, continued throughout the week. From Thursday the feature film was *Framed,* with Evelyn Brent and also *British Movietone News*. Admission prices of 6d to 1/3 were reduced to 4d, 6d and 8d for matinees. Still under the same company, but known as the Metropole Theatre (Bootle) Ltd, performances of cine-variety were presented until April 1934, then reverting back to revues and variety shows.

The shortage of variety acts in the early war years resulted in a return to cine-variety on 7 October 1940, with the film *Keep Your Seats Please,* starring George Formby, together with a star variety bill and quick-fire talent show. But this type of entertainment proved to be short lived, and on 23 November 1940 it was announced that the Metropole had closed until further notice. The Grand Gala Reopening took place on Monday 5 May 1941, with *Rations Unlimited,* including full variety at 6.30pm and 8.30pm. In celebration, Monday night was Gift Night, when 10/- notes were given away. Sadly this proved to be the shortest of opening periods, as it was the last week of nightly German air raids on Merseyside, known as the May Blitz, and during one of these, on 7 May, the theatre was destroyed. Two large hoardings filled the site until redevelopment in the early-1980s with the present café and amusement arcade.

1931
King's Hall Cinema • Gaumont Palace • Gaumont
Oakfield Road, Anfield

The Gaumont Palace, 1930s.

Silent films with orchestral accompaniment had continued successfully at the King's Hall until 14 July 1930, when the All Talking, Singing, Dancing sensation, *Mirth and Meldoy,* featured former Broadway Star, Lola Lane. The talkies lasted for a limited time only, as the cinema closed on 17 July 1931. The last film shown at the old cinema was the William Fox production, *Women Everywhere* (1929), a Hollywood production directed by Alexander Korda, the film starred J Harold Murray, Fifi D'Orsay and George Grossmith. The building was later demolished to make way for the New Gaumont Palace. Taken over by GB and acquired by the GTC in March 1928, the considerably larger new building cost £50,000.

The Gaumont Palace was built to the plans of well known cinema architects Gray and Evans, who also occupied land previously allocated to an adjoining billiard hall and two shops. It was designed to seat 1,600, compared to about 1000 in the old building. Work started early in 1931 by the noted contractors, George Platt & Son Ltd, Liverpool, and was completed shortly before Christmas.

The striking 79'-wide facade of brick and black and buff terracotta had red and black adornments. Over the wide main entrance was a lacquered gold verandah with a lettering display on the facia advertising the current attraction and a panel above bearing the name. The 152' side elevation to St Domingo Vale included an imposing separate entrance to the front stalls, fitted with oak doors, marble steps and terrazzo floor. The main entrance, in the centre of the frontage, had five pairs of glazed oak doors with stainless steel fittings at the top of marble steps. These led into an entrance hall with walls panelled in lime oak, floors laid with marble mosaic and a ceiling of ivory relieved with touches of blue. The foyer ceiling and beams were finished in soft iridescent metalled colours, the walls in tones of brown with touches of green and silver and window curtains of green silk. On leaving this seemingly sun-warmed atmosphere, one entered the 96' by 72' auditorium, likened to a rose-coloured drawing room – a drawing room for 1,100 people downstairs and 500 upstairs.

Decoration of the auditorium and foyers was most striking, with fine modelling of the fibrous plaster to ceilings and walls, domed plaster enriched ceilings under the balcony and in the entrance hall. Fine ornamental ventilation and organ grilles, beautiful decorations and lighting effects, together with luxurious seating and drapery, all blended to justify the comparison to a large drawing room. The walls were treated with an attractive fibrous plaster finish in festoons of Marblcote in soft tones of dull red and gold with metalled green dado. The ceiling was in textured plaster, painted a soft green with rust red beams and mouldings picked out in green, black and red, into which were incorporated the attractively designed grilles, cleverly concealing the ventilation system.

A stage and dressing rooms provided for cine-variety, with space available for an orchestra due to a movable floor. The 40'-wide by 33'-high proscenium opening was fitted with a pelmet in rich autumnal silk velour. Curtains of a similar material in rich gold with a central motif of brown silk velour, stepped up in pylons and lent height to the opening. The curtain bases had a lavish silk bullion fringe. The fireproof projection suite, above the balcony, was cut off from the auditorium, with access via a separate staircase from street level.

The local press announced on 21 December 1931 that Liverpool had received the Christmas gift of a luxurious new cinema. Under the ownership of the GTC and the management of the GB Picture Corporation, the Gaumont Palace was opened on that date by the Lord Mayor, Alderman JC Cross. He declared that Anfield had what was virtually a West End theatre and pointed out that all the materials used in the building were British. After the National Anthem, sung by Miss Mary Fawcett, there followed a full programme consisting of *The Devil to Pay* with Ronald Colman and Loretta Young, supported by the comedy feature *Oh! Oh! Cleopatra*, with the famous comedy team Wheeler & Woolsey and also the *Gaumont British News*.

As at the opening performance, matinees thereafter were to be daily at 2.30pm and continuous evening performances from 6.30pm, except for Saturdays and Bank Holidays with separate performances at 6.30pm and 8.45pm. Screening first runs in the district of GB circuit release films, the cinema was popular during its earlier years in competition with numerous older cinemas, despite strong opposition from the Astoria, Walton, opened by ABC in 1930.

The word 'palace' was dropped from the name in 1937, and 10 years later the Gaumont was controlled by CMA after the amalgamation of the Odeon and GB circuits. During the decline in cinema admissions, which accelerated in the early-1950s, the Gaumont was at a disadvantage in that films of Odeon circuit release were screened following the Astoria, Walton. Those of GB release continued to be concurrent with the Bedford, Walton and Empress, Tuebrook, fourth runs in Liverpool. Despite the acquisition of CinemaScope beginning 28 March 1955 with *Sign of the Pagan*, featuring Jeff Chandler, admissions continued to fall. From 16 June 1958 matinees ceased altogether, with continuous performances in the evenings only. Less than 4 years later, the Gaumont was closed, the last performance being on 26 November 1960 with *The Unforgiven*, starring Burt Lancaster, and in support, *Delta 8 – 3*. The building was taken over by Appleton's Household Stores Ltd, as their regional depot. It was a DIY store in 1993, and in September 2000 it became a Community Centre and remains so to date, with the principal external features unchanged.

1932
Carlton Theatre • ABC
Green Lane, Tuebrook

So rapid had been the appearance of new cinemas up to the 1930s that by 1932 it was felt that there was little scope for originality of design. However, in June of that year, when the Carlton Theatre had been completed on a commanding corner site, with frontages to Green Lane and West Derby Road, it was found that the new building embodied innovations in design and decoration, and was one of the most striking examples of the designs of architect Ernest A Shennan. Set well back from the original line, the new building allowed for a considerable widening of West Derby Road, which was to come 30 years later. For its external effect the building, erected by contractor CJ Doyle of Liverpool, depended largely on well balanced masses of sand-faced brickwork with stone dressings. Spanning the wide main entrance in Green Lane was an impressive steel canopy with a changeable lettering display on the facia, affording shelter for a large number of patrons. An open porch with a line of swing doors of limed oak in five pairs gave access to the wide vestibule, in which the central main paybox, in metal with embossed glass, was flanked on either side by two pairs of doors leading to the main foyer. Here the flooring was of manu-marble, with a prominent linear design guiding the eye to the principal entrance to the stalls and balcony. Opposite the entrance doors, a long wall between the stalls entrances was adorned in the centre by a large, gold-edged sunray design. At the extreme left and right separate areas each contained two pairs of doors leading to crossover, centre and side gangways of the rear stalls.

The stalls had a capacity of 1,280 in three sections across. All seats were upholstered in golden brown mohair velvet and 2000 yards of blue and golden brown Wilton carpet covered the whole auditorium. From the left-hand side of the foyer and the right-hand side of the vestibule, stairways led up to the first floor café directly above. The crush hall, a lounge under the rear of the balcony, had settees set in recesses along one side. This area connected the circle entrances at either end, where beyond the swing doors a short flight of steps led up to the crossover gangway dividing the front and rear circle seats, numbering 252 and 408 respectively. Next to the crush hall was the spacious café with a decorative Chinese willow pattern motif in a series of etched glass panels in the screen walls. The main colour scheme was jade green lacquer, with embossed Chinese figures in gold. A complete range of kitchen equipment was installed with the latest type of automatic gas water boiler, milk urn and coffee machine.

The auditorium walls were in the plain, modern 1930s-style, finished in rough cast plaster, incorporating leaping stags above circle level, and the lower part of the walls was adorned by a dark wooden dado. The focal point, the wide proscenium, had wings containing a series of vertical gold ribs, lit by concealed lighting. Set on the splayed walls, the ornamental inlet grilles were floodlit by lighting in large decorative bowls at the base. The weighty, handsome curtain effectively displayed the vari-coloured lighting thrown upon it. Dressing rooms at the rear provided for stage shows. In the centre of the orchestra well was a lift for the three-manual Christie organ console encased in polished walnut with gold bronze mouldings.

The projection room was rarely given a thought but in the Carlton it was designed on very generous lines, with access by a separate door on West Derby Road via a metal spiral staircase, to which there was also access at first floor level. As at most ABC cinemas, the equipment consisted of Ross projectors and RCA sound system. The large free carpark from Green Lane was an important amenity of the super-cinema.

The ABC's Grand Opening of the Carlton Theatre by the Lord Mayor of Liverpool, Alderman JG Cross, took place on 11 June 1932, with a reception for the invited guests from 2.30pm to 3pm. The British comedy, My Wife's Family, starring Gene Gerrard, was supported by a programme including Pathé Gazette and an interlude by a famous BBC organist, on the mighty Christie organ. Performances originally consisted of a matinee daily at 2.45pm and continuous in the evening from 6.30pm, but on Saturdays there were two distinct performances at 6.30pm and 8.45pm. Popular prices were: stalls 7d, 9d and 1/- and balcony 1/3 and 1/6, reservable at no extra charge.

At the time of opening, the Carlton, with a total capacity of 1,940, was Liverpool's largest purpose-built cinema. It was attended by large numbers for mainly ABC circuit release films, third run in Liverpool, second run being taken by the independently owned Majestic Cinema in the city, following the ABC Forum. Popular organ interludes were originally by James N Bell, and from 1934 until the early-1940s, by Vincent Parker. During the war, due to the 10pm closing time, performances were continuous from 2pm onwards and Sunday opening from 5pm was introduced. After the war a similar policy was maintained with weekdays as previously to 10.30pm. By the early-1950s the programmes were mainly double features of 3½ hours, and organ interludes were reintroduced as a regular added attraction, with guest organists such as Clifford Birchall, Trevor Willetts, Albert Brierley and Arthur Lord.

At about this time the anniversary of the opening was marked by a special Birthday Week, when, in addition to a leading film attraction, there was a stage show of about 30 minutes, with organ accompaniment by Clifford Birchall. The show was organised and introduced by AR Russell, a senior manager, who in a special souvenir programme, included an address to the patrons. Such added attractions helped to maintain the Carlton as one of Liverpool's leading cinemas, but with regard to screen entertainment, the latest system designed to bring back the missing patrons was CinemaScope, for which the Carlton, with its wide proscenium, was eminently suited. It was installed for the opening on 20 December 1954 of the Warner Bros picture The Command, featuring Guy Madison.

By the end of the 1950s the Carlton had lost two of its super-cinema elements; the café had closed and the organ had been sold and removed. The end of the decade also saw the conversion of the former café into the district offices of ABC. At this time also, dwindling audiences resulted in reduced opening hours from June 1959 to continuous performances in the evenings only, with separate matinees on Monday, Wednesday and Saturday, and a reduction in the stalls capacity by about 150 seats by the formation of a crossover gangway between the front and rear seats.

The cinema became known as the ABC in December 1962 and closed for extensive internal reconstruction on 22

January 1972. A licensed bar was built in the rear stalls with a separate entrance on West Derby Road, and the circle, with 636 seats, formed the cinema, styled as a luxury lounge. The original architectural features of the proscenium and walls were lost from view, covered by the new screen at a higher level and curtains extending to the side walls. The general effect was worsened by the fact that, to cut the cost, the flooring was not extended beyond the balcony front, which then overlooked the disused front stalls. In this austere style and reduced size, the ABC reopened on 27 March 1972 with *Love Story*, starring Ali McGraw and Ryan O'Neal, with supporting programme including *Pathé News*, with a 2pm matinee and continuous evening performance from 6pm. The bar opened as a western-style saloon called The Painted Wagon. At this time the ABC was in a solo situation in the district, but with competition from the Abbey, Wavertree, in which interest had been greatly renewed during the 1960s by the introduction of Cinerama.

In 1975 the ABC was reduced to one evening performance only, Monday to Friday, with Saturday and Sunday continuous in the evenings. It became apparent in 1979 that the proprietors, Thorn-EMI, were preparing to close down the entire operation, for not only was the licensed bar relinquished and acquired by Tetley Walker Ltd for refurbishment and opened as the stylish Lord Derby, but also the company offices were vacated in favour of the city location. The cinema's fortunes continued to decline and Thorn-EMI ceased control on 9 July 1980, with a John Travolta double feature: *Grease* and *Saturday Night Fever*.

The cinema opened on 10 July, leased to an independent exhibitor, Major Young, who had also taken over the ABC, Stockport, from Thorn-EMI. The original name, the Carlton, was restored to show the first programme under the new regime, *Mission Galactica* and *Roller Force*. Screenings continued to be mainly concurrent with the few remaining suburban cinemas, with one evening performance and matinees during school holidays. The cinema was run by Major Young, until sudden closure on Saturday 4 December 1982 with the film *Cat People*. Since then the building, with the exception of the public house, has been unused and has become derelict.

1932

Granada

East Prescot Road, Dovecot

In January 1932 planning permission was sought for a cinema to be built on the Dovecot housing estate by Robert Wilkinson of Birkenhead. In support of the application it was stated that in the entirely new district, about 6 miles to the south east of the city, 1000 corporation houses had been erected, with approximately 4000 more due to follow. On a site adjoining the new shopping area, the Granada was to be one of the outposts of the Liverpool entertainment industry. The cinema was designed by architect AE Shennan, FRIBA, who also planned the Carlton, Tuebrook, and some similarity was noted, particularly in the entrance and foyers. Both theatres were built by CJ Doyle of Liverpool, and the Granada, at a cost of £40,000, was described as an architectural acquisition, providing a welcome relief from the comparative sameness of the nearby properties.

The cinema's tall, 80'-wide frontage in sand-faced brick, relieved by stone dressing, was lit by three large neon signs and decorative neon lighting in orange, red and green. Above the wide main entrance the decorative concrete and glass canopy provided shelter for large crowds in wet weather. Five pairs of swing doors in the main entrance led into the vestibule with the paybox in the centre, flanked on either side by two pairs of doors to the foyer and, at the extreme left and right, stairs to the balcony lounge and 593-seat balcony.

The entrance and foyer had brown floor tiles and lighting by pendant fittings with pale green glass panels. The foyer led to anterooms at either side, in which were two pairs of doors to the rear of the extensive auditorium, with 1,210 seats on the stalls floor. The seats, as throughout the theatre, were in green Lister moquette. At the left and right of the vestibule, staircases led up to the 42' by 37' balcony lounge, decorated in stippled Marblcote, finished in orange with broad lines and chevrons in red and black with matching doors and columns. The furnishings consisted of large green sofas with matching tables and chairs. Lighting was by two, 13' lay lights, and two, three-light pendants. Doors at either side of the lounge led onto wide corridors to the balcony entrances, beyond which a short flight of steps led to the crossover gangway between the front and rear seats.

153

The modern auditorium, with plain surfaces devoid of embellishment, relied on the brilliancy of its colour scheme. Near the front splayed walls carried the decorative style to the proscenium arch, flanked on each side by a spear pointed grille in green and silver with a crimson base. The arch, 50'-wide by 30'-high, then the tallest in Liverpool, was treated in a ribbing effect of red and black. The silver satin curtains were relieved with black bands and fringe, contrasting with the festooned orange satin pelmet. Like all modern super-cinemas at that time, the Granada was adaptable for live entertainment, having a 12'-deep stage, lit by overhead and foot battens in red, green, blue and amber, with large dressing rooms adjoining. The auditorium walls had a pale green dado matching the front of the balcony, with a modern design in black and silver, relieved by dull red with crimson doors. Above the green, the walls and ceiling were of stippled Marblcote, finished in shaded orange. The red and black valance had horizontal and vertical lines of the same colours.

Instead of the usual suspended ceiling fittings, the auditorium was illuminated by lay lights flush with the main and under balcony ceilings. Along the centre of the former were six chevron-shaped lay lights, each 14' by 2'3", they housed eight 100-watt lamps. Smaller fittings of the same type were fitted at either side of the ceiling. At the rear of the auditorium, the projection room was equipped with Kalee 8 machines fitted with Super C Kershaw lenses, and a picture 30' by 27' was obtained at a distance from the screen of 130', stated to be the largest screen in the Liverpool area.

Opened as a talkie theatre, sound equipment was installed by BTP Ltd. Christmas Eve 1932 saw the opening of the Granada, Liverpool's latest super-cinema under the ownership of the Granada Cinema (Liverpool) Ltd, whose directors were CJ Doyle and M Wilkinson. W Speakman of the Capitol, Edge Hill, was the General Manager, and the manager and licensee was Harry NK Hudson, who had formerly been the greatly esteemed manager of the West Derby Picture House. The inaugural ceremony at 2.30pm was performed by Alderman Edwin Thompson JP and an elegant souvenir brochure was produced for the occasion. The special programme of films, booked for the opening day only, began with a Mickey Mouse cartoon, then the *Universal Talking News*, with commentary by RE Jeffrey, followed by *Ideal Cinemagazine* and *Northern Lights*, the screen version of Courtauld's Arctic expedition. The feature film was *The Rosary*, described as an exquisite story of romance and beauty.

The cinema was open to the public in the evening with performances at 6pm and 8.40pm and patrons were offered the use of a large, free carpark. There was a complete change of programme on Boxing Day, when the feature film was *Good Night Vienna* starring Jack Buchanan and Anna Neagle. Normal performance times then consisted of a daily 3pm matinee, evenings continuous from 6.30pm, and on Saturdays, three distinct performances at 3pm, 6.40pm and 8.45pm. Tickets for the stalls were: 5d, 7d and 9d, whilst the circle and front circle were: 1/- and 1/3 respectively, with matinees at 4d, 6d and 9d. In its favourable, unopposed situation, the Granada was very well attended, probably resulting in the takeover by the ABC circuit in 1935, beginning a regular concurrency of film bookings with the Carlton, Tuebrook.

From the late-1940s mainly double feature programmes, including *Pathé News*, were shown at continuous performances throughout the day. Late in 1954 CinemaScope was installed concurrently with the Carlton, opening on 20 December with *The Command*, featuring Guy Madison. In spite of all this, attendances at the Granada continued to decline, and by the end of the 1950s, performances were reduced to continuous evenings and three matinees weekly.

A sudden change to full time bingo was made after closure as a cinema on 30 September 1961, with the programme *Gold of the Seven Saints* with Clint Walker and *White Warrior*. Reopened by ABC shortly afterwards as the Granada Bingo and Social Club, it flourished and after a few years was acquired by Mecca Ltd, by whom it was run until 1994, since which time the building has not been used, overtaken by a new purpose-built bingo hall on East Prescot Road.

1933
Reo
Longmoor Lane, Fazakerley

The completion of Liverpool's 74th cinema, the Reo, was announced in 1933. It was located in the new suburb of Fazakerley, about 5 miles north east of the city, where a large number of council houses had been built. It was stated that with the completion of this cinema, building programmes on new halls had reached their limit for the time being, but it transpired that two more were opened the following year. At a time when simplicity of design had become necessary to produce, for a modest cost, a scheme which would provide an adequate seating accommodation, and, at the same time allow scope for alterations to keep the theatre up-to-date in regard to innovations that might bring about a change in shows. At a modest cost, the Liverpool architect, Lionel AG Prichard, ARIBA, designed a straightforward, no-frills scheme with a 1,500 seating capacity and flexible use of space. Making the most of the site with a 124'-long frontage and length and width of 90', the cinema achieved a capacity of 1,500 and included a balcony, spacious ground floor waiting room and first floor café. The building and equipment came to a cost of £25,000.

Constructed of red rustic bricks with buff-coloured mortar joints and grey stone dressings, the Longmoor Lane frontage consisted of a main block at the right-hand-side including the large main entrance, whilst to the left a single storey elevation with separate entrance to the front stalls, provided two waiting rooms alongside the auditorium. The paybox was in the first auditorium, which extended over half the length of the building. The waiting room, with space for 800 patrons, obviated the need for external canopies. Over the entrance, an oblong stonework panel bearing the cinema name, was surmounted by brickwork relieved by a large, arched white area of stone, adorned at the highest point by a sunray design. At the head of a short flight of steps in the main entrance, the paybox was flanked on either side by a pair of doors to the 63' by 28' foyer, served by small anterooms at each end. The flooring was of white terrazzo, with walls in flame, blue and cream. Along the left-hand-side were three pairs of doors to the rear stalls and a sales kiosk, on the right, a wide, linoleum-covered staircase to the balcony and large café, with three large windows on the side of the building.

The auditorium was squarish, being 90' in length and 75' wide, and accommodated 1,120 in the stalls, with seats in old gold velvet, divided into three longitudinal blocks with four gangways. Extending over the rear stalls, the curved balcony had 388 seats with a similar arrangement to the stalls. Free from cornices and fibrous plaster mouldings, the decor revealed a brilliancy of colour, with modern motifs worked in plaster paint, of which 3 to 4 tons was used on the interior of the building. The wall colours merged into those of the steeply-arched ceiling, where a sunray effect was achieved in alternate rays of amber and blue, fading from deep tones at the extremities to pale shades at the centre.

Illumination was by the Holophane three-colour system, principally from two ceiling laylight fittings, each 7' square, with a battery of Holophane. Three-colour floodlighting equipment was mounted on frameworks above each fitting to flood the hall with light, controlled by colour regulators in the operating box. The stage, with a proscenium opening of nearly 50', was lit by batten and footlights in which a total of 132, 150-watt lamps were arranged, controlled by six regulators. In bold relief against the blaze of colour, the proscenium front was painted in old gold. The stage curtain was of richly coloured appliquéd velvet and the screen curtain of silk gauze embroidered with decorative motifs; both operated by electricity. The operating room had two of the latest Kalee machines with high intensity arcs, installed by the Kershaw Projector Co, Leeds, giving a picture 24' by 18', at 96' from the screen.

A point of interest was that the Reo was the first cinema in the area to open without motor generators, Hewittic rectifiers being installed. The company had concluded that rectifiers could effect a substantial saving in electricity, eliminate vibration and guarantee a brighter picture. Although during most of its life the Reo was an ABC cinema, it was opened by an independent company, the Reo Cinema Co Ltd, whose directors were: Frank White (chairman); H Kenton (managing director); J Williams; H Dewhurst; H Cubley and J Callaghan. FW Stollard, formerly in charge of the New Atlas Talkie Theatre, Rice Lane, with 20 years almost unbroken service both on the exhibiting and renting sides of the industry, was appointed manager.

The Grand Opening of the Reo took place on 1 April 1933 at 2.30pm, with a personal appearance of the British stage and film comedian, George Clarke, who was the star of his latest feature film, *Where's George?* supported by a mystery drama, *The 13th Guest*. The programme was booked for the opening day only, changing to *Back Street*, featuring Irene Dunne and John Boles and full supporting programme. The Reo was advertised as *The Bohemian Rendezvous of the North*, with a gorgeous café and lounge and free parking. Performances consisted of a matinee daily at 2.45pm, continuous Monday to Friday from 6.30pm and seats bookable for 6.30pm and 8.40pm on Saturdays and Bank Holidays, at no extra charge to the normal prices of 7d and 9d in the stalls and 1/- in the grand circle. At the matinees the normal prices were 4d, 5d and 7d and children were admitted at all times at reduced prices.

Although without nearby opposition, the Reo was not generally among the better attended of Liverpool's suburban cinemas, although taken over by the ABC circuit in 1936. By the late-1940s, performances were continuous throughout the day, but due to declining attendances were reduced to evenings only and three matinees weekly, then by the end of the 1950s to evenings only. The booking policy was very mixed, including, in addition to the ABC circuit releases, those of the Odeon and GB circuits, which, although shown for 3 days only, resulted in later screening dates than at the majority of circuit controlled suburban cinemas. CinemaScope was installed in 1955; the Reo's proscenium allowing an almost 40' screen. The new system opened on 7 April with *Knights of the Round Table* featuring Robert Taylor.

The cinema survived for almost 6 more years, during which time unruly elements caused disturbances and damage to furniture and fittings. In addition to increasing maintenance costs, this resulted in plummeting attendances until closure an 14 January 1961, with the double feature *Watch Your Stern* with Kenneth Connor, and *Clue of the Twisted Candle* featuring Bernard Lee. Derelict after many years of closure, the building was acquired by Mecca Ltd, and after extensive refurbishment reopened as a bingo and social club. This was later closed, but was reopened by Mecca in the mid-1980s, and although redecorated and the circle reseated, lasted only 18 months before final closure in autumn 1998. The building was later demolished to make way for housing.

1934
Tatler News Theatre • Classic Cinema
Church Street, Liverpool city centre

The Tatler, 1951.

The building of this cinema was achieved only by extensive and complicated reconstruction of existing premises fronting onto Church Street and Williamson Street, in Liverpool city centre. The contractors, John Rimmer & Son of Liverpool, were congratulated on their ingenuity in solving their complicated problems. Described as being unique outside London, the venture was due to the enterprise of Alderman Edwin Haigh, JP, and Captain JH Haigh, MC, the former having a successful association with cinema entertainment in the city dating back to 1912 when he became the managing director of the Lime Street Picture Co. Having decided that Liverpool needed a news theatre, the owners proposed to exhibit mainly world news, interest, travel, comedy and selected high class dramas in programmes of around one and a half hours duration, predicting that this would appeal to ordinary cinemagoers as well as those with less time to spare, such as shoppers, business people and visitors.

Constituting the frontage to Church Street, the main entrance, although small, stood out prominently between the adjoining stores. Lined with marble, surmounted by an attractive canopy bearing the cinema name, the frontage was brilliantly lit with tubular tiered lights and neon display signs. Set back in the entrance, two pairs of frameless glass doors, with handles in the form of lengths of film, led into a long foyer with multi-coloured rubber flooring and wall decorations, finished with brightly coloured panelling dusted with gold. At the far end of the foyer was the paybox, the stalls entrance and stairway to the mezzanine floor, where patrons could obtain light refreshments from the soda fountain on their way to the balcony. The total capacity was 600, with 200 seats allocated to the balcony, which extended over the rear stalls and along the right-hand-side to an exit and stairway to ground level.

Simplicity and comfort were the keynotes of the auditorium with its buff walls relieved by bands of coloured concrete and decorative panels in the balcony, and well-spaced, comfortably-upholstered seats. The hall was mainly lit by laylights with shades flush to the ceiling which sloped down over the front part to form the upper limit of the proscenium opening. Surprisingly, for such a small theatre, live entertainment was provided for, with retiring rooms for artists, although there appears to be no record of it having been presented.

At the Grand Opening on Monday 19 February 1934, Alderman E Russell Taylor paid tribute to the industry and enterprise of Alderman Haigh, who recalled his promise to the city magistrates that the cinema would fulfil a real need with the special type of entertainment it was to provide, and hoped that the public would justify him by their support. Performances were continuous from noon to 10.30pm, the last complete show starting at about 9pm, patrons being guaranteed a wait of no more than 10 minutes. Admission prices were: stalls 7d, balcony 1/- and the programmes – changed every Monday and Thursday – always included a Mickey Mouse cartoon. The opening programme consisted of six items and began with the latest newsreels, then *Pathétone Weekly*, followed by *Hollywood Premiere*, a colour musical short. *New Zealand*, a travelogue, led up to *Animal Gods*, an engrossing Indian drama, and the programme ended with a Mickey Mouse, Silly Symphony, coloured cartoon: *Babes in the Wood*.

After just over 2 years the Tatler was taken over by Capitol & Provincial News Theatres Ltd, London, the proprietors until it was acquired by Classic Cinemas Ltd, in 1968. During the war, in 1941, the theatre was damaged by a high explosive bomb at the stage end, and incendiaries on the roof, resulting in the upper part of the theatre being damaged by fire and blast. Under a temporary roof, the theatre continued to operate, but in 1951 it became evident that the time had come to effect permanent replacement.

The theatre was closed from Monday 27 August for war damage repairs and a major scheme of refurbishment. William L Lowe and Partners (including Gray, Evans and Crossley), architects of Eberle Street, Liverpool, prepared the plans and supervised the work, which was done under licence issued by the Ministry of Works at a cost of £25,000. The result was a more modern interior adapted to the special requirements of a news theatre. The new roof, constructed over the top of the temporary one, was of steel Gypelith slabs. The new auditorium ceiling, at a lower level to improve the acoustic qualities, was of Plaxstele construction consisting of steel T bars and plasterboard. The interior was modernised as much as possible without altering the existing structure, and the decorations, mainly in fawn and maroon, were speckled in gold. New seating, carpets, loudspeakers and heating and ventilating plant were installed, with warm air intake through ceiling grilles and extractors at the rear of the stalls and balcony. Minor alterations were also made to the projection room.

The contractors worked to ensure the reopening on Thursday 11 October 1951 at noon, advertising: 'One hundred percent entertainment in luxurious surroundings'. Thereafter, performances were continuous from 10.30am to 10.30pm, with programme changes every Sunday and Thursday and admission prices of: stalls 1/-, balcony 1/9. Only 3 months later the Tatler was in the forefront of Liverpool's cinema entertainment, when Capitol & Provincial News Theatres announced that, as in the case of other Tatlers of the company, the Liverpool hall was to be equipped with a special plastic screen, sprayed with metallic particles, for the United Kingdom premiere of 3D films as shown at the South Bank Festival.

For 2 weeks, starting on 13 January 1952, patrons received special glasses on entering, which they wore in order to experience the stereoscopic effects. This consisted of two abstract experimental cartoons by Norman McLaren, a zoo trip with commentary by Desmond Walter Ellis, and *Royal River*; a coloured landscape of the Thames. Performances were continuous from l0am to 11pm and Sundays from 5pm to 10pm, with one price of 2/1. 3D films returned on 12 July 1953 with *The Black Swan*, from Tchaikovsky's *Swan Lake* by the Sadlers Wells Ballet and *Around and About*. The season ended on 22 August 1953 with the 3D Metroscopix comedy thriller, *A Day in the Country*.

In competition with the Liverpool News Theatre in Clayton Square (formerly the Prince of Wales), the Tatler presented world news and short films until closure on 25 September 1968, having been acquired by Classic Cinemas Ltd, who announced extensive modernisation and redesign as Liverpool's smart new home for feature films. Reopened as the Classic on 4 October 1968, with a new larger screen, the feature film was *War and Peace* with Audrey Hepburn, Henry Fonda and Mel Ferrer, screened at two separate performances at 2.30pm and 7.15pm. This was followed by reruns of leading films, and, for a few weeks only, late night shows on Friday at 11pm when a special programme was presented.

However, the new programming policy proved unsuccessful and ended after less than one year, on 6 September 1969, with *Doctor Dolittle*, featuring Rex Harrison. The theatre then became the Tatler Cinema Club, showing uncensored films to members only, starting on 8 September with the Swedish film *I, A Woman*. This continued until 22 December 1972, when the club was moved to London Road, there to be known as the Curzon Club Cinema.

The Tatler was then renamed the Classic Cartoon Cinema, which opened on 23 December 1972, with non-stop cartoons and comedies from 11am to l0.30pm. This was unsuccessful, closing only 3 months later on 31 March 1973. After lying empty for some time, alterations at a cost of £150,000 were made to convert the building into a fashion store, Solitaire. In recent years it has been a boutique.

1934
Paramount • Odeon
London Road, Liverpool city centre

The Odeon, 1959.

When the boxing stadium at the corner of London Road and Pudsey Street closed in March 1931, a new cinema was already projected to be built on the site. This was planned to hold about 3000 people and Paramount intended to call it the Plaza, later the Stadium and then the Mayfair, before eventually becoming the Paramount; another spacious, impressive and beautiful addition to the luxurious Paramount circuit. Before it was licensed, unsuccessful objections were raised by proprietors of the Futurist, Scala and Palais de Luxe cinemas, mostly on the grounds that the same company producing, distributing and exhibiting films made competition virtually impossible. Even in those days of rapid evolution in cinema construction, it was described as the last word from every point of view. Designed by FT Verity and S Beverley, FRIBA, with the assistance of Paramount director of construction, EH Perkins, the building was erected on a site of 30,000 square-feet by William Tomkinson and Sons. The total cost was £240,000.

The structure was of steel and reinforced concrete with a frontage of reconstructed silica stone extending adjacent to Pudsey Street. Due to the remaining store on the left-hand-side of the site, the frontage was restricted to about half the building's width, but it was still tall and imposing, with attractive carved stonework and a central architectural feature. This incorporated the two-sided, electrically-lit Paramount display sign, whilst neon tubes effectively outlined the facade's main contours. Neon tubes also outlined the deep canopy over the main entrance, on the facia of which a two row lettering display advertised the current attraction, curving at the corner, where an electric sign was fitted. Numerous electric bulbs on the soffit of the canopy and in the main entrance brilliantly illuminated the approach to the theatre. In the centre of the entrance, the shining chrome-coloured paybox was flanked on either side by two pairs of doors. These led to a square vestibule with three pairs of doors at the opposite end, leading into the large rectangular foyer, from which four entrances led to the rear stalls crossover gangway. This area appeared spacious, the ceiling of the first floor lounge extending to a great height, with a line of elegant chandeliers above.

The upper floor was reached by a broad staircase with attractive centre and side metal balustrades, which were also used between the full length pilasters extending from the ground floor up to the cornice. The lounge, with its attractively-patterned carpet, was comfortably furnished and adorned with artificial flowers. The area led to the restaurant at the front of the building and the front and rear circle.

The elaborate staircase inside the Paramount, photographed around 1934.

The Paramount was Liverpool's largest purpose-built cinema, with a total capacity of 2,670 — 1,972 seats in the stalls and 698 in the royal and grand circle. Some idea of the impressiveness of the auditorium is provided by its dimensions: 120' wide and 70' high, whilst the width of the stage opening was 80'. Since it was the intention to present a weekly stage show, an orchestra pit was provided with a lift for the magnificent console of the silver Compton organ, decorated in harmonious colours. The two organ chambers were ornamented with handsome gilt grilles within the long, splayed walls flanking the proscenium.

The auditorium was painted in subdued tones of terracotta, blue, grey and cream, with delicate, Japanese-style wall designs in gilt. The walls were given a beautiful, super-imposed contour line, upon which were hung and fixed the fibrous plaster dado, pilasters, and panels for fabric. In accordance with 1930s practice, lighting was concealed throughout. On top of the pilasters along the side walls, mural lights were shaded by translucent sunshine glass, providing a restful and harmonious effect. The attractive ceiling in blue, grey, red and gold was unspoiled by unsightly grilles, since air which had been washed, cleaned and sterilised by the ventilating system passed into the auditorium through apertures in the ceiling and below the balcony, leaving the artistic design intact.

Speaking to the press at a luncheon in the Adelphi Hotel, prior to the opening of the new cinema/theatre, Earl St John, director of Paramount Theatres, stated that a new type of entertainment was to be provided and was to include a stage show with famous bands, stage and radio stars and an organ interlude. Film bookings consisted of first releases in the area of all Paramount pictures and other leading attractions of merit, both British and American. The sound equipment was the Western Electric Wide Range system with the latest improvements. The Paramount Theatre opened under the direct supervision of Leslie C Holderness, general supervisor of Paramount theatres, and the general management of Tony C Reddin, with LJ Harris in charge of house management, with the staff numbering nearly 200.

The Grand Opening took place on Monday 15 October 1934 at 8pm, when the ceremony was performed by The Right Honourable Lord Mayor of Liverpool, Councillor George Alfred Strong, JP. In the programme of cine-variety was Cecil B Mille's *Cleopatra,* featuring Claudette Colbert, Warren William and Henry Wilcoxen and a cast of thousands. Live entertainment consisted of a stage show by Teddy Joyce (described as Canada's 'stick of dynamite') and his band, a presentation by Francis A Mangan's Mirrors of Delight with The Five Bolgaroffs, John Kellaway (The BBC Artist), 24 Dream Girls and 18 Helliwell Girls and an organ recital by Rex O'Grady and personal appearance of the Paramount British film star, Ida Lupino. The resident organist thereafter was Rowland F Tims, who had gained worldwide experience and gave recitals daily. From the next day performances began at noon with any seat (except royal circle, 2/4) at 1/- until 1pm, from which time, until 4pm, seat prices ranged from: 1/- to 2/6, with evening prices at: 1/- to 3/6.

Stage shows ended in 1937, but organ interludes remained a popular added attraction, and except for about 9 months following the outbreak of war in September 1939, the organ was in almost continual use until it was removed when the theatre was twinned in 1968. The first organist in 1940 was Harold Westran, who was followed in September of that year by Charles W Saxby, resident organist for about 2 years. Then came Charles T Allen, followed from about 1946 by a succession of touring organists from the Odeon and GB circuits. Before this time the theatre had been renamed the Odeon, having been sold by Paramount in July 1942 to the Oscar Deutsch's Odeon circuit.

In 1954 the Odeon had the distinction of being the first Merseyside cinema to be equipped for CinemaScope films with four-track magnetic stereophonic sound, which the previous year had first been presented by Twentieth Century-Fox at London Odeon, Marble Arch. A curved Miracle Mirror screen was installed for a picture size of 51' by 21', made of plastic material encrusted with tiny lenses to direct light outwards, instead of up and down as in conventional screens. Stereophonic sound was delivered by three sets of eight speakers behind the screen and 12 more around the auditorium. Twentieth Century-Fox's first CinemaScope film, *The Robe,* opened with great success on 11 January 1954, and was shown for 5 weeks until 13 February and, except for the opening day, was shown with three performances from 3pm, and weekday showings 5 times daily from 10am. Because of a dispute between Fox and the Rank Organisation, no further films from that producer were shown at the Odeon for over 5 years.

The next important innovation at the Odeon was Todd AO. For the installation the theatre was closed from 24 to 26 December 1958, the even larger screen was 51.5' by 24.5', and the number of speakers was increased to 83. Reopening on Boxing Day with *South Pacific,* the film ran until 20 June 1959, and during this time the organ was played daily by William Hopper, also known as Cecil Williams. Then followed extended runs of major attractions such as *Can Can*, *The Alamo*, *West Side Story*, *Spartacus* and *Lawrence of Arabia* before the all-time long-running *The Sound of Music* from 6 June 1965 until 29 April 1967. By this time the restaurant was closed, in 1958 having been converted for use as the 19th Victor Sylvester Dance Studio, to be opened by the Rank Organisation.

The end of *The Sound of Music's* record run began the Odeon's last 2 years as a single-screen cinema, with film bookings including epics and some reruns, continuing the policy of separate performances for which seats could be booked, whilst other weeks were allocated for normal circuit release films with continuous performances. The theatre, being too large for its reduced audiences, was closed on 20 June 1968 for conversion to twin cinemas. Two separate auditoria were constructed. The entirely restyled circle area formed Odeon 1, with 989 seats including Pullman chairs in the centre and the stalls became Odeon 2 with 595 seats and a new projection room at the rear, equipped with a Cinemeccanica 8 projector and a long-running Cakestand system, the original projection room serving Odeon 1 with Philips DP 70/35mm and stereophonic sound.

The conversion resulted in the loss of all the architectural features of the auditorium and foyers, the new treatment being of plain painted surfaces, relieved in Odeon 1 by curtained areas. But the new cinemas provided comfortable surroundings and were ideal for the presentation of CinemaScope and wide screen films. In the area originally allocated to the café there was now a licensed bar. Advertised as: *The Big Screen Scene,* Odeons 1 and 2 opened on 21 March 1969 with, in Odeon 1, *Oliver* in Panavision and full stereophonic sound. All seats were bookable for

The Paramount exterior.

the two daily performances at 2.40pm and 7.40pm, to which admission was at 20/-, 15/- and 10/-. Odeon 2 opened with *Chitty Chitty Bang Bang* in super Panavision (35mm), for which seats could also be booked for the separate performances at 2.15pm and 7.15pm, with performances on Saturday at 12.30pm, 4pm and 7.30pm at 12/6, 10/- and 8/.

After only 41 years, Odeon 2 was closed on 2 September 1973, for division into three auditoria, a 167-seat mini cinema being constructed at either side becoming Odeons 3 and 4. These opened on 23 December 1973 with, in Odeon 2: *The Belstone Fox*, in Odeon 3: *A Touch of Class*, *A Nice Girl Like Me* and in number 4: *Live and Let Die*. The four screen complex obviated the function of the Gaumont, which Rank closed within 6 months. A further reconstruction came in 1979 when the licensed bar became Odeon 5 with 148 seats, which opened on 4 November 1979 with *Midnight Express,* of which there were two separate performances at 3pm and 8.15pm. The circle lounge then provided space for a smaller licensed bar.

During the following 20 years, three out-of-town multiplexes were opened, including the company's Odeon at Switch Island, Netherton, only about 5 miles away. In order to compete, the company decided to double the number of screens in their city location to ten. At a cost of £2.8 million, the conversion began in January 1999, and was completed in just over 6 months, during which time three screens were used, with performances from 5pm.

The wide proscenium and 53' screen of the 1968/69 conversion to twin cinemas were retained in auditorium 1, although the capacity fell from 989 to 480, due to reduced width at the rear. Auditorium 2, on the ground floor, was also divided into three, and the old stage, which had hosted Beatles concerts in the 1960s, was converted to form auditorium 10, with 180 seats. The scheme included a restyled foyer and retail area in silver and blue to match the new silver facade, with the name in large, silver letters, mounted on the canopy above the entrance. The ten auditoria opened on Friday 16 July 1999, when the principal attraction was *Star Wars – The Phantom Menace*. The Odeon remains the only location of film entertainment in the city centre, but in recent years other companies have announced plans for multiplexes in various areas of the city.

1936
Curzon Theatre • Curzon
Prescot Road, Old Swan

The Curzon was erected in 1936 as an addition to the comprehensive circuit of Merseyside cinemas controlled by Bedford Cinemas (1928) Ltd. The managing director, John F Wood, was one of the city's motion picture pioneers. The new venture, on a prominent corner site in Prescot Road, was another of the imposing 1930s cinemas designed by the well known Liverpool architect, Ernest Shennan, FRIBA and the construction was by John Lucas & Son Ltd of Prescot. The frontage was of sand-faced brick above a base of cream-coloured Brizolite granite. The streamlined effect created by the gentle curves of the facade was repeated in the massive tower, constructed of Lenscrete masonry. The true beauty of this feature was appreciated when lit from within, combining with an extensive installation of neon, emphasising the contours of the building against the night sky.

Inside the tower, lenses with attractive hammered patterns reflected and diffused the light and had a high light transmission value. Beneath the massive concrete and glass Lenscrete canopy, below which the main entrance was brilliantly floodlit after dark, sets of swing doors led to the spacious, extensively-glazed vestibule. A white marble floor set off the shining black glass, with which almost the entire wall space was covered, and upon which were etched embossed Shakespearian characters. The curvilinear design of the foyer was expressed both in the black lines relieving the floor and in the stepping of the ceiling. By a clever arrangement of mirrors, the area appeared almost circular, rather than merely elliptical in shape. Opposite the entrance doors were the paybox, advance booking office and chocolate kiosk. The stalls entrances and approach to the balcony were flanked by vertical pillars of green and silvered glass, whilst the walls on either side were panelled in quilted maple and figured mahogany. On the left-hand-side, the stairs led to a spacious mezzanine floor, decorated in warm peach and lit by concealed lighting.

The auditorium had 1,750 seats upholstered in amber and a fully carpeted floor which sloped from the stage to a main crossover gangway, from where it was stepped to the rear. The decoration consisted of horizontal mouldings, with the lower part of the walls banded in shades of green, the same colour repeated in a lighter tone in the series of moulded plaster ribs which constituted the ante-proscenium relief. The upper walls and the outer part of the ceiling were spray-textured in buff Marblcote and finished in speckles of metallic amber and gold. Flanking the proscenium, two large sets of green translucent glass panels were etched with designs of well known fairy tales and nursery rhymes. Floodlit from within, these formed attractive points of interest as the main house lights faded out. Except for the wall mounted light fittings, the house lights were in the form of tubes concealed in troughs above the cornice and outer part of the ceiling, which also included a circular central fitting with concealed lighting, providing a remarkably faithful representation of daylight. Two deep bronze columns on either side of the stage blended tastefully with the amber and green curtains.

The orchestra pit featured the handsome console of the Compton organ, which incorporated all modern advances, including the electrone unit. The organ chamber was behind the screen, a position which had not hitherto been used for this unit. The large projection room housed two Kalee projectors, Western Electric wide range sound system, spotlight lanterns and electrical equipment.

The Grand Opening of the Curzon at 2.30pm on 10 October 1936 was by the Lord Mayor of Liverpool, Councillor RJ Hall. Guests were admitted by invitation only. The cinema was open to the public in the evening when there were separate performances at 6.15pm and 8.40pm, beginning with the *GB News* presenting 'The World to the World', with commentary by EVH Emmet. This was followed by a Walt Disney Mickey Mouse cartoon, *Orphan's Picnic*. Then an organ interlude by Lewis Oddy, organist of the company's Plaza, Birkenhead. The film was Metro-Goldwyn-Mayer picture, *The Unguarded Hour*, starring Loretta Young, Franchot Tone and Lewis Stone. With the exception of Saturdays,

performances were continuous in the evenings from 6.15pm with matinees daily at 2.30pm. Admission prices: 6d, 9d, 1/- and 1/3, reduced to 4d, 6d and 9d in the afternoon. With regards to films bookings, there was to be a bi-weekly change of programme Monday and Thursday, with an occasional 6 day film.

The first manager of the Curzon, Samuel A Eaton, had been in the business for many years and was one of the most prominent and popular managers in Liverpool, having begun his career at the Tunnel Road Picturedrome in 1919. Following periods as manager of the Belmont Road Picture House and the Carlton in Tuebrook, Eaton resigned his managership of the Prince of Wales in the city centre to take over the Curzon. His main aim was to make it the social and entertainment centre of the district and he invited the co-operation of patrons, whose suggestions and criticism received his personal attention. After only 2 years, in 1938, there came competition on the opposite side of Prescot Road when ABC opened their new super-cinema, the Regent, replacing the old cinema of the same name. Until after the peak admissions years of the late-1940s, the Curzon was generally well attended, although normally with second suburban runs including many ABC circuit release films following their screenings at the Carlton, Tuebrook, and Granada, Dovecot, the Curzon being approximately midway between those ABC theatres.

With the introduction of the novelty 3D films, in 1953, the Curzon was one of the few Merseyside cinemas where these could be seen, and for the first time in the district began with *Sangaree*, starring Fernando Lamas, on 28 September. A number of 3D films, including the famous *House of Wax*, were screened, ending a year later with *Hondo*, on 25 September 1954. The rather short-lived novelty was then replaced by the more lasting CinemaScope and, with magnetic stereophonic sound pioneered by Twentieth Century-Fox, the Curzon screened first runs in the district, starting on 20 December 1954 with *How to Marry a Millionaire* starring Marilyn Monroe.

By the end of the 1950s, Rank suburban cinemas had taken over the Fox CinemaScope films, and as an independent remaining under the control of the JF Wood circuit, continued with a mixed run of mainly older films for 3 days only. International Wrestling was introduced in September 1959 on Monday evenings at 7.30pm, continuing until 7 December. This was resumed in February 1960 on Thursday evenings until April of that year, after which the entertainment was restricted to films, ending on 20 August 1960 with *A Woman Like Satan*, featuring Brigitte Bardot and *Vice Raid*. The building was then reconstructed as a row of shops, the major part in the centre of the frontage becoming a supermarket, flanked on either side by smaller stores. A similar use of the building continues, with the upper part of the frontage little changed.

1937
Gaumont
Park Road, Dingle

The old Dingle Picturedrome was closed in 1931 after its acquisition by Denman Picture Houses Ltd. Six years later the new Gaumont was built on the site at the corner of Park Road and Dingle Lane. An imposing building, it added greatly to the entertainment facilities of South Liverpool, where also in course of construction at that time for Bedford Cinemas (1928) Ltd, was the Mayfair, nearby on Aigburth Road. The compact site of the Gaumont resulted in the planning of a shallow, wide auditorium by architect, WE Trent, FRIBA, assisted by D Mackay, ARIAS. The brickwork elevations accentuated the sweeping curve of the corner site with a rectangular tower forming the corner feature adjacent to Park Road. Above the main entrance, which was surmounted by a canopy, the facing was of grey and cream faience, whilst the entrance and steps were framed in a surround of bright blue faience. Five pairs of doors led into the wide entrance hall, in which the paybox was located next to the rear wall, midway between the two main stalls entrances. A staircase on either side led to the first floor lounge and doors to the balcony, and the decoration of the foyer was notable for the use of linoleum as a lining on the walls. The auditorium had room for 1,500, of which about 600 were in the wide balcony, which extended over the rear stalls. The seats had upholstered backs and armrests in wine-coloured velvet and were fitted on both floors in three sections, allowing four gangways.

The decorations were in warm tones with a predominance of amber and flanking surfaces of textured Marblcote, while in the ante-proscenium were two large grilles of simple geometric design finished in silver, gold and green. The ceiling, bordered by a heavy moulding, had a deep square central dome with lighting concealed in three of its sides, the fourth side housing the apertures of the projection room. The ceiling, with two, three and four tier ornamental glass light fittings suspended over the balcony, was deeply stepped down to the 45'-wide proscenium,

167

Inside the Gaumont, Dingle.

which was finished in a copper and set in a wide, corrugated green surround lit by concealed lighting. In front of the stage was an orchestra pit in which was the Wurlitzer organ console, up to the mid-1980s was the only remaining cinema organ in the Liverpool area in a former cinema. The projection room, with dimensions of 32' by 18', held two GB machines and the first installation in Liverpool of Western Electric Mirrophonic sound system. Westinghouse rectifiers eliminated the use of noisy motors, and 'laundered' air was provided by a washing plant, which refreshed and changed the air every 10 minutes.

As the Lord Mayor was on holiday, the opening ceremony, at 2pm on 29 March 1937, was performed by JM Cannon, Chief Supervisor of the GB Picture Corporation, for which some patrons in the packed audience had been waiting outside since 8am. Following the National Anthem, the performance began with a colour cartoon, *Birds of Love*, then *Ravenous Roger and Vocalising*, an Edgar Kennedy comedy, followed by *GB News*. The audience then enjoyed an organ interlude by William Whittle at the Wurlitzer. The feature film was the popular comedy *My Man Godfrey*, starring William Powell and Carole Lombard. The performance was continuous from 2pm, but thereafter, a separate matinee daily at 2.30pm was followed by a continuous evening performance at 6.15pm, whilst on Saturday evenings there were two distinct performances at 6.15pm and 8.40pm, for which all seats were bookable at prices ranging from 6d to 1/3.

The Gaumont, South Liverpool's luxury theatre, was well attended for the first suburban showings of the GB circuit release films, which were normally concurrent with the Casino, Kensington and the Plaza, Allerton, although just over a month later, a theatre of equal status, the Mayfair, Aigburth Road, also opened and provided strong competition. At the beginning of the war anti-aircraft gunners were stationed on the cinema roof and requisitioned the women's staffroom as their quarters. Remarkably, the Gaumont escaped almost unharmed from the Blitz, with only slight damage to the roof caused by falling shrapnel, none of which landed during a performance. However, there was a lucky escape when a landmine fell 100 yards away in Grosvenor Terrace, near the home of the cinema manager, Norman H Lockett.

During the 1940s and 1950s the use of the organ continued with famous guest organists visiting the cinema, including Harold Thiems and Stanley Tudor, the BBC organist. By the end of the 1940s performances were continuous throughout the day, a policy which was retained until October 1965, when falling numbers prompted a reduction to continuous evening performance and matinees on Monday, Wednesday and Saturday only. This was consistent with the general decline in cinema admissions from the early-1950s. In 1954 the 45'-wide proscenium was ideally suited to the new CinemaScope screen, installed for the opening of *The Black Shield of Falworth* on 6 December.

Attendances continued to decline during the first half of the 1960s. Less than a year after the introduction of reduced opening times, the Gaumont closed on 17 September 1966 with *Those Magnificent Men in their Flying Machines*. The change was made to a Top Rank bingo club, which was operated by the company for the greater part of 25 years. The organ having been retained, an almost forgotten era of musical entertainment was recalled by organ interludes preceding the bingo sessions. In the mid-1980s nostalgia was unleashed by a special performance of theatre organ music, when the mighty Wurlitzer was played by the famous blind organist, Billy Ellis and Ron Curtis. Unfortunately, attendances decreased during the 1990s, resulting in closure in 1998. The building is now unused and for sale, presently under offer.

1937
Mayfair Super-Cinema
Aigburth Road, Aigburth

In 1937 this latest addition to the Bedford Cinemas was considered to have set a new standard in theatre design. On a site second to none for prominence and convenience, the Mayfair super-cinema was erected by Tysons Ltd, of Dryden Street, Liverpool. It was designed by A Ernest Shennan, FRIBA, renowned for his versatility and skill as a designer of entertainment houses. Whilst the well balanced masses of sand-faced brickwork and cream faience constituted an excellent elevation, it was in the entrance surround that Shennan concentrated the finest materials and best craftsmanship. As at the Curzon in Prescot Road, considerable and effective use was made of glass, the main entrance being divided by shining black plinths, flanked by cream-coloured glass relieved by a number of artistic etchings. This part of the frontage had a unique concrete and glass canopy; an example of the unlimited possibilities of Lenscrete construction, in which the strength of reinforced concrete was combined with the beauty of glass. A single row lettering display occupied the facia, with the cinema name at either side. Neon lighting outlined the highest part of the frontage, with the name sign immediately below and above canopy level, the signs were given prominenece by twelve short neon tubes, fitted horizontally.

The Mayfair Aigburth – auditorium and pay-box.

Four pairs of doors in the main entrance led into the large foyer in which the sweeping curves were admirably suited to the Arbele Burr wood panelling. The flooring was of small tiles forming a semi-circular design appropriate to the front of the paybox, booking office and chocolate kiosk, directly opposite the main entrance, and this area was lit by concealed lighting within ceiling recesses. At one end of the foyer the stalls lounge was decorated in bronze shaded to dark cream, with doors to the auditorium flanked by bronze metal and glass lighting features and, as in the foyer, the walls were panelled in Arbele Burr Wood.

The lounge followed the sweep of the balcony, with four deep alcoves having glass illuminated panels depicting marine life, and the ceiling in a series of stepped illuminated coves. A striking feature of the auditorium was the ceiling, which consisted of a series of lighting coves stepped down towards the 40'-wide proscenium, the two nearest the stage being continued down the side walls to meet the horizontal bands of blue and grey of the lower walls. Set within a huge, curved decorative area, illuminated by concealed lighting, the proscenium was outlined by a series of clearly defined ribs finished in silver and gold. Camouflaged ventilating ducts created a most attractive shadow effect in combination with the concealed lighting at either side of the stage.

The proscenium was adorned by a gold festoon curtain with contrasting deep red scalloped edge pelmet and side drapes. Before the stage, in the centre of the orchestra pit, was a Compton organ mounted on a lift. Seating for an audience of 1,750 was upholstered in a grey and blue floral pattern and fitted in three sections across the sloping stalls floor. The balcony was stepped, and at the rear of this floor, the projection room housed two Kalee 11 projectors, arcs and lanterns, and the latest Western Electric Mirrophonic sound system.

Described as Liverpool's most luxuriously appointed cinema, the Mayfair was opened by the Lord Mayor, Alderman William Denton, at a special, invitation only performance at 2.30pm on 1 May 1937. The feature film starred Max Miller as *Educated Evans*, with full supporting programme including a musical interlude by the popular radio organist, Sydney Gustard. Open to the general public in the evening, there were separate performances at 6.15pm and 8.40pm, to which admission was: stalls 6d and 9d and balcony 1/- and 1/3. With the exception of the 6d seats, all seats were bookable for the 8.40pm performance. The opening feature film was booked for that day only, after which the Astaire-Rogers musical, *Swing Time*, began on Monday 3 May. The closest competition came from the newly opened Gaumont, Park Road. Films shown at the Mayfair included many of the ABC circuit releases, on or about the same dates as the Carlton, Tuebrook, following the city runs at the Forum and the second run Majestic.

In 1953, as at the Curzon, Old Swan, Bedford Cinemas introduced 3D, starting with *Sangaree* on 12 October and then at fairly regular intervals, ending with *Phantom of the Rue Morgue* on 15 December 1954, after which the longer lasting CinemaScope opened on 20 December with *The Command*, featuring Guy Madison. Greatly diminishing the attractiveness of the auditorium, but in the interests of increasing the picture size from the existing CinemaScope, in 1969 a large unmasked screen was erected. Extending over the greater part of the auditorium in width and height, the entire proscenium and associated features were completely hidden. Instead of a curtain closing over the new screen during intervals, the plain effect was relieved only by the fading-in of concealed coloured lighting around the edges.

From 3 August 1969 films were advertised as being 'On the Giant Floating Screen', beginning with the epic western, *The Alamo*, starring John Wayne. Although by this time the only cinema in that area of south Liverpool, performances were normally in the evenings only, with the Compton organ covered over. It was later played in 1971 by Bertie Johnson, one of Britain's top broadcasting organists, and for the last time, a few weeks before the cinema closed in May 1973, at a screening of *The Ten Commandments*. In the early-1970s, the only full house was for *The Sound of Music*, but this aside, attendances declined until closure on 23 June 1973 with, appropriately, *The Last Picture Show*, the top half of a double bill, which included *Bullitt*, featuring Steve McQueen. The theatre was converted by the new owners, Mecca Ltd, into another bingo and social club in close competition with Top Rank's Gaumont. Closed in 1984, it was sold and demolished to make way for a supermarket.

1937
Mayfair
Derby Road, Huyton

The opening of the Mayfair on 18 September 1937 was seen as another page in Huyton's rapidly changing history. It had a population of 25,000, for whom the nearest cinema had been the Granada, Dovecot, about 2 miles away. Designed by the well known Liverpool architects Gray, Evans & Crossley, the building was erected at a cost of £25,000 by William Tomkinson & Sons, on an island site next to the Council offices near Huyton railway station.

The striking modern facade was of plum-coloured rustic brick and cream glazed faience, and the main features of the upper level were three tall arched windows in the first floor lounge. Spotlights floodlit the elevation and a number of circular shaded light fittings on the soffit of the canopy provided lit the wide, central main entrance. There was extensive use of neon tubes to outline the upper part of the frontage and name sign in the middle below the coping.

Three pairs of glass-panelled doors in the main entrance led into the spacious foyer, giving access to the promenade leading to the auditorium. Staircases led to the balcony foyer and balcony. There was another entrance from the frontage to the front stalls through a separate entrance hall, which, like the other foyers and steps, had flooring of Hopton Wood Terrazzo. The balcony did not extend over the rear stalls, thereby avoiding the depressing atmosphere generally felt beneath a low ceiling and also achieved better ventilation. Luxurious seating, by CR Harrison & Sons Ltd, in rose-coloured velvet, and wide gangways, were attractive features of the 1,009-seat auditorium (676 in the stalls and 333 in the balcony).

Inside the Mayfair, Huyton.

The decor had a dignified simplicity, the side walls being treated in a vertical shaded design in a golden rose, incorporating attractive grilles at increasing levels towards the rear. The beautiful electric fittings suspended from the ceiling, and concealed lighting from within plasterwork areas, enhanced the colour scheme. Flanking the proscenium, the splayed walls above the exits were adorned by a balconette, upon which was a circular standard supporting a light fitting for the illumination of a decorative recessed area. The focal point of the auditorium was the proscenium with draperies in gold satin, relieved with light Rose du Barrie and screen curtains in silver satin illuminated by a four colour lighting system, which blended and changed automatically. The operating room, with direct street access, was fitted with the latest projectors and sound system, styled as Truephonic, supplied and installed by British Talking Pictures Ltd. The operator also had control of the lighting, which allowed a combination of 25 colours to be played onto the stage. At the rear of this modern 1930s cinema was a 100-space carpark.

The Mayfair was owned by a private company, whose directors included: AE and JP Fortnam; G Fortnam Appleton and Joseph A Appleton, ACA (secretary). The first manager and licensee, Austin Durrans, formerly manager of the Carlton, Tuebrook, was then the longest serving licensee in the Liverpool area, having been connected with both theatres and the renting side of the business since 1907, when he began his career at the old Paddington Palace. Of the eight theatres he had managed, the Mayfair was the third new cinema he had opened for the company, since prior to his appointment by ABC at the Carlton, he had been at the Astoria and Victory cinemas in Walton.

Five hundred invitations were sent out for the opening ceremony of the Mayfair on 18 September 1937, by Councillor J Strathdene, chairman of Huyton Council, who was presented with a silver key by the directors. The guests were given afternoon tea and handsome souvenir programmes. The audience was entertained with two short films, then the Bing Crosby musical, *Mississippi*.

The Grand Opening to the public followed on Monday 20 September, with a matinee at 2.30pm and continuous evening performance from 6.30pm, starting with *British Paramount News*. After an interlude for the sale of ices came the feature film, the Paramount, Cecil B de Mille production, *The Plainsman*, starring Gary Cooper and Jean Arthur. Evening performances Monday to Friday were continuous from 6.30pm, with matinees at 2.30pm on Monday, Thursday and Saturday. On Saturdays and Bank Holidays two distinct performances at 6.20pm and 8.40pm were arranged, so that intending patrons could book their seats in advance, except for the 6d front stalls, for 9d and 1/3 in the rear stalls and balcony respectively.

Despite its initial promise, the Mayfair was one of the shortest surviving Liverpool cinemas, being open for just under 23 years, during which time there was a mixed run of film bookings for 3 days only, mainly of GB release and, during the 1950s, including many off circuit B pictures. The cinema then became known as 'The Ranch', as westerns were so frequently shown. Attendances declined until closure on 30 April 1960 with *I'm All Right Jack,* starring Ian Carmichael and Peter Sellers. Following use as a store the building was converted for use as a Boots chemists and remains in this use to date.

1937
Majestic
Daulby Street, Liverpool city centre

Majestic Cinema, 1937.

Erected at the junction of Boundary Place and Daulby Street, on the site occupied since 1914 by the cinema from which the New Majestic took its name. It was a most interesting scheme, completed in 1937 at a cost of, including land, approximately £40,000. Designed by Liverpool architects Gray, Evans and Crossley, the opening followed soon after that of the Mayfair, Huyton, which they had also designed. Additional land of 465 square yards alongside the old building had been acquired to provide, in addition to larger general accommodation, an increase in the seating capacity of 700, to 1,162 stalls and 632 balcony seats.

Two long, modern side elevations, presented a generous expanse of brickwork relieved by horizontal lengths of cream-coloured terracotta, bordering the windows at various levels. At decreasing width from the rear of the building, the side elevations narrowed to the imposing front elevation, the principal feature of which was the elegant tower rising 75' above street level. Constructed of white, glazed faience, it was illuminated by neon tubes, as also the vertical theatre name sign on the front. Below this was the main entrance, with flanking walls in cream, glazed faience tiles emphasising this elevation. Surmounting the main entrance, the canopy with lettering display on the facia and circular, shaded lighting fittings on the soffit, extended at either side above the tiled area. At a slightly lower level, plain, metal-fronted, glass-covered verandahs, to the rear of the building, provided cover for queueing patrons when waiting rooms were full.

Three pairs of glazed doors in the main entrance led into a vestibule with a central paybox, beyond which were further doors to the wide entrance hall with striking rubber flooring. Concealed lighting in the ceiling accentuated the clever contrast of the dark wooden dado below the light walls and ceiling. From the entrance hall there was direct access to the rear stalls, whilst a wide, carpeted staircase with wrought iron balustrades and coloured plastic

The Première
of the
MAJESTIC CINEMA
LIVERPOOL

OCTOBER 2nd, 1937

handrails rose to the mid-balcony lounge on the first floor above the entrance. This was lit by circular shaded light fittings in rich colours, contrasting with the pastel-pink walls and comfortable pastel blue settees. In this area were the entrances to the front and centre of the balcony, divided by a crossover gangway, and a continuation of the stairway led up to the top balcony foyer leading to the rear of the balcony. Each foyer was capable of accommodating 100 patrons.

Another entrance to the auditorium was provided at the stage end from Boundary Place, from which patrons could enter the front stalls or descend a staircase to a waiting room. The architects excelled themselves by setting the proscenium within a large recessed area, lit by concealed lighting. The walls were decorated in soft tones of rose and gold with relief by delicate horizontal shading. Further concealed lighting came from troughs in the ceiling, and windows provided daylight when the cinema was not open to the public. A stage was included with artists' rooms nearby since it was the intention of the manager, Ellis Williamson, to include occasional variety turns in the programmes. The festooned stage curtains were of silver satin, with crimson satin drapes at either side, toning with the plush covered seats with pneumatic armrests supplied by CR Harrison & Sons Ltd, of Newton-le-Willows. At the back of the auditorium the fine operating room was equipped with the latest projectors by J Frank Brockliss Ltd, and Western Electric Mirrophonic sound system by the Western Electric Co Ltd.

The contractors, William Tomkinson & Sons, were justifiably proud of their achievement in demolishing and rebuilding the cinema in 6 months for the Grand Opening on 2 October 1937. The opening ceremony was performed by Sir Samuel Brighouse. For many years the cinema was under the control of Ellis Williamson as general manager and licensee for the owners, The Liverpool Majestic Picture House Ltd. The policy of continuous performances from 1pm to 11pm was retained and for the opening day, Saturday, also during the following week, the feature film was the Paramount musical *Waikiki Wedding*, starring Bing Crosby, supported by the espionage drama, *The Girl from Scotland Yard*, with Karen Morley. The admission prices of 6d and 1/- to the stalls, and 1/3 in the balcony were reduced to 6d stalls and 1/- balcony between 1pm and 5pm.

The Majestic was a city cinema offering suburban prices with the advantage of up-to-date films, since except for occasional first runs, these were no later than second run in Liverpool. These included Paramount Pictures, Warner Bros and British films released on the ABC circuit. On the fringe of the city, the cinema was generally well attended for mainly double features at continuous performances, a policy which had proved successful from the late-1920s.

Patronage consisted of visitors to the city as well as residents of the nearby suburbs. A wide screen for CinemaScope was installed but the equipment did not include stereophonic sound. The first film in the new format, *The Command*, opened on 17 October 1954. Despite falling admissions, the policy of continuous performances remained until 30 March 1968, when opening hours were reduced to continuous in the evenings only and matinees on Monday, Wednesday and Saturday. Only 2 years later the building and site were sold for redevelopment in connection with the building of the new Liverpool hospital.

On Saturday 20 June 1970 the local press advertised the last 7 days of the Majestic: 'Be in at the finish and see Alfred Hitchcock's most terrifying film: *The Birds* with also *The Day of the Triffids* at performances from 4.50pm and matinees at 1.20 on Mondays, Wednesdays and Saturdays.' The building was difficult to demolish due to its sturdy construction and the site was incorporated into the grounds of the new hospital.

1937
New Regent
Prescot Road, Old Swan

The erection of the New Regent, for ABC Ltd, began in 1937 to the plans of the company architect, W Glenn, FRIAS. It replaced the old Regent cinema on an adjoining site. The contractor was Charles J Doyle, Liverpool, who 6 years previously had erected the Carlton, Tuebrook and the Granada, Dovecot for ABC.

At a cost of over £30,000, the dark brick building with stonework relief was constructed lengthwise to the main road, with the facade in Baden Road. The design represented an interesting departure from normal practice; projecting out from the main building line in a slight curve, to the right-hand-side of the frontage, was the main entrance, flanked on either side by the large windows of the foyer. This part of the frontage was surmounted by a canopy, above which the curved section extended upwards in the form of a stone-faced area. Relieved by a three-row lettering display advertising the current programme, at the highest point of this feature metal railings enclosed a flat roof. Stonework was also used for the lower part of the elevation. With the exception of the principal, curved feature, the construction was of dark brick, upon which was fitted at the highest point of the frontage towards the left side, a large neon name sign, with an ABC triangle lower down. The canopy also advertised the current feature film by lettering display, on the facia, whilst the soffit was fitted with neon tubes. The main entrance was lit by overhead circular shaded light fittings, with a stills frame at either side, leading, via three pairs of doors, into the foyer, which had a cream-coloured terrazzo floor. With a high ceiling, the balcony lounge extended across, approached from either side by a stairway. The steps were of a reddish, patterned rubber, and the attractive metal balustrade and handrail extended across from the head of the stairs along the lounge.

The foyer and lounge were lit by several light fittings but attention was immediately drawn to the huge, suspended, metal and glass fitment consisting of a central section covered by opaque glass, internally lit by neon tubes. Several external subsidiary light fittings were at the highest point, with glass discs spaced all around. In the centre of the foyer, two pairs of doors, flanked on either side by a one-cashier, curved fronted paybox, led into a waiting room with doors at either side to areas giving direct access to the rear stalls crossover gangway. On this floor, with four gangways, 1,208 seats were fitted in three blocks across the auditorium, and with a similar arrangement, extending over the stalls approximately half its length was the 516-seat balcony, approached from either side of the lounge via short stairways leading to a crossover gangway at the rear of the front circle.

The Regent was a classic example of 1930s Art Deco-style; decorated mainly in a delicate shade of peach, with the plain surfaces above the balcony relieved by horizontal areas separated by silver-coloured lines. Beyond the balcony front, the walls, relieved at the upper level by pilasters, curved towards the proscenium, featuring at either side, a large, patterned grille within a light vertical ribbed area. The 45'-wide proscenium was adorned by a floral patterned curtain, the lower part of which was festooned. With the exception of several glass shaded fittings above the sides of the balcony, illumination was by lighting concealed in the ceiling troughs, the principal feature being the large oval dome at the front. As at many ABC theatres, the projection room was equipped with the latest Ross machines and RCA sound system. The Regent was at a disadvantage having no organ, but otherwise was equal in status to its close opposition, the Curzon, on the opposite side of Prescot Road.

Two days after the closure of the old Regent, the new cinema was opened unceremoniously at 2pm on 9 May 1938, attended by: AS Moss, general manager of ABC; Rowland Lea, general supervisor; PF Inkester, area supervisor and EG Nicholls, supervising engineer. The manager, FW Stollard, who had formerly managed the Capitol in St Helens, had also opened the company's Reo cinema, Fazakerley, in 1933 and had held several positions as a cinema manager. Screened at the 2.30pm matinee and continuous evening performance from 6.15pm, the first programme consisted of the feature film *Double Wedding*, starring William Powell and Myrna Loy, supported by short films and the *Pathé Gazette*. On Saturdays seats were bookable for the two performances at 6.15pm and 8.40pm. Admission prices were: 6d to 1/6. In a similar situation to that of the nearby Curzon, between two ABC cinemas (the Carlton in Tuebrook and the Granada in Dovecot, which shared a concurrency of first suburban showings of the company release films), ABC therefore provided the principal competition to the Regent. There, the alternative film booking policy included many of the GB (later Rank) release films, but following that company's suburban cinemas.

Although fully justifying the description of a super-cinema, especially from the early-1950s, the Regent was not one of the better attended in the suburbs. In the mid-1950s, CinemaScope was belatedly installed, starting on 19 May 1955 with *The Black Shield of Falworth*, but by that time, much of the system's novelty had been lost. From 13 February 1956, ABC allocated to the theatre a week-long visit by Hubert Selby with the Hammond Electric organ, in a country-wide tour of ABC cinemas. Patrons were given a leaflet describing the organ and inviting requests. After leaving the services in 1946, Hubert Selby resumed broadcasting on the company organs and the BBC theatre organ, and in 1952 founded the Cinema Organ Society.

Despite the fact that there was suburban competition only from the Carlton, Tuebrook, attendances at the Regent continued to decline into the 1960s, and in an attempt to revive its fortunes, ABC undertook refurbishment which reduced the capacity to about 1,500. This was carried out in week beginning 18 February 1962. The reopening as a luxury suburban cinema was on 25 February, with the epic western, *The Alamo*, featuring John Wayne and Richard Widmark, screened at a continuous performance from 4.20pm.

The boost to attendances was not sustained and in November 1965 opening hours were reduced to one evening performance, Monday to Friday, and continuous on Saturdays and Sundays. This policy continued during the cinema's last 18 months, when it remained unprofitable, if not actually operating at a loss, the large capacity being far in excess of requirements. In 1967, ABC sold the building and site for redevelopment, and the last performance was on Saturday 25 March with a double feature: *First Man on the Moon* and *The Stooges in Orbit*. The building was demolished to make way for a row of shops with living accommodation above.

1939
Abbey
Church Road, Wavertree

The Abbey was the first of three cinemas opened in the Liverpool area during 1939 prior to the outbreak of World War II. It was generally considered to be the finest of the super-cinemas, designed by Alderman AE Shennan, JP, FRIBA. The cinema was erected on a prime suburban site, facing the well known Picton Clock Tower at the junction of Childwall Road and Church Road North, formerly known as the ancient Wavertree Green, part of the common land of the old Manor of Wavertree. The cost, excluding the site, was £50,000, the enterprise of a local concern, the Regal Cinema Co (Liverpool) Ltd. Their secretary, WL Hampson, was well known in the local entertainment world for his successful launching of both the Casino, Kensington, in 1923, and in 1930 of the Regal, Norris Green, from which the company then derived its name.

The plans of the new cinema were approved by the Liverpool Licensing Justices in September 1937, and from mid-1938, 200 men were engaged for about 9 months on the construction. The most striking external feature was the main entrance and its semi-circular sweep continuing upwards to the apex of the building, the whole bay consisting of windows, which diminished in height as the structure ascended. These were separated vertically by five columns of black faience tiles, whilst grey faience tiles were used to form the horizontal separation of the windows. The small side windows near the roof were styled with Norman arches, whose lines were pleasingly carried downward in the mellow brickwork. A canopy with lettering display on the facia to advertise the current feature film, and well designed neon lighting followed the contours of the corner entrance. Three pairs of doors led into the circular vestibule, in which was the paybox and swing doors to the main foyer. This conveyed an immediate impression of size and dignity, with the ceiling and one wall completely mirrored, whilst the opposite wall was in Australian walnut. The flooring of wood mosaic had a decorative motif of musical notes.

Leading up from the foyer, the magnificent 10' wide staircase in green terrazzo had an ornate balustrade in polished copper and aluminum. At the head of the staircase, with flooring similar to the foyer, the lounge had a ceiling formed in a series of large fluted domes, giving additional height to the room in which patrons could enjoy light refreshment in comfort. Two pairs of doors led from the lounge to the balcony, the most advantageous position from which to view the magnificent ceiling, composed entirely of large domes in iridescent gold, each individually illuminated.

The main walls were treated in wide, horizontal bands of primrose, orange, and gold speckle, separated by bands of silver. These bands led the eye to the main grilles on the long, curved walls flanking the 42'-wide proscenium, an interesting feature being the illuminated columns of multi-coloured lights which acted as a frame. Contrasting with the light-coloured stage and screen curtains, the pelmet was festooned and the appearance of the proscenium and flanking walls was enhanced by a deep lighting trough which illuminated the ceiling above. The auditorium seated 1,126 on the ground floor and 744 in the balcony, and special attention was given to lines of sight from every part.

Duosonic, full-range, sound equipment and Magnus projectors were installed by GB Equipment Ltd, together with public address system, arc lamps, special effects projector and the marvellous Multitone Telesonic deaf aid equipment, which did not require electricity, being a small radio instrument which could be carried to any seat. Facilities also included the serving of coffee throughout the auditorium, as well as chocolates, cigarettes and ices and adjoining the building was a spacious carpark.

For the Grand Opening a brochure was produced, in which the manager, WJ Grace, introduced himself to the patrons, describing the numerous attractions of the Abbey and inviting both criticism and compliments. The local press announced 'The Perfect Cinema at Last', although there was no organ.

The opening ceremony at 2.30pm on Saturday 4 March 1939, was performed by WT Lancashire CC. This was followed by the gala performance, with the feature film, *Joy of Living*, starring Irene Dunne and Douglas Fairbanks Jr, *British Paramount News* and full supporting programme. Music was by Mrs Wilf Hamer and her band, by kind permission of the Grafton Rooms. In the evening there were two separate performances at 6.30pm and 8.40pm. The circle seats could be booked in advance, the normal policy for Saturday evenings during the first 6 months up to the outbreak of war on 3 September 1939, when the Abbey began continuous performances from 2pm to 10pm.

Initially, Monday to Friday performances were continuous from 6.30pm, with a matinee daily at 2.30pm, and in this way the first complete week began on 6 March 1939, with Anna Neagle in *Sixty Glorious Years,* in Technicolor. Popular prices ranged from comfortable front stalls seats at 6d, back stalls at 9d and circle 1/- and 1/3, reduced at matinees to 4d in the stalls and 6d in the circle.

After only 4½ years under the ownership of the Regal Cinema Co, it was announced in October 1943 that the Abbey had been sold to John F Wood, coming then under the control of Bedford Cinemas (1928) Ltd, whose small circuit included the Mayfair, Aigburth, and the Curzon, Old Swan. The film bookings thereafter continued to include many of ABC's circuit releases, but in the 1950s, as at the company's other super-cinemas, the Abbey was to the fore in the presentation of the latest projection systems. A new wide screen was installed in 1954 for 3D films, which started on 15 August with *Kiss Me Kate,* featuring Kathryn Grayson and Howard Keel. Another film in 3D, *Hondo,* starring John Wayne, was shown before the wide screen came into regular use for CinemaScope. The first film for this screen was *The Command*, a Warner Bros western, screened on 19 December 1954 for 7 days.

In 1960 the Abbey was among the few Liverpool cinemas equipped with stereophonic sound and screened a second run, following the Odeon in Liverpool, of *South Pacific.* The film ran for 5 weeks from 11 September, at one evening performance at 7.30pm and a matinee at 2pm on Monday, Wednesday and Saturday. This was followed by showings of *The King and I* and *Carousel.* However, the most important year in the Abbey's history was 1964, for on 25 January it was closed for conversion into Liverpool's only Cinerama Theatre, entailing work costing £75,000, with an extra £30,000 for equipment. Due to the fact that the Cinerama picture was almost a half circle, extensive reconstruction of the auditorium was necessary, involving the hiding from view of the proscenium and flanking walls with attractive grilles. These were covered by the giant Cinerama screen and deep red curtain. The rear stalls seating was drastically altered by the construction of a new projection room to house the three projectors, with straight picture throw and synchronised to screen the Cinerama picture.

Due to the rearrangement of the seating and the altered sight lines in both the stalls and circle, the capacity was reduced to 1,260. On the first floor the lounge was converted into a licensed bar, making the Abbey the first Liverpool cinema with this facility. A preview of the first Cinerama film, *This is Cinerama,* was given on 17 March 1964 at a charity performance in aid of the King George V fund for Sailors. Among the guests were the chairman of Litherland UDC, Councillor and Mrs Lawrenson, and the Mayor and Mayoress of Bootle, Alderman and Mrs J Morley. Music was by the Liverpool Scottish Pipe Band and the Liverpool City Police Trumpeters. On the following day the first public performance was given and the film ran for 7 weeks with nightly performances at 7.45pm, a matinee on Wednesday and three performances on Saturdays at 2pm, 6pm and 8.30pm. All seats were bookable at 5/6, 7/6, 10/- and 12/6.

Although Cinerama was a great initial success and included the Merseyside premieres of *How the West was Won* and *The Wonderful World of the Brothers Grimm,* only a limited number of the productions were to follow and projection by the three lens system ended in April 1965, when the cinema was closed for several days for the alteration of the equipment to single lens Cinerama, using 70mm film with Panavision and stereophonic sound. The reopening on 15 April was with the all star film *Its a Mad, Mad, Mad, Mad World*.

Cinerama films at the Abbey ended on 6 March 1971, after an 11 week run of *Song of Norway.* Following this, the film bookings included many reruns of epic films in 70mm, advertised as 'on the giant Cinerama screen'. Other dates were allocated to normal circuit releases retaining the policy of one evening performance and matinees on Wednesday and Saturday, except for school holidays. The fact that advance booking ceased from 12 January 1974, is an indication of decline, but the cinema survived for a further 5 years, the final performance on 4 August 1979, with the epic disaster film *The Towering Inferno* in 70mm. Shortly afterwards the entire contents of the cinema (a total of 294 lots) was sold by auction.

Within a short time the ground floor was sectioned off for use as a Lennon supermarket. Unfortunately, a proposal to construct two mini cinemas in the former circle did not materialise and the area was unused until 1984, when Coral Leisure Ltd obtained a bingo licence. The Coral Bingo and Social Centre was officially opened by comedian Ken Dodd on 18 October 1984. The building has since been used for similar purposes but by different companies.

1939
Regal
Church Road, Litherland

The interior and exterior of the Regal.

During the 1930s, the district of Litherland, about 4^{1}/$_{2}$ miles north of the city, was the location of a considerable private house building programme. The number of houses increased from 3,700 to 5000 between 1934 and 1939 in the area north of the Leeds & Liverpool Canal. This divided Litherland into two separate areas, with the older properties south of the canal and access between the two by a small, hand-operated, wooden bridge. In the mid-1930s, with the development of the district and increased road traffic, this was replaced by an electrically-operated road lift bridge. The architect, George E Tonge, FRIBA, had designed many entertainment houses, including the Garrick Theatre and Grand Cinema, Southport, one of the most beautiful and palatial provincial cinemas and the Regal was designed on similar lines.

The building was constructed of sand-faced rustic bricks and facings in cream-coloured terracotta, which was used to emphasise the curved corner, and also the lower part of the flanking wall across the width of the building which incorporated a small shop. In the centre of the corner elevation the main entrance was surmounted by an illuminated canopy, above which, a tall fin carried on either side the cinema name in neon lighting, which also outlined this elevation. Flanked by large still frames, the main entrance included on the left, a doorway, leading to a wooden staircase to the first floor company boardroom above the entrance and the projection room. Directly ahead, in the main entrance, three pairs of doors led into the spacious foyer, both areas with a flooring of green and cream terrazzo. Horizontal bands of pastel shades in green and cream, divided by vermilion strips, conveyed a dignified modern effect, enhanced by the principal lighting from a large glass shaded light fitting suspended from the high ceiling.

On the far side of the foyer, opposite the entrance, was the paybox, set into the wall with a front of polished walnut. This area of ceiling was considerably lower than that of the main foyer, and led at either side onto a wide, sweeping corridor, painted in soft buff. Two illuminated showcases were incorporated, intended to be let to local firms to display samples of their goods but were normally used to advertise forthcoming attractions. The corridors curved to give access at the head of a flight of stairs to the sides of the auditorium where a crossover gangway divided the front stalls from the centre and rear.

The auditorium was nearly 100' in length and 75' across at the widest point, at the rear. Seating an audience of 1,100 in two sections, the front stalls stood on a well raked floor, whilst the centre and rear was stepped, ensuring the entire audience a perfect view of the screen. The heavy green and red carpet was also fitted in the corridors. The walls at the front of the auditorium included an exit at either side and curved to the attractive proscenium with partly-festooned, silver-grey curtain. The walls curved up to the ceiling, both textured in peach, overshot with silver, producing a charming sunlit effect, with illumination from four large, glass-shaded light fittings flush to the ceiling. The plain walls were relieved by several artistically-patterned, richly-coloured grilles, and lined with two-inch-thick Gypklith acoustic tiles, adding to the natural effect of the Western Electric Mirrophonic sound system. The provision of backstage dressing rooms made it possible for variety entertainments and concerts to be given if required.

The Regal, at a cost of £30,000, was originally owned by an independent company, Plaza Cinema (Preston) Ltd, who also controlled several cinemas in the Preston and Southport areas. The experienced managing director, JG Johnson, was to be responsible for the film bookings, having been engaged in the business for about 30 years, including 9 years managing the Southport Opera House. A representative gathering of Litherland residents was present for the opening on Monday 12 June 1939, by Councillor J Eaton, JP, Chairman of the Council. The feature film was the Gracie Fields comedy *Keep Smiling*, with full supporting programme shown for 3 days only, there being a change on Thursday to *Algiers*, featuring Charles Boyer and Hedy Lamarr.

Evening performances were continuous from 6.30pm, and a matinee daily at 2.15pm, with admission prices 6d, 9d and 1/- to the front, centre and rear stalls respectively. Although generally considered to be the most attractive and comfortable cinema in the area, the Regal was not in a particularly favourable position with regard to film bookings, being barred from first run films by ABC, GB and the Southan Morris circuit, who controlled the nearby Coliseum, Litherland. This resulted in a mixed selection of films including many of ABC circuit release. In order to keep up with the latest presentation methods, a screen of almost CinemaScope proportions was installed in 1955. Films were advertised as 'On the Panoramic Screen', but when screening films in the old ratio (4:3) this had the disadvantage of a considerable loss of the upper and lower part of the picture.

The Regal was taken over by ABC, who commenced film bookings on 25 July 1955 with *The Love Match*, starring Arthur Askey, with *Invaders from Mars*; a concurrent showing with the company's Gainsborough, Bootle, which was to be the normal policy. The screen proportions were adjusted to normal wide screen, increasing in width via adjustable masking to CinemaScope, which began on 22 August 1955 with *A Star is Born*, featuring Judy Garland and James Mason. ABC introduced continuous performances throughout the day, but during the late-1950s, except for Saturdays and holidays, these were reduced to evenings only.

In the early-1960s attendances continued to decline despite the fact that the only remaining opposition cinemas in the area were the Essoldo, Litherland and the Gaumont, Bootle. The popularity of ten pin bowling, at that time, following the opening by ABC of the Tuebrook Bowl was apparently the reason for the company decision to open a second centre at Litherland. The cinema closed on 28 July 1962 with the double feature *A Cry from the Streets*, with Max Bygraves, and *Inn for Trouble*. During the following 6 months the interior was converted into a luxurious bowling centre with 23 lanes, 11 on the lower, and 12 on the upper floor, with refreshment and licensed bars. The opening of the centre on 26 January 1963 was shown on ABC Television.

The popularity of ten pin bowling declined during the 1960s and ABC disposed of the building, which then became Allinson's Theatre Club with an extension in length to accommodate Wispa's discotheque. These continued to operate until 1984, when, after a period of closure, the building was acquired by a new company, Firehurst Leisure, proprietors of several Liverpool nightclubs. Reopening with the new name, Secrets, it was described as one of Liverpool's plushest nightclubs, with a 1920s-style bar and adjoining disco renamed Clouds. For many years the outside has borne little resemblance to its original attractive appearance as the Regal Cinema, particularly the curved corner, which has had a plain, dark plaster treatment, and is minus the fin and canopy.

1939
Plaza • Odeon • Classic • Cannon • Apollo • Plaza
Crosby Road North, Crosby

The Plaza, 1930s.

This cinema has the unusual distinction of opening and closing on the same day. Opening on 2 September 1939, the outbreak of World War II on the following morning meant that all places of entertainment were closed until further notice by Government order in anticipation of air raids. The Plaza, as it was originally known, was opened by a local company, Crosby Entertainments Ltd. The managing director, Philip M Hanmer, with 17 cinemas under his control, was well known both on the exhibition side of the industry, and as a former chairman of the North Western branch of the Cinematograph Exhibitors Association. The board of directors consisted of Bryce Hanmer, Arthur D Dean, George D Vickers, Ernest Spencer and Ben Cohen. Designed by Lionel AG Prichard, FRIBA of Moorfields, Liverpool, a specialist in cinema design whose projects included the Ritz, Regal and West Derby, Liverpool. The Plaza embodied the most modern ideas in cinema construction, and the architect's plans were skillfully implemented by Ernest Spencer, building contractors of Aintree, specialists in cinema construction.

The imposing modern facade was constructed of golden brown rustic bricks and reconstructed Darley Dale stone dressings, the latter being used to form five tall, panelled architectural features, which at the base included the windows of the first floor balcony lounge, and horizontal lengths at the apex. These features were accentuated by 1,100' of fluorescent tubing in pastel shades of red, blue and green, and a double line of tubing outlined the name Plaza, set high in the centre, with 45" Staybrite steel letters. In the middle, the wide main entrance was surmounted

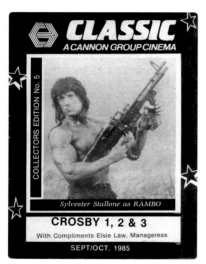

by a canopy with facia of a single row lettering display advertising the current feature film, for which the main advertising was a stills frame and large poster site at either side of the entrance. Covered queueing areas to the front stalls were provided at each side of the entrance, and on the left-hand-side of the building, a spacious free carpark. Extensive neon tubing on the canopy soffitt brilliantly lit up the wide main entrance, in which four pairs of glass-panelled doors gave access to the wide foyer with flooring of red and gold Terrazzo, to tone with the general decorative scheme. Similar treatment was given to the brass-railed, metal balustrade stairways at the extreme sides of the foyer, and also the first floor lounge.

A feature used effectively in the entrance hall was Mirroflex flexible, silvered glass, patented and manufactured by Arthur Holt & Co Ltd, Seaforth, who undertook all the glazing. Concealed lighting was used throughout; in the foyer from lamps within elegantly designed shaded light fittings, and at the rear, a full-width trough illuminated a separate area of the ceiling. At either side of the modern, 1930s-style paybox and kiosk, two pairs of entrance doors in series led to the rear stalls crossover gangway, from which four gangways gave access to 1,000 seats, arranged in three sections across the auditorium. The raked floor gave an uninterrupted view of the screen.

Luxury red plush seats, with padded armrests, were supplied by specialists, CR Harrison & Sons Ltd, Golborne, Lancashire. The first floor lounge extended across the greater part of the frontage, and at the left-hand-side, a short flight of steps led up to the balcony, where a crossover gangway divided the 450 front and rear circle seats. This floor only projected a few feet over the rear stalls, giving a feeling of spaciousness and improving ventilation.

The 52'-wide proscenium was flanked by two plain columns, and in front of the large screen, the draperies consisted of an elaborate proscenium curtain of gold and petunia satin, and a screen curtain in silver satin, illuminated by foot and top batten lighting in four colours. At each side of the proscenium the splayed walls included the front stalls exits with a balconette and patterned grille above. The simple but dignified 1930s Art Deco decor was enhanced by concealed lighting. This was installed in troughs above the proscenium and splayed walls, and also for a short distance along the side walls, and in the panelled features extending from the balcony front. The plain, straight ceiling was relieved by longitudinal designs, which included the ventilation grille and lighting in recessed panels giving a soft glow.

Extending for a short distance above the rear of the balcony, supported by columns, the spacious projection room was equipped with the latest projectors and sound system by BTP. Music lovers were excellently catered for by the installation of a Melotone Compton organ, the only cinema organ between Liverpool and Southport. This modern organ had the full range and volume of a cathedral organ and could also produce the effect of a symphony orchestra or the vivid rhythm of a dance band. To correct the information in *The Dream Palaces of Liverpool* (1987), the console was in a fixed position in the centre, with the top at stage height. The resident organist, George Dawson, was reputed to be one of the best in the North of England. On a number of occasions he had broadcast from the Albert Hall, Sheffield, and had held resident appointments at the Gaumont Palace and the Broadway super-cinema, Hammersmith, relinquishing his position at the former to take up his engagement at the Plaza.

The resident manager, William Gandy, had considerable experience in the business, having been in charge of various theatres under the same direction as the Plaza. As well as his widespread cinema interests, the managing director of the company, Phillip M Hanmer, was a member of the Waterloo Hospital Board of Management, which prompted him to ensure that all those attending the opening night paid a donation to the hospital. They could secure their seats for a minimum donation at 1/6, 2/6 and 3/6 for the front stalls, rear stalls and balcony respectively.

Advertised as Crosby's Luxury theatre, the Plaza was officially opened at 8.30pm on 2 September 1939 by the Mayor of Crosby, Alderman Herbert Williams, JP. The entire proceeds were donated to the hospital for x-ray equipment and better nursing accommodation. The capacity audience put war worries behind them as they settled down to enjoy, *A Farmyard Symphony*, a Walt Disney cartoon, the latest *GB News*, George Dawson at the Compton organ and *South Riding*, starring Edna Best and Ralph Richardson.

On the following day came the announcement of the outbreak of World War II, resulting in the closure, for about 2 weeks, of all places of entertainment throughout the country. The Plaza then reopened on 18 September with *The Count of Monte Cristo*, featuring Robert Donat. Performances consisted of a matinee daily at 2pm and continuous in the evening from 5.45pm to 10pm. Although with the advantage of a modern luxury cinema in competition with several far older cinemas in the area, during the first 3 years as an independent, the position with regard to bookings was not very favourable. ABC and GB were both being represented in the district at the Regent and the Corona, Crosby, respectively. The Plaza was therefore barred from screening first runs in the district of many leading films. The problem was later relieved by the inclusion of Odeon circuit release films. Then in mid-1943, the cinema was acquired by the Odeon circuit, whose release films, usually for 6 days, brought formidable competition to the long established circuit cinemas. The name 'Plaza' was retained until June 1945.

The stage was brought into use, with occasional live entertainment in addition to the film programme, for the first time in January 1947, when Blackpool organist Reginald Dixon was engaged to play the Compton organ for a national talent competition entitled 'Starlight Serenade'. Also during the late-1940s, famous artists of stage and radio, Arthur Askey, Tommy Handley and Hilda Baker appeared at the Odeon. Live entertainment in the 1950s began on 2 July, with a Celebrity Concert in aid of the Bootle Police Benevolent Fund. The musical programme consisted of: Walter Midgley, a tenor direct from his huge success at Covent Garden; Olive Groves, a frequent radio soloist, and the Jack Byfield Trio.

In the early-1950s the Odeon's manager, WA Howarth, was succeeded by Kenneth Lloyd, one of the company's top showmen, and during his time there, until taking over the Odeon in Southport, one of the highspots was Queen Elizabeth's Coronation. On Coronation Day, 11 June 1953, the doors were opened at 9.45am to admit, free of charge, local pensioners and the blind to hear a broadcast relay of the ceremony. During the following week, ending 20 June, 40,000 people watched the film of the Coronation, *A Queen is Crowned*. Nearly 2 years later the screen was replaced by a much wider one for CinemaScope, on which the first feature film, *Sign of the Pagan*, starring Jeff Chandler and Jack Palance, was screened on 7 March 1955 for 6 days.

The Odeon continued to be the best attended of the district cinemas, against strong opposition only from ABC Regent, Crosby, but a reduction in opening hours was put into effect in July 1965, with afternoon performances on Monday, Wednesday and Saturday only. The Rank Organisation relinquished control on 10 December 1967, when the cinema was taken over by the Classic cinema circuit, and the name was changed accordingly.

The Classic continued to be a single-screen cinema for almost 9 years then, in June 1976, work began on the expensive conversion to a triple. A mini cinema with 100 seats was constructed at either side of the stalls, each with a projection room equipped with a Westar projector, Westrex sound system, and Westrex Tower long running film projection system. These auditoria were styled as Classics 2 and 3, whilst the central area of the stalls and the balcony, with a total of 670 seats, formed the Number 1 cinema, served by the original projection room with Gaumont Kalee Duosonic projectors and Westrex sound.

The Classic triple had a gala opening on Friday 6 August 1976, when at 2.30pm there was a procession from the cinema, a jazz band, the Classic Junior Morris Dancers, the real *Chitty Chitty Bang Bang* car and the dinosaur from *One of Our Dinosaurs is Missing* and from 3.30pm it was open house at the cinemas. The first film was shown at 4.30pm and the opening attractions consisted of, on Screen 1: *One of Our Dinosaurs is Missing*, on Screen 2, *Gone with the Wind*, and *Young Frankenstein*, and *John and Mary* on Screen 3. The Classic circuit came within the Cannon group in May 1983, resulting in a further change of name to the Cannon.

Seven years later the company announced its intention to close, since its interest lay in multi-screen cinemas. A campaign to save it was launched by cinema enthusiast Janet Dunn, who set up a special committee and organised a petition which was signed by thousands of local people. Although this did not change Canon's decision to close the cinema, it was saved in March 1990, having been bought by Apollo Leisure Ltd, by whom film bookings were continued from 30 March, and it was then known as the Apollo.

The opening films were *The Rescuers*, *War of the Roses*, *Steel Magnolias* and *Always*. The ambitious £750,000 redesign and expansion plans, announced by the Apollo group in October 1991, unfortunately did not materialise. In the Autumn of 1995 they stated their intention to sell the property to a developer for demolition and replacement by DSS offices. Then Janet Dunn began a second campaign to save the cinema and she formed the Crosby Community Cinema Committee. Various fund-raising activities were instituted, including a local charity shop, in an

Inside the Plaza, Crosby.

attempt to raise £300,000 to buy the building and site by the end of 1996 but the cinema was saved only by the strength of local opposition, indicated by a 10,000 signature petition. The council refused planning permission for redevelopment, and although the CCCC were then given first refusal to purchase of the building, time for fundraising was too short and the Apollo announced closure on 7 November.

The building's future as a cinema was then only secured by the negotiation of an 18 month lease with new owners, Derwent Lodge Estates, after which, during the summer of 1997, campaigners and volunteers raced against time to finish the massive task of cleaning and redecoration in time for the reopening of the main auditorium on 18 July. This consisted of the lower floor with 200 reupholstered seats, and the balcony with approximately 400 seats. The former projection equipment having been removed, a new Philips projector and platter cakestand long running projection system had to be bought. Discerning patrons were impressed by the amazing sound quality of the DTS digital system. After over 50 years of ownership by major circuits, the cinema's original name, the Plaza, was reinstated on 18 July 1997, when it was officially reopened by Crosby Labour MP, Claire Curtis-Thomas. Many invited guests attended the 8pm performance of Steven Spielberg's monster movie *The Lost World*.

A month later, on 15 August, after considerable refurbishment, comfortably reseated to a capacity of over 70, a second auditorium reopened with *Speed 2 – Cruise Control,* concurrently with nationwide release. The elimination of curtains provided for the installation of the widest possible screen, and except for digital sound, similar equipment to that of Number 1 was installed.

The Plaza regained its former status as a triple-screen cinema on 13 February 1998, with the new release, *Paws,* in the other mini auditorium, with similar projection equipment and screen. Ninety reupholstered and seats in two sections were installed between a central gangway.

The Plaza's diamond jubilee was celebrated on 2 September 1999 with a night of nostalgia, attracting a capacity audience of 600. Volunteer staff dressed in period costume to sell refreshments, and a commissionaire paraded in the foyer. The performance began with the return of David Nicholas, resident organist at the Philharmonic Hall in Liverpool, who played the original Compton organ at the Crosby cinema in the late-1950s and 1960s. For this performance he played music from the golden age of the cinema organ, on an instrument loaned by Rushworth's music store in Liverpool, to create an authentic atmosphere. The vice-chairperson, Jean Plant, was thanked, as well as all concerned for their great efforts in the restoration and reopening of the Plaza. Chairperson, Janet Dunn introduced the Deputy Mayor of Crosby, Councillor Paul McVey, who launched an appeal for funds to purchase the cinema at a cost of £325,000, which elicited a generous response. The programme included one of the Look at Life series, *The Cinema Steps Out*, which illustrated the great change in cinemas of the 1960s as well as vintage trailers and advertisements. The main feature was David Lean's classic 1945 love story, *Brief Encounter*.

Later in 1999, the owners of the building advised that the option to purchase would end on 16 January 2000, by which time the lessees would be required to buy or vacate it. Only 3 days before the deadline, the situation was saved by an award of £66,500, by the Esmee Fairbairn Trust, a charitable group which distributes funds to worthy causes throughout the country, achieved by a last gasp telephone call to the charity by Janet Dunn. At the time, the company only had about £140,000 from the council and about £9,000 from local fundraising. The bank then loaned £60,000 until a similar amount arrived from the charity's aid foundation.

So, on 13 January 2000, after months of uncertainty and frantic fundraising, Crosby Community Cinema exercised their option to buy the building. Since then the company have bid for Capital 2 Lottery money from the North West Arts Board, to significantly improve the cinema's facilities.

1955
Albany • Astra Entertainment Centre
Northway, Maghull

Due to building restrictions imposed during World War II, the Albany was the first new cinema to be opened in the Liverpool area for 16 years, in a location where previously there had been no cinema. The £100,000 enterprise was promoted by Maghull Cinemas Ltd, a private company with offices in Liverpool. They were closely associated with the Leslie Blond Group which controlled several North West cinemas, including the then newly-opened Phoenix, Wallasey, upon which Alexander Webber, ARIBA based the planning of the Albany. The company was also responsible for the building of many private houses in Maghull and received congratulations for providing entertainment for the residents.

The frontage was mainly of rustic brick, relieved at the windowless upper level by narrow, vertical, stone sections, also forming the coping. The lower part included the main entrance in the centre, with a large display window at either side. Three pairs of doors opened into the spacious foyer, with the central paybox adjacent to the opposite wall. On the left-hand-side, a rare amenity was the refreshment buffet, where patrons could obtain tea and coffee in addition to the normal cinema kiosk items.

The Astra Entertainment Centre, 1980s.

The Albany was described as a cinema of surprises, although the ideas were considered most practical, and on entering, the first of these was the siting of the manager's office between the foyer and the rear of the auditorium, providing the occupant with a one way view into both areas. At either side of the paybox, doors led onto a short corridor at the end of which were entrances to the rear of the stadium-type auditorium. Ahead of these a gangway divided the staggered seating into three sections. The seats, with Dunlopillo upholstery, were Royal blue with standards in gold, fitted to the flooring with a rake of 1:14. The auditorium being 150' by 70', there was no difficulty in placing 1,400 seats, even allowing for a clearance of 2'9" between rows.

This was one of the few cinemas which did not have a proscenium, the directors having provided, in the mid-1950s, for the distant future when it might be necessary to have space for the picture to be partly spread around the walls. In later years, the reverse proved to be the case, but at that time the aim was to achieve the largest possible CinemaScope screen, 47' in width, which could be varied by telescopic masking down to 34' for normal format films. The metallic screen gave improved reflectivity, whereas previously screens were rubberised, and in the interests of sound realism, loud speakers were placed in the closest proximity. Experts were called in to deal with the issue of perfect acoustics, trying to break up the sound so it did not reverberate against the walls. This was achieved by installing ceiling covers of special acoustic plaster in nine slanting sections across the curved ceiling, breaking up the sound before it reached the listener. This also provided nine recesses for concealed lighting. Emergency lighting was confined to the walls, concealed in glass shades. Also in the interests of acoustics, there was special expensive wallpaper in wine and gold.

There was a quite well-proportioned stage about 8' deep, fitted more for the reason that it was expected in an up-to-date cinema rather than for the presentation of theatrical performances, but no proscenium. Adorning the stage, the wine-coloured drapes and screen curtains in old gold, blended with the general decoration, which was enhanced by the Hollophane lighting system, by which a varied range of mingling colours could be operated from the projection room over the foyer, bestowing on the interior the effects of a passing rainbow.

The somewhat experimental and revolutionary heating system was the brainchild of managing director, Leslie

Blond; warm air being supplied from the roof downwards, in the hope that this would eliminate the common complaint of cold feet. There was a spacious, self-contained operating suite above the foyer, with access to a flat roof behind the frontage, equipped with two GB Kalee 21 projectors, which, like the sound and associated equipment was supplied by the J Arthur Rank Organisation. Patrons were well catered for in bad weather, for, in addition to the foyer with room for about 400 people, sheltered areas along the sides of the building were enclosed. The large area of land around the building became a carpark for about 200 cars.

In the presence of a large gathering of invited guests, the Albany cinema was officially opened on the evening of Wednesday 28 September 1955, by Douglas Glover, MP for Ormskirk. The film chosen for the occasion ideally demonstrated the effectiveness of the 47'-wide screen: the 20th Century-Fox CinemaScope picture, *There's No Business Like Show Business*, shown in De Luxe colour with star cast including Ethel Merman, Donald O'Connor, Marilyn Monroe and Dan Dailey. The company was granted a 6 days only licence to William Ronald Bremble, stating that there would be a continuous performance Monday to Saturday from 6pm to 10.30pm, with admission prices: 1/3, 1/10 and 2/4. On the following Saturday, the first children's matinee at 2.30pm featured *Texas Terror,* starring John Wayne, supported by two serials and a cartoon, with admission at 7d, 9d and1/-.

A Sunday licence was not granted until 15 April 1956, when the first programme of old films for Sunday only was shown once from 8pm. Despite the expertise that went into the planning of the Albany and the fact that it was quite far from any other suburban cinema, it did not attract anything like the anticipated number of patrons, and by the end of the 1950s, the large capacity was significantly in excess of requirements.

Surviving for nearly 20 years as a single screen cinema, it was more or less restricted to continuous evening performances with film bookings of ABC and Rank release following the showings at the circuit suburban cinemas. However, with one of the largest CinemaScope screens on Merseyside, it was eminently suitable for the presentation of epics and big musicals such as *The Sound of Music* and *South Pacific* during the 1960s. Having been taken over by the Hutchinson Leisure Group of Burnley, the last performance at the Albany as a single screen cinema was on Saturday 1 February 1975, with a double feature consisting of *Enter the Dragon* starring Bruce Lee, and *King Boxer*.

Work then began on the construction of two mini cinemas, each with 193 seats side by side in the rear half of the auditorium, whilst the front part was converted into a bingo hall with a separate entrance via a long corridor from the new entrance at the right of the frontage. The two GB Kalee 21s were replaced by a Westar projector and Tower long-running film system for each auditorium which were approximately half the length of the original with appropriate reduction in picture size.

Reopened on 5 June 1975 as the Astra Entertainment Centre, there was room for about 500 for Surewin Bingo. Cine 1 screened *Man About the House* and *The Best of Benny Hill,* at one performance from 7pm; in Cine 2 was *Freebie and the Bean* with supporting shorts at 7.30pm. With the exception of the following week, when the cinemas were open continuously throughout the day, the Astra reverted to evenings only, except in school holidays.

After a further 6 years, the bingo section was closed due to falling demand. The company then confirmed its faith in the future of cinema by building two more cinemas, each with a capacity of about 300, in the old bingo hall. At a cost of £100,000 – the entire cost of construction in 1955 – the interior was completely refurbished and recarpeted. At the rear of the new auditoria the projection room was fitted with equipment similar to that of cinemas 1 and 2, and the entire work was completed without closure.

The Grand Opening of Cines 3 and 4 took place on 20 December 1981, with *Assault on Precinct 13* and *Halloween* in Number 3, and in Number 4 *One Flew Over the Cuckoo's Nest.* The Astra came under the ownership of the Apollo Leisure group in June 1986, but little more than 2 years later, the company stated that it was no longer viable despite an increase in takings, and there was a 700-strong petition to keep it open. It was operated by that company for almost 9 years until closure on 27 April 1995, when it then lay unused. Planning permission for conversion to a supermarket was refused mid-1997, but granted in 1988, and the cinema was demolished to make way for it.

1956
Gaumont • Odeon
Stanley Road, Bootle

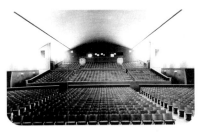

The exterior and interior of the
Gaumont, 1950s.

The Gaumont was erected on the site of the old Broadway cinema, the interior of which was destroyed during an air raid in May 1941. Costing £120,000, it was part of a £1m rebuilding programme by the Rank Organisation. Although after the war many attempts were made to obtain permission to rebuild it, this was not granted until 1955.

Due to the deteriorating condition of the remaining frontage and walls, these were demolished to make way for a completely new theatre. The method of construction was a big departure from normal practice, being in the form of a huge, reinforced, concrete barrel vault, the first of its type in the country. The long, low, windowless frontage was principally of dark, rustic brick relieved by the stone and faience tiles of the lower part, with the Gaumont neon sign at the upper left-hand-side. Bordered by grey stone, the wide main entrance had a canopy illuminated by neon tubes with the cinema name on the facia, along with two streamer advertising displays, angled to left and right with details of the current programme. The soffit of the canopy included numerous circular recesses containing electric bulbs lighting the approach to the main entrance. This was flanked on either side by a recessed area of faience tiles in a maroon and white striped pattern, which extended with the stonework above a base of black tiles.

The entrance was supported by two circular stone columns with illumination from the ceiling similar to that of the canopy. The paybox in the centre was flanked by two pairs of frameless doors to the foyer in crimson relieved by blue, a cheerful space, with a clean uncluttered design. In this area, adjacent to the wall opposite the entrance, the bright confectionery kiosk was panelled in sapele and Indian laurel, with lighting from three long electric fittings hanging from the ceiling, each with shaded electric lamps at various levels.

From the foyer, a short flight of stairs rose to the rear of the upper floor of the auditorium. Corridors led to the stalls at either side, where a crossover gangway with wooden partitions divided the two seating areas. There were

1,350 of the latest type of seat, upholstered in rust moquette, on the raked stalls floor and stepped upper floor, styled as the front and rear balcony, and separated by a crossover gangway. Simplicity and modernity were the two immediate impressions gained on entering the auditorium. The red and blue colour scheme, with deep red carpeting, created a most pleasing, warm and comfortable atmosphere. Soft, diffused lighting came from a row of metal, bowl-shaped shades, set at an angle, each throwing light forward to the front of the auditorium and to ensure perfect sound reproduction, the side walls and ceiling were lined with special acoustic tiling.

The proscenium, adorned by a gold curtain with patterned relief, enclosed a revolutionary, high definition CinemaScope screen, 50' wide, the side masking of which could be adjusted for films of lesser width such as wide screen and normal ratio, by a remote control system in the projection room. This was said to be the last word in technical equipment and included a pair of GB Kalee 21 projectors costing around £3,000. Thermostatically-controlled ventilation and heating systems, the latter oil-fired and believed to be the only one of its type in the Liverpool area, provided an even temperature at all times. Selected seats on both floors had plug-in sockets for the latest type of hearing aid device and there was parking next to the theatre.

Under E Larrosa, former manager of the Cameo, Liverpool, a well known figure in the local entertainment world, the Gaumont began its rather short life as a cinema on 23 January 1956. There was a gala opening by the Mayor of Bootle, Alderman TA Cain, and personal appearance by film star, Anthony Steele. The opening ceremony at 6.15pm was followed by a programme consisting of *Simon and Laura*, with Kay Kendall and Peter Finch and *Running Wild* starring William Campbell. Performances thereafter were continuous throughout the day, except Sundays, when the opening time was 4pm. Admission prices were: 1/6 and 1/10 to the stalls, whilst at the rear of the auditorium, at a higher level, styled as the balcony, the seat prices were 2/4 and 3/-. Film bookings were first suburban showings of Rank release films to the GB circuit, and the theatre was among the better attended in the suburbs for several years.

The major wave of name changes to Odeon started in 1952, when the practice of separate film release to the GB circuit came to an end, at Bootle on 26 April 1964. By this time, even the leading cinemas were poorly attended, resulting, from July 1965, in a reduction in opening hours at the Odeon to continuous in the evenings only on Tuesday, Thursday and Friday. The Odeon continued in this way until the more drastic reduction from 1 July 1974, when the cinema was closed every Tuesday and Wednesday, except in school holidays. The Odeon was finally closed the following year, the last performance being on 1 November 1975 with *Shampoo*, starring Warren Beatty and Shirley MacLaine. The auditorium was then used for a short time as a skateboard park, and in 1982, the property was acquired by Golden Leisure Ltd for conversion into a snooker centre. With appropriate internal conversion and considerable restyling of the frontage, it reopened in 1996 as a licensed house named Qudos.

1975
Studios 1, 2 and 3 • Ritz • 051 Cinema
Brownlow Hill, Liverpool city centre

The triple-screen cinema were part of a £1.4m entertainment centre, which included a Hofbrauhaus Bavarian Beer Hall and Scamps discotheque. Developed by the Star group in 1975, who at that time operated a nationwide chain of 140 cinemas, and also beer halls, discotheques and restaurants in addition to three other entertainment centres. The building was erected at the corner of Brownlow Hill and Mount Pleasant, on a site formerly occupied by the Mardi Gras night club. The architects were Gillinson, Barrett and Partners, Leeds, and the principal contractor was Holland, Hannen and Cubitts of Bromborough, Wirral.

The plain exterior of dark brickwork relieved by tiles, featured a tall tower at the junction of the two roads. Mounted high on this was an internally-lit display sign advertising the current films. From the Mount Pleasant frontage an external turning stairway led up to the main entrance, in which two pairs of doors gave access to the small carpeted foyer with paybox and sales kiosk along the right-hand-side and entrances to the cinemas on the left. Seating in Auditorium 1 was for 215, in Auditorium 2 for 130 and in 3 for 140. They were very basic, minus screen curtains, stage, or proscenium. The black screen masking was bordered by the splayed side walls at either side, and below was a slope from the front crossover gangway, whilst screen illumination during intervals was by spotlights mounted on the side walls.

The press stated that the cinemas reflected the clean, modern lines of the 1970s, with the emphasis on comfortable seating and bold colour schemes. Projection equipment consisted of Westrex 7000 projectors, Westrex sound and Towers long running system. In charge of the studios at the opening, Arthur Cullimore had gained considerable experience at Star Quintuple Centres in Manchester and Chorley. Advertised as 'Liverpool's New Entertainment Centre and New 3-screen Scene', Studios 1, 2 and 3 opened on the evening of 9 October 1975. The double features were: *Confessions of A Window Cleaner* and *Blazing Saddles* on Screen 1; *Emmanuelle* and *Secrets of A Door to Door Salesman* on Screen 2 and *The Legend of Bruce Lee* on Screen 3.

The Star circuit stated its intention to offer a contrasting choice of programmes continuous from 2pm Monday to Saturday, and from 4pm on Sundays, but with ABC and Rank cinemas in the city, the new cinemas were disadvantaged having no first runs of the leading films. To provide an alternative, an increasing number of adult, X-certificate films were shown. By September 1984, all programmes comprised of this type of film at an admission price of £2.50. This policy was continued until February 1985, when the lease was assigned to Dinoheath Ltd, a company owned by Anne Robertson Devlin, Rik Prowse and Robin Price.

The new owners began a major refurbishment of the cinemas at a cost of several thousand pounds. Part of the move to present a new image was the change of name to the Ritz. A new film booking policy was introduced to include the very best British, European and American art films not previously shown in Liverpool, whilst Screen 1 was to specialise in extending the city runs of the more successful films, following their termination at the ABC and Odeon. The cinemas closed as the Studios on 9 February 1985. They reopened as the Ritz on 11 February, with continuous performances of *The Missioners* and *Privates on Parade* on Screen 1, *Swann in Love* on 2, and *The World is Full of Married Men* and *The Story of Linda* on 3. Despite the fact that admission prices were below the city average, adults paid £1.80, and concessions were £1 until 4pm Monday to Friday, when there was a further reduction to 50p for children, senior citizens and UB40 holders. After only 6 months, the reduction to only 75p for all performances was an indication of declining admissions.

Dinoheath Ltd operated the cinemas for a further 2 years until 11 March 1988, when it closed for 3 weeks and the lease was taken over by two employees, T Cartwright, the chief projectionist, and Mrs J Johnstone, who formed Run Trend Ltd. They invested £8,000 in reseating and redecorating the foyer, including new light fittings.

Ritz 1, 2 and 3 reopened on 4 April 1988 with three performances of *The Aristocats*, followed by *Robocop* in Studio 1. *Teenwolf* and *Wish You Were Here* were shown in Studio 2, whilst Studio 3 presented adult movies from noon until 7.50pm, as well as one showing of *Housekeeping*, a PG film, at 8pm. All seats were £1.50, concessions £1. Despite the improvements, this proved to be the shortest period during which the cinema was open. After only 4 months, the lease was suddenly terminated, followed by closure on 25 August 1988, with continuous performances from 1pm of *The Jungle Book* and *Vice Versa*. A continuous performance of adult movies from noon to 7.45pm, was followed by *The Exorcist* at 8.15pm.

The cinemas were closed until early in 1991, then taken over by London-based Robins Cinemas. They had become aware of the local outcry at the closure of the 051, mainly from Liverpool's then expanding student population, with added concern that an independent cinema remained to show films not booked by the major circuits. The new manager, Adrian Kai, formerly with the Bluecoat Chambers-based Merseyside Arts marketing consortium, considered this remarkable in a city with strong artistic traditions, so well provided with every other form of entertainment. A multi-thousand pound refurbishment included new seating and a new sound system. Retaining the name 051, the company stated that the policy was to show new release and rerun independent films together with quality mainstream films, for a regular full price of £3 and reduced price of £1.99 for concessions and all day Monday.

The film attractions for the opening on 15 October 1993 consisted of Ken Loach's new film, *Raining Stones*, with ex-*Brookside* actor Ricky Tomlinson, on Screen 1; the futuristic, sub-titled Spanish satire *Accion Mutante*, on Screen 2 and Quentin Tarantino's cult offering, *Reservoir Dogs*, on Screen 3. Despite previous indications of demand, continuing losses resulted in the withdrawal of Robins Cinemas and closure on 19 October 1995. In the following month an agreement was reached between the staff and the landlord, that, in return for a share of the profits, they could run the cinema rent free.

Still known as 'The 051, the home of unusual films', it opened for the last time on 17 November 1995, with two evening performances of *La Separation*, *The Silences of the Palace* and *Gunhed*. At this time the admission price was £3.50, with concessions at £2.50. Matinee performances at 3pm were added on Wednesdays from 6 December 1995 and also on Sundays from 14 July 1996. This policy of operation continued until final closure on 25 September 1997. The night club, also called the 051, closed recently.

Following the opening in 1975 of Studios 1, 2 and 3 in the city centre, there were no further cinema openings in the Liverpool area for over 24 years, by which time cinemas were never again to bear any resemblance to their forerunners. During this period there were conversions of three 1930s super-cinemas: the Odeon, Liverpool, twinned in 1968-69, later increased to four, five, then ten auditoria; the Classic, Crosby, tripled in 1976, and the ABC, Liverpool, also tripled in 1982. Although adding to the choice of films, the advantage in this respect was considerably diminished by a completely new style of single-storied building, the multiplex, in most situations providing between eight and twelve auditoria. The first of these in Britain, named 'The Point' due to its eye-catching pyramid structure, with ten auditoria, opened at Milton Keynes on 29 November 1985. It was a £10m joint development by Bass Leisure and American Multi Cinemas Incorporated.

The number of multi-screen cinemas thereafter increased to 21 by 1989. This included Liverpool's first multiplex, the 12-screen Showcase Cinema, East Lancashire Road, Norris Green, which opened on 13 December 1989. The climate-controlled auditoria offered relaxation in the comfort of seats described as rocking-chair loungers. Being on one floor they provided easy disabled access and were also fitted with a sound system for the hard of hearing. State-of-the-art film presentation included Dolby and THX stereo sound. Each projector was fitted with the long-running cakestand platter system, eliminating the previous necessity of rewinding. A large floodlit carpark provided an important amenity in this out of town location, near the M57 motorway. Access to all auditoria was from a spacious foyer, preventing outside queueing.

Liverpool's second multiplex opened on 30 August 1991. It was the latest of the 143 cinemas operated nationally by Metro Goldwyn Mayer. About 2 miles from the city centre, the building is in the heart of a retail park, which also offers a choice of eating places, large DIY stores, garden centre, bowling alley and free parking. The spacious foyer with large attractive sales kiosk, leads into the eight auditoria, with luxury seating varying in number from 200 to 400. A festoon curtain rises and falls over the 25' to 36' screens.

The latest sound projection technology included the advanced Bose speaker system providing unrivalled sound quality. It also boasted a computerised booking system and the Hard of Hearing Loop System, by which patrons using hearing aids could tune in to the telephone frequency, enabling them to hear the film soundtrack with ample volume and clarity. Credit Lyonnais reluctantly became the new owners in 1992 when they foreclosed on the Italian financier, Giancarlo Paretti, who then controlled MGM.

Richard Branson's Virgin group became Britain's biggest cinema owner in 1995, a deal giving them control of the MGM chain of 166 cinemas, including the Liverpool multiplex, which became known as Virgin Cinemas in July 1996. Since the end of March 2000, this multiplex has been under the control of the UGC group of cinemas. The foregoing provides an appropriate end to this history of Liverpool cinemas, now not far from 100 years since the opening of the city's first, the Aigburth Assembly Picturedrome, in 1906.

Index

A

ABC (Plaza • Gaumont • Odeon • Classic • Cannon), Allerton **123**

ABC (Forum • Cannon • ABC), Liverpool city centre **140**

ABC (Carlton Theatre), Tuebrook **150**

Abbey, Wavertree **176**

Adelphi Picture Palace (New Adelphi Cinema), Liverpool city centre **32**

Aigburth Assembly Picturedrome (Rivoli Theatre • Rivoli Cinema), Aigburth **8**

Albany (Astra Entertainment Centre), Maghull **185**

Alhambra (Electra Palace • London Road Picture House • King's Picture House • Essoldo • Curzon Club Cinema • Tatler Club Cinema • Classic • Eros Club Cinema), Liverpool city centre **30**

Apollo (Plaza • Odeon • Classic • Cannon), Crosby **181**

Apollo Theatre (Winter Gardens Theatre), Bootle **19**

Astoria (ABC), Walton **131**

Astra Entertainment Centre (Albany), Maghull **185**

Atlas Cinema (Rice Lane Picture House), Walton **65**

Avenue Cinema (Tunnel Road Picturedrome), Edge Hill **69**

B

Bedford Hall (Bedford Cinema), Walton **17**

Belmont Picture House (Lido Cinema), Anfield **63**

Beresford Cinema, Dingle **90**

Bijou Theatre (New Pavilion • Bijou Electric Palace • Bijou Cinema), Waterloo **20**

Bootle Picture Palace (Palace Cinema), Bootle **46**

Broadway Cinema (Picture House), Bootle **35**

Burlington Cinema, Vauxhall **113**

C

Cabbage Hall Picture House, Anfield **58**

Cameo Cinema, Wavertree **112**

Cannon (Odeon • Classic • Apollo • Plaza), Crosby **181**

Cannon (ABC • Forum • ABC), Liverpool city centre **140**

Capitol Cinema, Edge Hill **129**

Carlton Cinema, Orrell Park **134**

Carlton Theatre (ABC), Tuebrook **150**

Casino Cinema, Kensington **103**

Century Cinema (Mount Pleasant Hall), Liverpool city centre **10**

City Picture House (Lime Street Picture House • Futurist Cinema), Liverpool city centre **40**

Classic (Plaza • Gaumont • Odeon • Cannon • ABC), Allerton **123**

Classic (Plaza • Odeon • Cannon • Apollo • Plaza), Crosby **181**

Classic (Electra Palace • London Road Picture House • Alhambra • King's Picture House • Essoldo • Curzon Club Cinema • Tatler Club Cinema • Eros Club Cinema), Liverpool city centre **30**

Clubmoor Picture House **109**

Coliseum Cinema, Walton **100**

Coliseum Picture House (Essoldo), Litherland **88**

Coliseum Picturedrome (New Coliseum), Paddington **23**

Commodore, Bankhall **135**

Corona Cinema, Great Crosby **79**

Cosy Cinema (Graphic Cinema), Kensington **96**

Crosby Picture House **58**

Curzon Club Cinema (Electra Palace • London Road Picture House • Alhambra • King's Picture House • Essoldo • Tatler Club Cinema • Classic • Eros Club Cinema), Liverpool city centre **30**

Curzon Theatre, Old Swan **165**

D

Derby Picturedrome (Derby Cinema), Liverpool city centre **45**

Dingle Picturedrome, Dingle **49**

Doric Cinema (Westminster Hall), Kirkdale **18**

E

Electra Palace (London Road Picture House • Alhambra • King's Picture House • Essoldo • Curzon Club Cinema • Tatler Club Cinema • Classic • Eros Club Cinema), Liverpool city centre **30**

Electric Picture Palace, Litherland **25**

Empire, Garston **72**

Empire Picture Theatre (Picture Palace of Bootle), Bootle **9**

Empress Picture House, Tuebrook **71**

Eros Club Cinema (Electra Palace • London Road Picture House • Alhambra • King's Picture House • Essoldo • Curzon Club Cinema • Tatler Club Cinema • Classic), Liverpool city centre **30**

Essoldo (Coliseum Picture House), Litherland **88**

Essoldo (Electra Palace • London Road Picture House • Alhambra • King's Picture House • Curzon Club Cinema • Tatler Club Cinema • Classic • Eros Club Cinema), Liverpool city centre **30**

Essoldo (Victoria), Anfield **104**

Everton Electric Palace (Everton Palace) **44**

Everyman Cinema (Hope Hall Cinema), Liverpool city centre **51**

F

Forum (ABC • Cannon • ABC), Liverpool city centre **140**

Futurist Cinema (Lime Street Picture House • City Picture House), Liverpool city centre **40**

G

Gaiety Cinema, Liverpool city centre **57**

Gainsborough, Bootle **91**

Gala International Film Theatre (Liverpool Picture House • Prince of Wales • Liverpool News Theatre • Jacey Film Theatre), Liverpool city centre **47**

Garrick, Kirkdale **74**

Garston Picture Palace (Wellington Picture Palace) **24**

Garston Picturedrome (Rink Cinema) **25**

Gaumont (Plaza • Odeon • Classic • Cannon • ABC), Allerton **123**

Gaumont (Odeon), Bootle **187**

Gaumont, Dingle **167**

Gaumont (Trocadero), Liverpool city centre **93**

Gaumont Palace (King's Hall • Gaumont), Anfield **148**

Gem Cinema, Everton **114**

Granada, Dovecot **153**

Granby Cinema (Prince's Cinema), Toxteth **45**

Grand, Wavertree **59**

Grand Tivoli (Tivoli Palace • Palais de Luxe), Liverpool city centre **11**

Graphic Cinema (Cosy Cinema), Kensington **96**

Grosvenor Picture House, Kirkdale **97**

H

Hippodrome Cinema (Royal Hippodrome Theatre), Tuebrook **143**

Homer Cinema, Everton **68**

Hope Hall Cinema (Everyman Cinema), Liverpool city centre **51**

I

Imperial Cinema (Sun Hall), Bootle **28**

J

Jacey Film Theatre (Liverpool Picture House • Prince of Wales • Liverpool News Theatre • Gala International Film Theatre), Liverpool city centre **47**

K

Kensington Picturedrome (Kensington Cinema) 26

King's Picture House (Electra Palace • London Road Picture House • Alhambra • Essoldo • Curzon Club Cinema • Tatler Club Cinema • Classic • Eros Club Cinema), Liverpool city centre 30

King's Hall Cinema (Gaumont Palace • Gaumont), Anfield 148

L

Lathom Hall Picture Palace, Seaforth 34

Lido Cinema (Belmont Picture House), Anfield 63

Lime Street Picture House (City Picture House • Futurist Cinema), Liverpool city centre 40

Liverpool Picture House (Prince of Wales • Liverpool News Theatre • Gala International Film Theatre • Jacey Film Theatre), Liverpool city centre 47

London Road Picture House (Electra Palace • Alhambra • King's Picture House • Essoldo • Curzon Club Cinema • Tatler Club Cinema • Classic • Eros Club Cinema), Liverpool city centre 30

Lyceum Cinema (Lyseum Talkie Theatre), Garston 101

Lytton Cinema (Prince's Picture Palace • Prince's Picturedrome • Prince's Picture Hall), Everton 32

M

Magnet Cinema, Wavertree 68

Majestic Cinema, Liverpool city centre 173

Majestic Picture House, Liverpool city centre 66

Mayfair, Aigburth 169

Mayfair, Huyton 171

Mere Lane Picture House, Anfield 79

Metropole Theatre (Metropole), Bootle 146

Moulton Picture Palace (Tivoli Cinema), Everton 24

Mount Pleasant Hall (Century Cinema), Liverpool city centre 10

N

New Picture Hall (Waterloo Picture Playhouse • Winter Gardens Cinema), Waterloo 20

New Pavilion (Bijou Theatre • Bijou Electric Palace • Bijou Cinema), Waterloo 20

New Premier Picturedrome, Old Swan 52

New Prince's Theatre (Strand Cinema), Bootle 38

New Regent, Old Swan 175

O

051 Cinema (Studios 1, 2, 3 • Ritz), Liverpool city centre 188

Odeon (Plaza • Gaumont • Classic • Cannon • ABC), Allerton 123

Odeon (Gaumont), Bootle 187

Odeon (Plaza • Classic • Cannon • Apollo • Plaza), Crosby 181

Odeon (Paramount), Liverpool city centre 160

Olympia Theatre/Super-Cinema, Tuebrook 105

P

Palace, Aintree 60

Palace Cinema, Bootle 35

Palladium, Seaforth 61

Palladium, Tuebrook 56

Paramount (Odeon), Liverpool city centre 160

Park Palace Kinematodrome (Park Palace Cinema), Dingle 15

Picture House (Broadway Cinema), Bootle 35

Picture Palace of Bootle (Empire Picture Theatre), Bootle 9

Plaza (Gaumont • Odeon • Classic • Cannon • ABC), Allerton 123

Plaza (Odeon • Classic • Cannon • Apollo • Plaza), Crosby 181

Popular Picture House, Everton 111

Premier Picture Palace, Wavertree 34

Prince Picturedrome, Liverpool 33

Prince of Wales (Liverpool Picture House • Liverpool News Theatre • Gala International Film Theatre • Jacey Film Theatre), Liverpool city centre 47

Prince's Picture Palace (Prince's Picturedrome • Prince's Picture Hall • Lytton Cinema), Everton 32

Prince's Cinema (Granby Cinema), Toxteth 45

Princess Cinema, Kirkdale 138

Q

Queen's Picture House, Walton 53

Queen's Picture House, Waterloo 54

R

Regal Cinema, Litherland 179

Regal Cinema, Norris Green 126

Regent Cinema, Old Swan 114

Regent Picture House, Crosby 85

Reo Cinema, Fazakerley 155

Rialto, Toxteth 117

Rice Lane Picture House (Atlas Cinema), Walton 65

Ritz Cinema, Anfield 126

Ritz • (Studios 1, 2, 3 • 051 Cinema), Liverpool city centre 188

Rink Cinema (Garston Picturedrome) 25

Rivoli Theatre (Aigburth Assembly Picturedrome • Rivoli Cinema), Aigburth 8

Roscommon Picture Palace (Roscommon Cinema), Everton 33

Royal Cinema, Anfield 81

Royal Hippodrome Theatre (Hippodrome Cinema), Tuebrook 143

S

St James' Picturedrome Cinema, Dingle 64

Savoy Picture House, Tuebrook 70

Scala Super-Cinema, Liverpool city centre 75

Sefton Park Picturedrome, Wavertree 27

Smithdown Picture Playhouse, Wavertree 72

Stella Picture House Cinema, Seaforth 82

Strand Cinema (New Prince's Theatre), Bootle 38

Studios 1, 2, 3 (Ritz • 051), Liverpool city centre 188

Sun Hall (Imperial), Bootle 28

Swan Picturedrome (Swan Cinema), Old Swan 78

T

Tatler Club Cinema (Electra Palace • London Road Picture House • Alhambra • King's Picture House • Essoldo • Curzon Club Cinema • Classic • Eros Club Cinema), Liverpool city centre 30

Tatler News Theatre (Classic Cinema), Liverpool city centre 158

Tivoli Cinema (Moulton Picture Palaces), Everton 24

Tivoli Palace (Grand Tivoli • Palais de Luxe), Liverpool city centre 11

Trocadero (Gaumont), Liverpool city centre 93

Tunnel Road Picturedrome (Avenue Cinema), Edge Hill 69

Victoria Cinema (Essoldo), Anfield 104

Victory Picture House, Walton 98

W

Walton Vale Picture House 99

Warwick Picturedrome (Warwick Cinema), Toxteth 50

Waterloo Picture Playhouse (New Picture Hall • Winter Gardens Cinema), Waterloo 20

Wavertree Picturedrome 62

Wellington Picture Palace (Garston Picture Palace) 24

West Derby Picture House (West Derby Plaza) 116

Westminster Hall (Doric Cinema), Kirkdale 18

Winter Gardens Theatre (Apollo Theatre), Bootle 19

Winter Gardens Cinema (Waterloo Picture Playhouse • New Picture Hall), Waterloo 20

Woolton Picture House 121